ADVANCE PRAISE

'On the pitch or off the pitch, millennials with their sheer number and presence rule the roost. They represent the youth of today full with energy, enthusiasm and potential. They need to be engaged better, their boundless energies need to be channelized, but first they need to be heard and understood. Unfortunately, we see a lot of rough edges between the previous generations and millennials, whether in cricket or outside, mostly owing to misunderstandings. The result is often counterproductive for organizations and societies, the cricket equivalent of caught-behind or stumped. This book is one of its kind; it not only allays the myths about Generation Y but also comes out with very clear and practical strategies to engage them. A sure Sixer! I wish the book and the author all success'.

Syed Kirmani
Cricketing Legend (Represented India 1971–1986)
Recipient of Padma Shri and Arjuna Award

'From the first time I spoke with Debashish, I was amazed by his knowledge and passion for engagement. That's why I invited him to judge The Lotus Awards. Engaging with millennials will be one of the biggest challenges businesses face, and we are lucky that Debashish has shared his extensive research to help make this easier for us all'.

James Murphy FRSA
Founder, Engage International Ltd, UK
(The Blue Lotus Awards)

'This book is an exhaustive study of a dilemma facing every organization on the planet—how to motivate and retain Generation Y employees and consumers. The young entering the workforce today bring new and exciting skills that open up new possibilities for organizations and by 2030, Generation Y staffers will account for two-thirds of all employees in the global workforce.

However, this generation is unlike any other having grown up in an age of technology, greater access to education and a much freer lifestyle which fosters different motivators, needs and priorities than previous generations. These new motivators are at odds with what employers have traditionally expected.

Dr Sengupta skilfully explores this nexus in greater depth than most other research available. Moreover, he goes further by providing a step-by-step guide to winning over millennial staff and consumers—something not covered in any other research that comes to mind. This book is essential for leaders of organizations, talent acquisition and management staff as well as sales and marketing experts trying to reverse declining sales trends. This book must be on your desk!'

Bernard O'Meara
Marquis Who's Who since 2009, Australia

'The author's work is an insightful treatise on a contemporary reality which has started impacting many a social and business landscape globally. One can experience the painstaking research effort and the authentic enquiry adopted by Debashish as we immerse in its thought-provoking and gripping content. The book is rich with facts and feelings ascribed to this cohort aptly called now as the most disruptive population to inhabit the world. It makes the much needed and timely contribution to the global imperative of millennial engagement not just within organizations and workplaces but also in the burgeoning social and formal marketplace as consumers of products and services. In fact, millennials are becoming the biggest spending generation, but many corporates fail to tap into their buying power because of not just ineffective marketing strategies but also in failing to realize that they are a unique lot with some distinctive characteristics. A classic contribution has been made by the author to guide organizations and professionals discover practical ways to engage millennials through some revealing behavioural insights and workplace culture design strategies. It indeed enables crucial paradigm shifts by uncovering the truth behind some myths and stereotypes about millennials. This is not just a good-to-know content but also a serious read to shape and sharpen our competitive edge and to ensure sustainability for the present and future'.

R. Yuvakumar
Learning and Development Adviser,
Executive Coach and Corporate Mentor UAE,
Head Mashreq Learning Systems,
Mashreq Bank, Dubai

'The rapid advancement of science and technology has greatly enhanced our understanding of the universe. This book delves deep into the universe of the human mind with Generation Y at its core. Rapid pace of change has the potential to widen the disconnect between generations in various spheres of life disturbing peace at personal and societal levels. Understanding, as rightly pointed out by the author, is a prerequisite for effective and fruitful engagement across generations. Rarely do we come across a book like this. Usefulness of this book extends far beyond workplace and marketplace. It will change the way we look at the youth in general and millennials in particular'.

Jeethendra Shetty
Deputy Director (Administration),
Department of Youth Empowerment and Sports,
Government of Karnataka

'This is the book I have been waiting for, as an employer. The importance of this subject is widely known, but mostly spoken with individual perceptions. This book will help us to understand millennials while defining the workplace policies and practices, taking into account the fact that by 2020 half of the population in India will be below 25 years of age. This book will also help the millennials understand how they are perceived with clear analysis for them to integrate with society. I congratulate Dr Debashish for this book'.

Ramesh Sampath
Country HR Director, Valeo India Private Limited

'This is a very important book in our context. Millennials are a force that cannot be ignored. It is important, therefore, that everyone who interacts with millennials gets some understanding of what drives them—and their drivers are really unique. This book by Dr Debashish, the culmination of close to a decade of research, tries to decode millennials and their thinking—a start to engaging with this generation in a more meaningful manner'.

RJ Jimmy
Mirchi 95, Bengaluru

'Dr Debashish has written a must-read primer for organizations to reach out, understand and engage with millennials. *The*

Life of Y is a well-researched, timely publication that will help build a bridge between organizations and Gen Y to better the quality of engagement'.

K. Sivakumar
Co-founder and CEO,
Saluto Wellness Private Limited

'All the new generations, in my opinion, always felt that they were one step ahead when compared to their predecessors. And, obviously, the "previous generation" thought the opposite and bemoaned the watering down of values, work ethics, etc. But, in the current scenario of baton handover to the "millennials," we are witnessing an upheaval which is still being probed into and many are clueless. While, we, in the pre-millennial generation, are learning to grudgingly accept the sweeping changes brought about by technology, social media, human relationships, etc., somewhere there is a disconnect when we approach the "millennial" human factor which is a product of these new waves. This book aims at unravelling that mystery and suggests to us the way forward. Must read!'

Kumar Krishnaswamy
Group Head, Human Resources,
Medwell Ventures

'A timely analysis and thorough exploration of the "Y" factor, the book charts a strategic path for engaging millennials'.

Anitha Moosath
Associate Editor, *The Smart Manager*

'Millennial puzzle is a global challenge today. There is certainly a sense of excitement as millennials populate workplaces and marketplaces and become more dominant players in the society. However, there is also a sense of uncertainty as to how to engage them, aggravated by the widespread myths that prevail about this generation. This book not only spectacularly busts those myths but also introduces us to the "real" millennial as never before. Actual life narrative accounts of millennials make it even more lively and gripping. A must-read for everyone, including millennials themselves!'

Ranjini Manian
Author of *Make It in India*
Founder, Global Adjustments

'This is a very relevant topic across the world. It is even more pertinent in India given the demographic profile. Dr Debashish Sengupta is passionate about this topic and has covered all the key aspects of it'.

Mohandoss T.
Senior Executive in a large MNC firm

The Life of Y

The Life of Y

Engaging Millennials as
Employees and Consumers

Debashish Sengupta

SAGE | Response
Business Books

Los Angeles | London | New Delhi
Singapore | Washington DC | Melbourne

First published in 2018 by

SAGE Publications India Pvt Ltd
B1/I-1 Mohan Cooperative Industrial Area
Mathura Road, New Delhi 110 044, India
www.sagepub.in

SAGE Publications Inc
2455 Teller Road
Thousand Oaks, California 91320, USA

SAGE Publications Ltd
1 Oliver's Yard, 55 City Road
London EC1Y 1SP, United Kingdom

SAGE Publications Asia-Pacific Pte Ltd
3 Church Street
#10-04 Samsung Hub
Singapore 049483

Published by Vivek Mehra for SAGE Publications India Pvt Ltd, typeset in 12/14 pt Garamond by Zaza Eunice, Hosur, India and printed at Chaman Enterprises, New Delhi.

Library of Congress Cataloging-in-Publication Data

Name: Sengupta, Debashish, author.
Title: The life of Y : engaging millennials as employees and consumers /
    Debashish Sengupta.
Description: Thousand Oaks, California : SAGE Publications India Pvt Ltd, [2018]
    | Includes bibliographical references.
Identifiers: LCCN 2017030002 (print) | LCCN 2017037895 (ebook) |
    ISBN 9789386602756 (Web PDF) | ISBN 9789386602749 (print (pb))
Subjects: LCSH: Generation Y—Employment—India. | Employee motivation—
    India. | Personnel management—India. | Generation Y—Mental health.
Classification: LCC HQ799.8.I53 (ebook) | LCC HQ799.8.I53 S46 2017 (print) |
    DDC 305.20954—dc23
LC record available at https://lccn.loc.gov/2017030002

ISBN: 978-93-866-0274-9 (PB)

SAGE Team: Manisha Mathews, Apoorva Mathur, Syeda Aina Rahat Ali and Rajinder Kaur
Illustrations Courtesy: Reetika Mukherjee

This book is dedicated to my beautiful
better half Vandana,
my son Arnab and
the countless millennials around the world.
I love you all.

Thank you for choosing a SAGE product!
If you have any comment, observation or feedback,
I would like to personally hear from you.

Please write to me at **contactceo@sagepub.in**

Vivek Mehra, Managing Director and CEO, SAGE India.

Bulk Sales

SAGE India offers special discounts
for purchase of books in bulk.
We also make available special imprints
and excerpts from our books on demand.

For orders and enquiries, write to us at

Marketing Department
SAGE Publications India Pvt Ltd
B1/I-1, Mohan Cooperative Industrial Area
Mathura Road, Post Bag 7
New Delhi 110044, India

E-mail us at **marketing@sagepub.in**

Get to know more about SAGE

Be invited to SAGE events, get on our mailing list.
Write today to **marketing@sagepub.in**

This book is also available as an e-book.

BRIEF CONTENTS

DETAILED CONTENTS

FOREWORDS

———————◆◉◆———————

Baby boomers are great. However, if they're the only people leading your company, you'll lack leadership talents crucial for tomorrow. It's a premise I hear over and over: the most important job of the CEO and the board of directors is to pick the next CEO. Succession is critical. Picking the next CEO and future leaders is about the future. So why do most companies go about picking their next generation mired in the past?

In *The Life of Y: Engaging Millennials as Employees and Consumers*, Dr Debashish Sengupta describes the typical millennials, how leaders can engage and develop this important and abundant group, and what the future will look like when nearly 75 per cent of the workforce will be composed of this interesting and unique generation.

In 2028, says Dr Sengupta, 'the last of the boomers will be at retirement age, Millennials will make up three-quarters of the workforce and the oldest millennials … will be entering leadership positions'. It's crucial that leaders today know the criteria based on which they can select, develop and engage these future leaders to ensure that they are well suited to lead us into tomorrow.

Think about it. What are the chances that the typical current CEO, likely a baby boomer, is well positioned to identify all the crucial characteristics of the organizations' future leaders? And, should that CEO be joined in picking those CEO characteristics with a board filled with people in his or her age demographic?

This is where you will find *The Life of Y: Engaging Millennials as Employees and Customers* absolutely invaluable. Based on years of research, Dr Sengupta takes us on a journey through the depiction and many narratives about millennials, helping us understand them, their hopes and dreams, quirks and challenges. And if you are a millennial and read this book, it may help you understand yourself and your own generation in ways you had never contemplated.

Read this book, expand your horizons, look to the future and enjoy the experience you will have when you let Dr Debashish Sengupta take you on this journey into the understanding of Generation Y.

Life is good.

Marshall Goldsmith
The Thinkers50 #1 Leadership Thinker in the World

We are living in the most exciting and best of times ever in terms of the potential we have to change the world with the help of technology. We are witnessing the birth of technologies that will fundamentally alter the way we live, work and relate to one another. The scale, scope and complexity of the transformation is unlikely to be like anything humankind has experienced before.

The first three industrial revolutions have seen the displacement and disruption of businesses by locomotives, electricity and computers. Now a fourth industrial revolution is underway, wherein technologies are converging to blur the lines between the physical, digital and biological spheres.

Compared with previous industrial revolutions, the fourth one is evolving at an exponential rather than a linear pace. Moreover, it is disrupting almost every industry in every country.

At the same time, we are witnessing the entry of a vast number of millennials into the workforce. Millennials, also known as the Generation Y (Gen Y), born between 1980 and 2000, are expected to account for roughly 75 per cent of the global workforce by 2025.

To thrive and not only survive in this brave new world, corporates need to attract, train and retain the best of these millennial workers. For this, employers will have to understand millennials' career aspirations, their attitudes about work and the factors that provide them job satisfaction.

Interestingly, several recent surveys have found that most young workers around the world viewed 'commitment to making the world a better place' among the top attributes they are looking for in prospective employers. One survey by Deloitte has shown that millennials are likely to commit to their organization if they share its sense of purpose.

As the influence of the millennial generation grows in the workforce, human resources professionals would need to respond to the change in employee composition and its potential in determining the future of the organization.

Job security, professional development and pay are not the main motivating factors for Gen Y. Rather, they are likely to find fulfilment in the purposeful pursuit of their passions. Organizations that are able to successfully channel this creative passion into crafting products and services that 'make a difference' will be the ones that come out on top.

The publication of Dr Debashish Sengupta's *The Life of Y: Engaging Millennials as Employees and Consumers* is timely as the book not only provides valuable insights into the way Gen Y thinks but also disproves some of the perceptual myths and stereotypes associated with it.

This book is a must-read for organizations that are looking to positively engage with the millennial generation. It boldly attempts to define the rules of engagement for a generation that will reshape our future.

Kiran Mazumdar Shaw
Chairperson and Managing Director, Biocon

PREFACE

It is hard to describe the moment when you are completing a manuscript. Although this book in a way marks the culmination of years of research work, the last three months especially have been exhilarating. During these three months, I spoke to more millennials than I would have spoken to all put together in the last many years. It has been a tremendous experience listening to their stories, feeling their emotions and sensing their highs and lows! With every conversation, I made an even stronger connect with them, understanding their lives to be able to showcase to the world the real *life of Y*. All these years, I have been living their life through their stories. It has been one of the most thrilling journeys that I have ever undertaken! And not to forget the early-morning and late-night writing sessions, the manuscript completion deadline by the publisher seemingly approaching faster than it should and the innumerable cups of coffee and tea that fuelled me on and on in this exciting writing voyage. And so, when the manuscript nears completion, there is a sense of relief but also a feeling of vacuum that you feel after your most enthralling holiday is over. I hope this book reaches to those millions of millennials to whom this book is dedicated and they find meaning in the words, but I will remain eternally thankful to the almighty that he gave me this opportunity to live these moments, which have been priceless.

Yet, this book is just a beginning! Beginning of how corporations, leaders, societies and families would view millennials differently and how they would interpret their behaviours as they have never done before, develop a genuine empathy for the first time, and begin to change their organizational designs, leadership styles, social norms and more importantly their mindsets to engage the phenomenally talented yet grossly misunderstood 'digital natives'.

This book is also for millennials themselves. I have spoken to some of them, even known some of them, and so this book is a way of talking to many more of them in a more direct manner. And so, I hope 'You' find this book a slice of your life and at the same time know how many members of your generation share the kind of life you live, the exciting crests and also the trials and tribulations you ride on and also realize that 'You' are not the only one who has been misunderstood! I sincerely hope this book becomes your voice to the world.

Debashish Sengupta
ThelifeofYbook@gmail.com
Bengaluru
May 31, 2017

ACKNOWLEDGEMENTS

When a book gets completed, the author gets all the credit and attention, which I feel is a sort of over-amplification. Without the significant and invaluable contributions from many, this book would just have been at best a good idea.

First and foremost, I owe thanks to millions of millennials around the world who have inspired me to take up this work and do my research and especially to those who have been very forthcoming in sharing their stories, trusting me, confiding in me and helping me to understand them better. I feel honoured at such a response. Thank you 'Y'.

I would like to thank Reetika Mukherjee who has done the beautiful illustrations for this book. Reetika, who will appear for her secondary school exams in 2018, has amazed me with her brilliant artistry and talent at such a young age. Her illustrations fill this book with life.

I would like to make a special note of Dr Ray Titus and Dr Bernard O'Meara whose brilliant observations at various stages of my research work have been an incredible support. My special thanks to all those special people who have said very kind words about the book. Thanks for all those words of encouragement.

In addition, I would like to thank P. Upendra for his superb lensman support.

Finally, I am thankful to the good providence of marrying Vandana who after 12 years of our marriage continues to put up with all my idiosyncrasies and has given me the space and time to pursue my writing and passion. My young boy Arnab has been such a sport to let me steal some of his vacation time to complete this book. Both life and this book would have been incomplete without them.

PART I

Unravelling Millennial Behaviour

1

THE MISUNDERSTOOD GENERATION!

*R*anjini, a 23-year-old, works as an information technology (IT) professional in Bengaluru. She is of the opinion that her company has no clue about managing people like her. She wants personalized appreciation and recognition for what she does. She feels that her contributions are not valued and everything in her company is just another process. She expects flexibility at work. On the contrary, she finds the rules and regulations in her company very rigid. Everyone is expected to fit in the 'system'. Even for a simple work-from-home or early-leaving permission, she has to answer a dozen questions. She finds such questions and explaining her point frustrating, to say the least. Ranjini is the typical millennial who thinks and behaves differently than previous generations or organizations do.

Are organizations ready for this burgeoning new generation that is entering the workforce in large numbers? Do they have strategies to engage them? Facts suggest on the contrary that most companies are struggling to keep the millennial workers happy and engaged. The 2016 millennial survey by Deloitte on India has alarming news for companies in India. Almost 66 per cent of the millennials or millennial workers in India are likely to change their companies by 2020. That works out to be two out of every three millennial workers in India. While world over similar trends are visible, India ranks third where there is largest probability of millennial workers leaving their current companies. The survey also points to the fact that this lack of loyalty may be a sign of neglect that millennials might be facing in their organization.

Such poor level of engagement of millennial workers in India and rest of the world is a huge red flag for all companies. Poor engagement will not only have cost implications but will also have huge negative implications on the growth, profitability and sustainability of the companies, especially when going is not particularly easy for most of the industry sectors.

Millennials, also known as the Generation Y (Gen Y), born between 1980 and 2000, cannot be ignored. By 2025, they will make up roughly 75 per cent of the world's workforce. India will have the largest number of millennials anywhere in the world by the year 2021. In the USA, millennials already comprise largest percentage of the workforce. By 2028, the last of the baby boomers will be reaching retirement age, millennials will make up roughly three quarters of the workforce by this time and the oldest millennial, still quite young at just 47, will be entering leadership position. They double up as customers. To think of that 65 per cent of India's population which is below 35 years of age is enough to establish the significance of this generation for companies. They are not only present in large numbers, but they are also where it counts most—impacting both the workplace and the marketplace.

Any short-sightedness in engaging millennials can affect a business firm adversely in both the short term and the long term. Research also points to the facts that many leaders and companies are oblivious to the changes in the workplace due to the change in the composition in the workforce and that there is a renewed need to understand the new workforce to engage them better. The fact is that most of the organizational designs are obsolete and do not match with the behaviour, mindsets or aspirations of the new generation. Companies need to urgently revisit and transform their organizational designs to engage millennials.

BARMY Times

Violent clash between the Army soldiers and officers in one of the northern districts of the country some time back cannot be ignored as a one-off incident. Neither should it be read as an impending mutiny. Army is a great bunch of brave people defending the nation and has time and again demonstrated extreme gallantry in the face of adversary. But definitely, the times are changing and it seems that Army has to do some catching up with the new generation to keep its house in order.

The incident happened during an inter-company boxing match when a solider, despite trying his best, lost a friendly boxing match. One of his officers confronted him after the match, publicly ridiculed him and thrashed him. The soldier did not take the insult lying down and retaliated. A prolonged physical clash ensued between soldiers and officers. The ugly incident left Army red-faced and embarrassed.

The Army must have penalized the ones who broke discipline after due enquiry. But will that really put an end to what seems to be a systemic issue brewing inside the organization.

This is not the first of such incident in recent times where the soldiers have given back a fist for a fist. Although the top brass of the Army have come down heavily against such errant soldiers and have handed them exemplary punishments, the question is whether that will suffice. The repetition of such incidents, nevertheless, indicates that the problem may be lying elsewhere.

Millennials are populating the Army, like many other organizations, in big numbers. Reports suggest that the new-age soldiers are not only better educated but also more aspirational. A more educated, aspirational and high-on-self-esteem millennial soldier may be expecting greater respect and more egalitarian treatment.

Millennials accept authority by example and for a limited time frame. In other words, the superior gets respect not for his position but for the exemplary performance that he/she exhibits. And the respect lasts as long as such behaviour of the superior lasts. In the coming years, as more millennials enter the Army, managing these new-generation soldiers will be a challenge.

Organizations all over the world are experiencing the phenomena of multi-generations at work. The increasing tension between Gen X bosses and millennial employees is not only the problem of the Army but also of many organizations around the world. The organizations that are able to recognize the fact are trying to decipher Gen Y and in the process trying to find out newer and better ways to manage and engage them.

A seminal work done as a Manekshaw Paper highlighted the need to change the organizational design of the Indian Army

(Mallick, 2011). There are enough indicators to show that the Army's ability to attract quality officers has declined sharply following the globalization of the Indian economy.

Poor design is a result of poor understanding about the millennials and the widespread myths about them. Criticism of millennials by the previous generation, also known as millennial bashing, is very common. They are termed as lazy, entitled, impulsive, lacking work ethic and loyalty towards their employers, and gadget freaks, to just list a few. A recent survey of American Express and Millennial Branding found that most managers think that millennials have a poor work ethic; they are the ones who can be easily distracted and they have unrealistic compensation expectations. A different study from the Conference Board of Canada (2014) found that the majority of previous-generation members, that is, Gen X and baby boomers, think that millennials are overconfident in their abilities. Such myths about millennials show that they are a hugely misunderstood generation.

Mandatory Picnic

Purva, a millennial herself, works as a management trainee in the human resource department in a premier IT company in the country. She had been recruited by the company through the company's annual campus recruitment drive. Her excitement when she bagged this opportunity was palpable, as she had always dreamt of working for a top technology company. However, over the past six months, her excitement has sort of abated. Today, when she reached the office, a mail from her boss stumped her. The mail was addressed to the team and read as follows:

Dear team members,

The company has organized a picnic for all the Facility-2 employees to Banbara National Park on coming Saturday. It is mandatory on part of all my team members to participate in the picnic as it is an excellent opportunity to do team building. All members are also required to contribute ₹3,000 towards picnic expenses. See you all at the picnic.

Cheers,

AK

Purva's temper shot up after reading the mail. This was not the first time she had received such mails. Her mind was raging with questions—How can they make picnic mandatory? That too on a weekend! And then they are asking us to pay as well. This is like extortion! She had an engagement party to attend on Saturday. Besides, she had visited Banbara National Park twice before in the past, with her friends. She had no intention of going there again.

Purva had enough with these mandatory-marked mails. She decided to have a talk with her boss.

AK: Hi Purva, please tell me. You wanted to have a conversation with me?

Purva: Yes, ma'am, regarding the picnic.

AK: Purva, it has been six months since you have been a part of our team and you still haven't got over the habit of calling us by ma'am and sir. Please, Purva, call me by my name. I am comfortable that way.

Purva: Sorry, AK, actually I do not want to go for the picnic.

AK: Chill, Purva, I hope you read the mail properly. I want my entire team to go.

Purva: But, ma'am, this Saturday I already have something very important and personal planned. Besides, I have already been to that National Park!

AK: No, no you must go Purva. This is a good team-building opportunity as well.

Purva: I am sorry, AK, but you are kind of imposing this on me. And it's a weekend for God sake! How can you say that it is mandatory? Besides, I even have to pay for something that I do not want to do. Do you think that all this will lead to team building?

AK: Hmm. You seem quite worked up on this. Anyway, get back to work. You will hear from me soon.

AK quipped and then left her cabin, leaving Purva with no time to react.

Purva returned to her cubicle, looking quite exasperated. She couldn't concentrate on her work. She decided to call her friend and classmate during her MBA programme, Sania. She had always been someone whom Purva had trusted and called especially whenever she was tense. Purva and Sania spoke for a long time and Sania agreed that these team-building exercises were very superficial. Sania told her that it was a good thing that she confronted her boss. While talking to Sania, she saw another mail from AK. The 'mandatory' clause had been removed and it was now optional to go for the picnic. A sense of relief was clearly evident on Purva's face but all this had left a bitter taste in her mouth. Anyway, for now the trouble had been averted. But Purva wondered when she would gain receive a similar 'compulsory' directive. After all, the day had just started.

In all likelihood, Purva will get one of those infamous labels from her manager that millennials have usually been branded with—arrogant upstarts, who don't want to work hard or persevere and who are generally irritating at workplace… and what not! In most of such behavioural interpretations, the bias of the earlier generation against millennials is clearly visible.

Is Purva's conflict with her manager an isolated incident? Studies suggest that there is a widespread disconnect between the previous-generation managers and leaders and millennial employees that often surfaces in its ugly form.

Between Real and Virtual

Such misunderstandings and conflicts are not only happening at workplaces. They are occurring in social and family spheres as well. Over the past few years, I had several invited opportunities in the corporate world to share my findings on the millennial workforce. In a well-known, reputed and rapidly growing chain of birthing hospitals in Bengaluru, after one of my talk sessions, a senior nurse walked up to me and said that now she knew why her son behaved the way she had never been able to understand before, his needs and friends. That was when I started to realize the immense impact right understanding of millennials could have on society and workplaces.

A radio jockey (RJ) on an afternoon show on a local radio FM was audibly quite surprised by the fact that 72 per cent young Indians login to their Facebook (FB) page at least three times a day. Her astonishment grew further as she interviewed a 'listener' on her show who told her that she was always online on FB and she checked her updates every now and then, even at times in the middle of the night. That was too much for the RJ and she teased the listener a bit on her behaviour.

Most people, like the local RJ, do not understand the changing demographics of our nation. The millennial generation has grown up in a 'connected' world, unlike all other previous generations, and do not necessarily see the 'real' world and 'virtual' world (or the online world) as two different realms. They have almost parallel existence on both these worlds, which seamlessly merge for them. They effortlessly glide from one to the other, back and forth, and not necessarily shut down 'one' and then switch to the other world, like most older-generation people do.

This parallel existence of the Gen Y makes them always 'connected'. However, since they are constrained with time, even as they call themselves a bit 'socially lazy', they prefer 'online' to stay connected. They are hanging out with their friends both at a café and on FB at the same time and sharing updates both offline and online.

The new generation is heavily connected on social media for personal, social and professional reasons.

Here are the top 15 reasons why millennials use FB:

1. FB helps quench their curiosity. It also helps them know personal things about other people in a very impersonal way.
2. It helps them stay abreast with the major life events of their friends and acquaintances.
3. It helps them to bridge the gap of distance and time with their friends and stay in touch.
4. It helps them to forge and nurture relationships. Birthday and anniversary wishing on FB is very common.
5. Many use FB to engage with brands that they follow or like.
6. It helps them improve their networking skills.
7. They use FB to maintain close friends-group camaraderie.
8. It helps them live an aspirational life.
9. It allows them to brag, boast and make others jealous or simply get the 'likes'. It makes one feel good about oneself. Every time we get a like, our body releases a hormone known as dopamine. In the brain, dopamine functions as a neurotransmitter—a chemical released by neurons (nerve cells) to send signals to other nerve cells. The brain

includes several distinct dopamine pathways, one of which plays a major role in reward-motivated behaviour.

10. It helps them to know and share interesting stuff (updates—information, photos, selfies and jokes).
11. It helps them earn virtual currency (e.g., FB Credit, Farmville Cash and Microsoft Points).
12. It promotes their work and interests (through FB pages).
13. It helps them search for lost friends.
14. It helps them seek help during times of crisis or seek information from a large pool of people on different aspects.
15. It is also a tool for them to beat loneliness.

Appy Generation

Gen 'Y'ers have been termed as those who are driven by money, who spend without thinking and who do not save enough; who are demanding and self-serving and who delay taking major decisions; who have a misguided notion of superiority, outrageous sense of dressing and least respect for timeliness; and who are too busy tweeting, blogging and texting, all at the same time. Their behaviour has often been misinterpreted and misunderstood.

'Gen Y space is not always a place!' Employers, marketers and retailers all over the world are slowly realizing this fact.

When McDonald's recruited Atiq Rafiq, an ex-executive of Amazon, as the chief digital officer sometime back, many wondered what was a digital officer doing in a fast food retail chain! But the answer lies in McDonald's attempt to reach out to the millennial customers in the USA.

Falling sales and rising competition have forced the 'aging giant' to learn different 'ways'. Suddenly, the lesser known fast food retail chains such as Five Guys Burger, Fries and Chipotle are attracting far more millennial crowd and moolah! The new retail chains are offering mobile apps to Gen Y that helps them to customize orders, place orders, get 'deals' and even make payments.

Traditional methods do not seem to be working for most companies, including McDonald's. Due to the fact that millennials are highly digital and 'mobile', the more than 70-year-old fast food retail chain giant is changing the way it does things, and all for good reasons. McDonald's is like a baby boomer who wants to learn the tricks of engaging and attracting more millennials!

No prizes for guessing that McDonald's has developed an app 'McD' and is attempting to go the extra mile to be more digital and mobile-friendly and attract Gen Ys in their stores. What started initially for the US market is soon spreading to other locations, given the global nature of this generation and high degree of similarity in their behaviour.

Data clearly show that the number of people buying smartphones and tablets is enormously high and is increasing at an increasing rate. For 2017, the number of smartphone users in India is estimated to reach 340.2 million, with the number of smartphone users worldwide forecasted to exceed 2 billion users by that time. The new generation is especially on mobile all the time. It makes every logical sense to be where they are if one intends to engage them.

The development of 'mobile HR applications' is a step in the direction of engaging the Gen Y or the millennial employees. Mobile HR apps can offer applications like mobile learning applications, workforce communications, workforce analytics, etc. on mobile without necessitating a portal or a browser.

Appreciating the cause of millennials' behaviour is only the first step towards understanding millennials. This is however a good first step but not enough. Their life and their dilemmas are still not understood. A look at Tanya's story gives an idea how even good intentions of this generation are often misunderstood by the older generations.

What's interesting is that the line between online and offline is blurring for the new generation and for them, it is parallel existence in both these worlds. They find it strange when their parents, teachers or employers ask them to give up their gadgets, or come out of the online world or restrict their social media usage. For them, the online and offline worlds are one and the same, one diffusing into the other.

Calendar Life

Tanya is a young MBA professional, fresh out of the college, working, independent and a gadget-addict. She works as a manager with a reputed brand and loves to flaunt her professional status. Financially, she is secure and despite being a fresher feels that she has career security. However, by her own confession, she leads a 'calendar life'. She hardly has enough time for herself, her friends and her family. Birthdays, festivals and even calling home have to be accommodated during weekends, since the 'calendar' simply does not allow anything except work schedule. Nobody to go back to at home and not enough social bonding with friends make loneliness a habit for her.

Tanya is a bold girl, who works and lives independently in Bengaluru. She has resisted her parents' attempts to get her married. She feels that it is too early for her to make such a serious commitment. Her refusal to marry has not gone down well with her parents who live in Jaipur. Tanya is quite headstrong to fall to such pressures. She has been successful in negotiating some more time for herself and in avoiding the marriage bait.

Tanya's childhood friend Sameer has been a bit troubled lately. Sameer works as a mechanical engineer in an automobile company. He is of the same age as that of Tanya. She has been postponing meeting with Sameer for quite some time now. However, today he sounded really worried. So, Tanya decided to meet over coffee at the Burroughs Café.

At the café, Sameer's troubled expression told Tanya that he has been going through a lot of late. Sameer has been engaged for about three months now. After he updated his relationship status on his FB page, all of a sudden someone started writing all sort of bad things about him on the social networking site. Most have been warnings meant for his fiancée to desist from marrying Sameer. The person, whoever was doing this mischief, it seems had created some anonymous accounts on FB. His fiancée had also been getting all these messages that often told her that Sameer was a devious guy, who was not trustworthy, and warned her against marrying him. Tanya promised to help Sameer.

In next two weeks, Tanya tried to connect with such 'accounts' without really revealing that she knew Sameer. With the help of FB and WhatsApp, she was able to track down this person. She turned out to be a girl called Meera. Tanya decided to meet Meera. After meeting Meera, she came to know that sometime back, Sameer's marriage proposal had been sent by Sameer's parents for Meera. Both families had met as well, after which Sameer rejected the alliance, although Meera was willing to go ahead. Stung by the rejection, Meera decided to avenge the humiliation by tormenting Sameer and sabotaging his other possible marriage alliances. Tanya gave a piece of mind to Meera and warned her to desist from doing such things. Social media had helped Tanya track the culprit and set things alright before they turned murkier. After this episode, all those defaming messages stopped and Sameer was relieved.

During her next visit to her hometown, Tanya narrated this incident to her mother and told her proudly how she could unearth the person by using social media. Even before she could complete, her mother blamed the social media for all such troubles, 'That is why I ask you not to put your pictures and other things over FB. But you youngsters would never listen. You will write everything on that site. This is why you have all these problems...'. Tanya's mother went on lecturing her and her attempts to explain how FB and WhatsApp had actually helped in this case went futile. Tanya lamented her decision to share the developments with her mom. She is perplexed by her mom's reaction and is ready to give up any hope that her parents will truly understand her world. Tanya's mother does not quite understand her desire for freedom, her 'calendar life', her desire for space, her loneliness, her desire to be 'herself' or for that matter her online life. Being misunderstood is painful and causes immense stress at times.

Millennials report highest levels of clinical anxiety, stress and depression than any other generation at the same age. According to the American Psychological Association, 'Adults aged 18–35 are experiencing more stress than any other generation. College students in particular seem to grow more stressed with every passing year. Nearly half attend counselling for various mental health concerns, with anxiety being by far the most prevalent one'.

To Be or Not to Be!

Nina, much like Tanya and Sameer, is misunderstood. Nina Thomas comes from a conservative Christian family. She hails from a southern state of India,

Kerala, and 'God's own country'. She was in the final semester of her MBA and was specializing in human resource management. Nina was excited about the upcoming placement season but when she called home, her dad told her that once the exams were over, he wanted her to get married and had already started looking for alliances.

It is not uncommon for millennials to find their parents trying to dictate their choice of discipline that they should study or their choice of career. Often called as 'helicopter' parents, their constant habit of 'hovering' over the kid's lives often leaves millennials exasperated.

Nina felt a surge of anger and frustration within but she could do nothing. She wanted to break free from the shadow of her dad, but it was not so easy. Nina quietly prepared for her final semester examinations. She could not let her academic performance flounder at any cost, although she had lost her enthusiasm and motivation. Nina completed her final examination and left for her hometown.

Nina had been a bright student all throughout her academic life and had dreamt of a great career. Her mother had always been her emotional anchor. Nina knew that her father's wishes would finally prevail. She wanted to get away from home and work. Her father always told her that she was too ambitious. Nina just wanted to follow her dreams though. Seeing her resoluteness, her father finally offered her a deal. She could take up some small job for about a year. In the meantime, he would search a suitable boy for her and once the marriage was finalized, she would marry and settle down. Nina agreed as this was the best she could negotiate.

Luckily for Nina, she got a job in a metro city that was 600 km from her city. She loved her family but this assignment would give Nina her own space. She started to work as a research assistant in a private university.

It was now about 18 months that Nina had been working. Her marriage had been 'fixed' by her parents. Luckily for her, the boy to whom she was supposed to get married worked in the same city as she did. She had met her fiancée a couple of times and he seemed to be a nice, understanding person. The marriage was solemnized. Nina returned to her workplace after her leaves were exhausted. Nina's husband James was working as a techie in an IT company. They took up an apartment in a location that was more accessible to Nina's workplace. James office was in ITPL, Whitefield. He was having a tough time commuting every day. Around this time, Nina also switched from her university job to a corporate HR job with a reputed Indian IT company that was among the top 10 in terms of revenues. Getting this job was not easy as Nina's initial experience of about two years was not being considered as a relevant experience. Nina was hired as an HR executive for an entry-level HR job. The compensation offered to her was not very attractive, but it was still better than her research assistant's one. She decided to take up the job as she thought that it was a gateway for her into the corporate world.

Nina started to get the real hang of her job after just about a month into her new job. Her official 9-hour workday often got stretched to 12 hours. She would reach home only by 9 p.m. Then, she would cook and do other household chores. All this left her completely exhausted. There was no flexibility on reporting hours at office. She would also be called on weekends. In the last 35 odd days, she hardly had one-day break. James also had a demanding week at his work schedule. They hardly had time for each other.

A day off was a lucky break! The pressure was getting a bit too much for Nina. She tried to speak to her manager about her problem, but he hardly seemed to understand her point of view. Instead, he lectured her on becoming more professional in her approach to make her mark in the corporate sector.

Two more months passed. Nina was finding it difficult to balance her professional and personal lives. This would have been far easier to handle had she started this job two years back when she completed her MBA and was a single. But now, she was feeling the pressure.

Nina was contemplating quitting. She discussed her plans with James. He was fine with her quitting her job but was worried that her career plans may be stonewalled by her move. She also knew that if she resigned from this job, it would be very difficult to resurrect her corporate dream. She was once again at crossroads— should she choose her career over life or otherwise? Couldn't she have both?

Nina's dilemma is the predicament of most Gen Y members. Their life is far more complex than we think. The pulls, pressures and demands are at times both contradictory and excruciating, which more often than not the previous generation finds difficult to comprehend.

Money and work continue to be one of the biggest stressors for millennials. They have entered the workforce at a difficult time. Job market is not growing fast enough, economy is still not doing great and job instability is very high. Snapdeal, one of the well-known e-commerce retailers in India, recently laid off over 600 employees while the founders took a 100 per cent pay cut. Financial and job-oriented success is often driven by fear.

Deeper Dive

There is a need for a deeper dive into the lives of millennials. They are misunderstood in families, societies and organizations. Their life is far more complex and layered than we understand. There is a need for a deeper dive into their lives and their experiences to truly understand them and their behaviour.

Millennials can't be just counted in a limited fashion as the next generation of workers, as they also double up as the next generation of consumers, and more importantly they will be the key to determining whether businesses succeed or fail. Research also points to the fact that many are oblivious to the changes needed in the workplace due to changes in the composition in the workforce. As the economy recovers and companies return to the challenge of engaging highly capable professionals to drive renewal and growth, there is a renewed need to understand the new workforce (millennials) to engage them better.

Whether they are employees or consumers, students or just individual members of the society, millennials are a powerful segment and engaging them and winning them is very important. However, expecting millennials to conform to previous ideals of the organizations or society will be a mistake. Instead, companies and the society raising the bar of their own capabilities to adjust their standards to fit this generation will be critical in winning them over.

Understanding is the first step towards winning and understanding the life of Y is critical in engaging them. Capturing their life experiences is the best way to create a right understanding about this generation.

There is an urgent need to change our understanding and capabilities to engage this generation. The other way round is a futile attempt and a losing battle. Faced with indifference, Gen Y will simply disconnect—something that companies, society and nations can ill afford.

Are millennials kids of the times? Have the times that they have grown shaped them in a different way compared to the previous generation and hence they behave differently? Could the resultant generational affect behind the different behaviours and mindsets that millennials exhibit?

The next chapter takes readers to a 'deep dive' and helps them to fathom the reasons behind millennial behaviour.

2
UNDERSTANDING
MILLENNIALS

For being a part of a French TV show, some participants inflicted electric shocks of 460 volts on fellow contestants. 'Le Jeu de la Mort' or The Game of Death, telecasted on 'France 2' TV, was like any other quiz show, complete with a host and list of questions except that if a contestant gave an incorrect response, then they would be inflicted with an electric shock. Among the chants of 'punishment' from the studio audience, most contestants ignored the screams of the zapped contestant and repeatedly gave electric shocks until the contestant fell down appearing dead. Out of

80 contestants, only about 20 per cent refused to obey such 'orders'. Rest 80 per cent of the contestants agreed to inflict the 'punishment'.

Shocking! How could normal everyday people agree to do something so cruel to their fellow human beings, and all of that just for being part of a TV show!

A fact unknown to the participants was that the show was rigged. All this was actually part of an experiment. The ones on whom the electric shock was being inflicted and were screaming were actually actors, faking shock and pain. In reality, no electric shock was being given to them. However, the participants who were inflicting such shocks were unaware of this fact. They were under the impression that they were giving real electric shocks. Why would someone agree to do something so brazen and terrible?

Considerable research evidence shows that the environment, shaping situational variables, becomes a huge determinant in shaping and transforming human behaviour. The human psyche gets exhibited through behaviour that is again a function of attitudes. The attitudes that people harbour are a result of learning, especially social learning. This learning is conditioned by the environment or the contextual factors. Could environment have also played a role in the way millennials turned out and the way their behaviour became markedly different from previous generations? Can insights into human behaviour become critical in understanding why millennials behave the way they do?

Power of Context

To find answers to our queries, we have to go half a century back and see what happened then. Way back in May 1962,

Stanley Milgram carried out an infamous and controversial experiment at Yale University, one that changed the view of the world regarding human behaviour. Milgram, a Jew himself, was searching answers to holocaust and Nazi's brutal and inhuman oppression of Jews. He wanted to study that under what conditions would a person obey authority who commanded actions that went against conscience.

For the purpose of the experiment, normal male volunteers in the age bracket of 20–50 years were selected to become the 'subjects' in the experiment. The 'subjects' were told that the purpose of the experiment was to find out whether people learn better and with greater accuracy when they are punished.

What the 'subjects' did not know was that the experiment was also rigged. The 'learners', who were actually actors, pretended to be tied to an electric shock generator. According to the plan, each of them would give incorrect responses to seemingly simple questions. The 'subjects' selected for the experiment were to act as 'teachers'. The 'teacher' was seated in front of the shock generator that had lines of electric switches, right from 15 volts to 450 volts. For every incorrect answer, the 'teachers' were supposed to give an electric shock to the 'learners', the intensity of which would keep increasing progressively with each incorrect response. The 'teacher' and 'learner' were made to sit in separate rooms in a way that that they could not see but hear each other.

The teacher was then given a list of word·pairs that he/she would have to teach the 'learner'. The 'teacher' would begin by reading a word and four possible answers. The 'learner' was expected to pick the correct matching word from the four options given to him/her and on every incorrect response, the 'teacher' would press a switch on the shock generator that would inflict electric shock to the 'learner', each time increasing the intensity up to 450 volts.

The experiment began and subjects acting as 'teachers' started giving electric shocks to 'learners' as they kept giving incorrect responses. The 'learner' would give out shrieks of pain that would go on becoming shriller and louder as the intensity of the shocks increased. The 'learner' could even be heard screaming 'Please let me out of here...'. These cries were actually pre-recorded sounds made by the shock generator, but the 'teacher' (or the subject) actually believed that for each wrong answer, the 'learner' was receiving real electric shocks and that the cries were for real.

Another unique feature of the experiment was a 'man' wearing a white coat and reading glasses was seated behind the 'teacher', who was actually a part of the team of researchers and acted as the 'authority' figure in the experiment. At times, when the 'learner' would howl in pain because of the intensifying electric shocks and make desperate requests to be let off, the 'teacher' would pause and look behind the man in the white coat. He would in turn 'order' the 'teacher' to continue, irrespective of the cries of the 'learner', by saying things such as 'Please go on', 'Continue please', 'This is required for the experiment, please continue' and 'It is essential that you continue'.

When the experiment ended, Milgram found, shockingly, that 65 per cent of the people who acted as 'teachers' went on giving electric shocks right up to 450 volts, if there was some pressure, even when the 'learner' fell silent presumed to be unconscious or dead.

The experiment not only exhibited 'obedience' but showed that normal everyday kind of people could do unimaginable things when put under pressure from authority figures. In both Milgram's experiment and the experiment conducted in the guise of French TV show, the 'subjects' were under the impression that they were giving real electric shocks.

During Milgram's experiment, people noticeably cringed, shook their heads as they administered shocks, some even left their seats to protest the experiment, yet when instructed, they continued to administer what they believed to be a terrible pain to a helpless person. It is amazing that these two experiments separated by almost 50 years produced similar results.

In Milgram's experiment, the man in the white coat, the voluntary participation of the 'subjects' (they were even getting paid @ $4 per hour for being part of the experiment) and the fear of spoiling the experiment created a pressure on them. The 'teachers' and 'learners' could not see each other that created a sort of de-personalization. What also added to the 'situation' was the fact that 'learners' were giving incorrect responses to seemingly very simple and mundane question that most people ought to know!

In the French TV show, the show presenter, the studio audience, fear among the 'subjects' of spoiling the TV show and perhaps even the fear of losing their participation on a show that gave them instant fame created a situation that compelled them into the 'act'.

Ever since Milgram conducted his experiment, many variations of the same have been carried out, even using female volunteers. But the outcome has not been different. In fact, for a 2009 episode of a BBC documentary 'Horizon', when Milgram's experiment was replicated, only 3 out of 12 participants refused to continue with the experiment.

The context clearly played a significant role. Milgram's study gave valuable insights into the crimes committed during the Second World War, the holocaust when millions of Jews were subjected to cold-hearted and dastardly tortures by Nazis. Milgram began his experiment three months after the trial of Nazi war criminal Adolf Eichmann started in Jerusalem.

Why did hundreds and thousands of soldiers obey Hitler? Why did soldiers, who were generally well-educated ordinary people, decent and courteous in their everyday life, callously and inhumanely with almost no limitations of conscience commit such ghastly crimes?

Most of the Nazi generals were intelligent and successful, and had power and opportunity to refuse to follow the orders. Most of them could have escaped the country and gone underground to avoid being part of such atrocities, yet they chose to obey—why? Millions of Jews were massacred in gas chambers, women were raped and killed, newborn babies were thrown alive in burning ovens and hundreds were castrated or subjected to mindless medical trials, tested with drugs, frozen to death or exposed to various tortures. Many women were sterilized by the injections that resulted in inflamed ovaries and horrible pain. Ground glass and sawdust was rubbed on the wounds of people by Nazi doctors.

Were the Nazi soldiers, generals and doctors just obeying orders? Milgram had quoted in his 1974 article 'The Perils of Obedience' that

> Stark authority was pitted against the subjects' (participants') strongest moral imperative against hurting others, and, with the subjects' ears ringing with screams of victims, authority won more often than not. The extreme willingness of the adults to go to almost any lengths on the command of an authority constitutes chief finding of the study and the fact more urgently demanding explanation. (Milgram, 1974)

Did a combination of a powerful authoritarian dictator, a belief embedded in their minds by repetition that an inferior race needs to be eliminated, a systematic brainwashing and a mob mentality, all created a context so compelling that it drove hundreds and thousands of Nazis into obeying commands that led them to committing profoundly immoral and insane acts of violence against fellow human beings?

The context can indeed become very powerful and if it is made compelling enough, it can drive and even shape human behaviour.

Late Sumantra Ghoshal, ex-professor at London School of Business, had once talked about 'Smell of the Place'. His brilliant concept that he shared in a World Economic Forum (WEF) talk and his brilliant analogy underlined the power of contexts in shaping and influencing behaviour and mindsets of people. His concept explained why members of a company or for that matter of any organization behaved in a particular way. And many a time when we come in contact with any such organization and its employees, we at times feel delighted, happy and satisfied, while with others we feel disappointed, disillusioned and often cheated. 'Smell of the Place' is a concept that is powerful and enduring. It needs to be understood and discussed by people trying to decipher culture and behaviour of people in organizations.

While I think of the 'Smell of the Place', I feel almost a sense of compulsion to share an anecdote shared by an extremely close friend of mine. The concept could not be better explained in my opinion.

Lalit, a friend of mine who was prospecting a new school for his child, decided to explore a new school. Upon reaching the front desk, he expressed his desire to meet the admission counsellor and the principal of the school. He was given an application form to fill in all the details of the child and parents and to his utter surprise he was asked to pay ₹500 for meeting the admission counsellor. Why on earth he will have to pay to meet the admission counsellor? After all, he did not even know about the school and wasn't the admission counsellor supposed to provide new parents all the information related to the school?

He requested the lady at the front office, but she very curtly told them that this was the rule and they must first pay.

After Lalit paid the requisite ₹500, the counsellor gave them information about the school and took them on a short tour of the school. Some of the things that my friend was learning about the school were surprising him. The kids had lunch in their classrooms and they were not allowed outside. The classes, lunch time, activities, all were supervised. There was no time for the kids to play free or to socialize without the supervision of the teachers. The atmosphere appeared too controlled! We all had a free play time in our schools when we learnt to be on our own. We had our friends, our fights, our laughter and our sobs too. Until today, we cherish those moments and some of our best friends may be our school friends. The safety of the kids also appeared to be compromised with not-so-high railings on each floor in the school building. Despite all this, Lalit decided to hold back his judgement for a while.

The academic engine of any educational institution was faculty and principal, the academic leader, who pretty much set the culture, context and direction of teaching, learning and disciplining. So, Lalit wanted to meet the principal to clarify the doubts in his mind.

Lalit was told that he will have to first pay another ₹1,500 towards some sort of registration fees and his child will have to appear for an entrance exam. Only then they could have an audience with the principal.

What? The principal will only meet a parent after paying ₹2,000! And why the child would be even forced to take an entrance test if the parents were not satisfied with the school. The school felt like some roadside eatery where you will have to first purchase coupons to get a masala dosa!

Additionally, the school had a different mode of teaching in which they integrated a few subjects and tested the students. So, how a kid who is not used to such integrated system of teaching, coming from some other school, could face an entrance exam on the same pattern? None of these questions were answered by the counsellor.

Lalit strongly insisted that he wanted to meet the principal and when he did not budge, the admission counsellor finally asked him to wait. After waiting for about an hour, Lalit, his wife and his nine-year-old child were ushered in the principal's office.

A middle-aged, very serious-looking lady greeted them rather coldly as they entered the office. Lalit and his family were offered seats. Without directly addressing the parent or the child, principal asked the admission counsellor (who had not been offered a seat) for the application form and the entrance result of the child. The counsellor replied that the child had yet not taken the entrance test. The principal looked at Lalit and told them that she would talk to them only after the child has appeared for the entrance test. Lalit tried to explain the reason behind his insistence to meet her before any further formalities but the principal continued to repeat her statement. Lalit understood that the principal was asking them to leave her office and come only after the requisite procedures had been followed.

Lalit's child who was excited about the new school expressed to the principal that he wished to be a scientist when he grew up and that he had done well in various science and maths competitions. He expected a few motivational words but the principal instead retorted, 'Ok, now let us see if you do well in our entrance exam', as if it was some kind of a challenge or a rebuke?

The counsellor, who already had an earful from the principal, further insisted that the child take the entrance test the very same day to avoid any further embarrassment for her. Lalit knew that the entrance test was set on a completely different pattern and that his child was not prepared. He, however, convinced his unwilling child to take the entrance test. And yes, he paid up another ₹1,500.

Lalit and his wife were tremendously disillusioned with the behaviour of the people whom they met in the school. The ultra-commercial nature of the school, the highly controlled environment, bureaucratic systems and scant respect for individuals (whether they were colleagues or guests) shocked them. The child who had gone to the school with heart full of excitement appeared wilted at this moment.

Lalit and his wife had unanimously decided that they will never admit their child in this school, irrespective of the test result. They already knew that the *entrance test was a trap which was meant to ridicule the abilities of a child and make parents feel obliged that despite their child not performing, the school was giving them another opportunity. Lalit came to know that parents besides paying a hefty fees had to buy everything from the school, from books to school bag, stationery and uniform! He also realized later that the entrance test would be waived off for kids who came from 'advantaged' families and whose parents' influence could help the school in some way.*

Predictably, the counsellor called after a week and told Lalit that his child had not been able to clear the entrance test and he will have to appear for a retest. Lalit asked the admission counsellor what they had inferred from the dumb test and why they did not interview the child to understand his thoughts, abilities and creative ideas. The counsellor, however, had no answer to his questions. Lalit simply hung up and sighed a sense of relief. After all, he had only lost ₹2,000 but did not bury the dreams and creativity of his child under the rubble of bureaucratic system that did not know how to treat people and respect them. He did not want his child to grow up in a mass production factory, straight-jacketed, a person who will be transformed to a robot who knows how to follow instructions but has lost power to think or create or dream!

Coming back to the 'Smell of the Place' concept of organizations, Sumantra Ghoshal very aptly stated that revitalizing people had lot less to do with changing people and lot more to do with changing contexts that companies, senior managers and leaders create in their organizations.

Why did the front-office lady or the admission counsellor treat them the way they did? Why did the principal, who was supposed to be an academic first, behave shabbily with her colleagues or with guests?

Sumantra Ghoshal gave a brilliant analogy of how one feels during summers in downtown Kolkata, compared to the feeling of an individual in the forests of Fontainebleau during spring. Kolkata, though being a wonderful place, during summer months transforms into a difficult place to live in. The heat and humidity saps energy and makes one feel tired and exhausted. While during spring, in the forests of Fontainebleau, the crispness in the air and the beautiful smell make one jump and run.

The problem is that most companies have created summers of downtown Kolkata inside their organizations and expect people to be engaged, to jump, to run, to contribute, to innovate and to be creative. The 'Smell of the Place' is that of constraint, compliance (fit in the system, stick by rules, do not question procedures), control (power is centralized, decision-making is controlled, people are not empowered) and contract (everything is just a transaction).

Companies that create the forests of Fontainebleau of spring have a different *smell,* that of stretch (everyone is inspired and motivated to go beyond the obvious), discipline (people are not supervised, not constantly monitored; self-discipline, accountability and responsibility prevails instead), trust (leaders create a culture of trust; people are not doubted for their actions and initiatives) and support (leaders exist to support their people).

I believe that Lalit smelt summers of downtown Kolkata in the new school.

The context can indeed be powerful in shaping mindsets and behaviours.

In 1971, when Philip Zimbardo conducted the Stanford Prison Experiment (SPE), little did he know that he will not only provide answers to the 'puzzles' of the past but also unlock secrets to the future.

For SPE, a mock prison was created at the basement of the Psychology department of Stanford University. Out of the 75 people who volunteered for the experiment, in response to a newspaper advertisement, 24 males were carefully selected and were randomly assigned guard and prisoner roles. All 24 males selected for the experiment were normal ordinary people with no criminal past. The 'guards' were given uniform, a baton, dark glasses and certain powers that allowed them to enforce discipline in the prison. The researchers held an orientation session for guards the day before the experiment, during which they instructed them not to physically harm the prisoners.

The ones who were assigned prisoner role were taken by surprise when they were arrested from their homes or public places, handcuffed by real police officers in full public gaze. They were taken to a police station and booked for petty crimes and taken through all routine procedures before shifting them to the 'prison'. At the prison, they were stripped naked and were given a prisoner cloak to wear. Each prisoner was assigned a number that would become their identity for the next few days. Zimbardo designed the experiment in order to induce disorientation, de-personalization and de-individualization among the 'prisoners'.

Zimbardo took on the role of the superintendent, and an undergraduate research assistant was assigned the role of prison warden. In the prison, while guards had shift duty, the prisoners had to stay in small prison cells for the entire period of the experiment.

Nothing eventful happened on the first day. But when some prisoners started disobeying the guards resisting their authority, the guards turned to the prison warden for directions. They were in turn asked to enforce prison discipline. From there onwards, the lines between experiment and reality started to blur. The prisoners started acting as real prisoners and the prison guards as real guards. The guards on their own started to physically reprimand the prisoners. As the revolt grew among prisoners, the guards progressively dehumanized and tortured the prisoners. Basic human privileges were taken away from some prisoners. Good and bad prison cells were earmarked. The prisoners who obeyed were put into good cell and given some privileges. While the prisoners who revolted were stripped naked, asked to sleep in bare floor, not allowed restroom breaks and even put in isolation cells. The prisoners started to act and feel like real victims—some showed signs of withdrawal, some revolted and others broke down.

Surprisingly, while all this was happening inside the prison, Philip Zimbardo, the principal investigator and the 'prison warden' were so absorbed in the experiment that they did nothing to stop it even as the conditions in the prison turned from bad to worse.

He aborted the experiment prematurely in six days instead of two weeks when Christina Maslach, a graduate student in psychology, whom he was dating (and later married), objected to the conditions of the prison after she was introduced to the experiment to conduct interviews. Zimbardo also noted that, of more than 50 people who had observed the experiment, Maslach was the only one who questioned its morality, while all others including the principal investigator had been absorbed in the experiment.

The symbols of power (uniform and wooden batons) given to the guards, a sense of legitimacy to their actions, dark glasses given to them and numbers assigned to prisoners that allowed for greater degree of de-personalization, the artificial helplessness created for the prisoners, all made the situation so powerful and compelling that the line between the experiment and reality completely blurred. The situation altered the behaviour completely.

Decades later, in 2004, when the first pictures and video of torture of Iraqi prisoners at the hands of the American prison guards at the Abu Ghraib prison started leaking, they sadly but surprisingly resembled the images of SPE.

Abu Ghraib prison near Baghdad, the capital of Iraq, that had been reportedly the centre of torture and mass execution under Saddam's rule had been (so-called) liberated by the US Army. In reality, however, the American soldiers committed serious human rights violations against Iraqi prisoners. They physically and sexually abused, tortured, raped, sodomized and killed prisoners. Many prisoners were illegally detained in the prison and were denied basic human privileges such as drinking water, washing facilities and fresh set of clothes. Despite the fact that between 2003 and 2004 American soldiers committed heinous tortures on Iraqi prisoners, it will be incorrect to assume that the USA and allied army personnel that included even female soldiers were evil. They were normal competent people carefully recruited through a standardized system. Then why did they resort to such dastardly acts of human rights violation?

A close look at the details makes clear how the situation played a powerful and compelling role. The acts of extreme humiliation and abuse were committed by the US Military Police Reserves. They were not the soldiers prepared for this mission at all. Additionally, all this happened at a single place—Tier 1A on the night shift. This place was the centre of military intelligence, the interrogation centre. The CIA and US Army were not getting any information on insurgency and they put pressure on the military reserves to elicit information from the prisoners. And this is how it was interpreted. That kind of thing gave them the power of oppression.

In short, the contextual forces brought the evil out of them. The ones who were outside the context and viewed it from 'outside' behaved contrarily. Schiendler in the case of Nazi oppression who single-handedly rescued 300 Jews from Auschwitz, Christina Maslach who stopped the SPE and Joe Darby, a lower level private who for the first time brought the

Abu Ghraib prison torture to the notice of US authorities were all heroes.

Behind all is the power of the context. Zimbardo calls this Lucifer effect. He argues that behaviour is a dynamic interplay between individual dispositions or what's inside people, situation or the external factors around the person and the system that alters political, economic, social and legal variables. Psychologists believe that behaviours are transformed because of the situation and situations are created by the power of the system.

Understanding foundation of human behaviour is at the core of understanding behaviour of millennials. Behaviour is determined by what people bring to the table or what's inside them but more importantly by what context brings out of them and how do the systemic forces alter the context.

Foundations of Millennial Behaviour

Every generation exhibits behavioural traits that are unique. More so if the era they live in is a transformed one in comparison to the previous one. Millennials in particular live in an era that has seen change far greater than any other. These changes have populated both the macro and micro contexts. The resultant generational effect has been unique.

Millennials have gained importance considering the fact that their numbers and influence shall grow phenomenally in the years to come. Also known as the Gen Y or echo boomers, millennials are the fastest-growing workforce segment. Millennial consumer's expenditures on cars, apparel and other items are growing and soon will exceed those of previous generations. A Speciality Equipment Market Association research says that millennials are purchasing vehicles in large numbers and more than 50 per cent plan on spending additional funds to personalize and modify their vehicles. The estimated spending power of millennials is $1.6 trillion and estimated discretionary non-essential spending is about $430 billion. Undoubtedly, millennials are the fastest-growing workforce and marketplace force. Increasing awareness and understanding of this group and adapting strategies to suit their needs will help us to attract and retain them. Millennials often evoke extreme reactions.

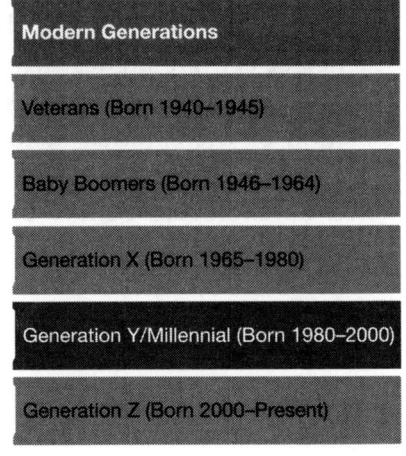

Modern Generations

Veterans (Born 1940–1945)

Baby Boomers (Born 1946–1964)

Generation X (Born 1965–1980)

Generation Y/Millennial (Born 1980–2000)

Generation Z (Born 2000–Present)

Generation Y, millennials to some, are those young workers who walk into the office with a digital assistant in one hand and a Starbucks latte in the other. They gladly accept the door keycard and PIN, wave hello to the security video camera in the lobby; arm themselves with the company laptops and connect them to their personal Blackberries. They quickly log in to Facebook and MySpace during the work day. They're not afraid to download new applications and fiddle with security and power settings. (Security Magazine, 2009)

There have been fancier descriptions of millennials' behaviour. Most of the contemporary researches have aimed at describing the behaviour of the millennials. Some of them describe millennials as consumers, as employees, as information-seekers, etc.

Interestingly, many of such observations have bordered or ventured in the realm of myth and have created a certain understanding or say rather misunderstanding about them. Many business managers feel that hiring millennial employees is as difficult as attracting millennial customers. Millennial employees and customers are considered to be smart, opinionated and have grown up with a multitude of choices. They are not afraid to challenge authority and are willing to confront the status quo. Because of this, they have often been branded as brash, too ambitious, impatient and the ones who lack wisdom, more difficult than the previous generation. They are also termed as high-maintenance and entitled generation, those who always have an opinion and want to be asked for it, even otherwise share it and want others to act on their opinion as well.

How Context Shaped Millennials

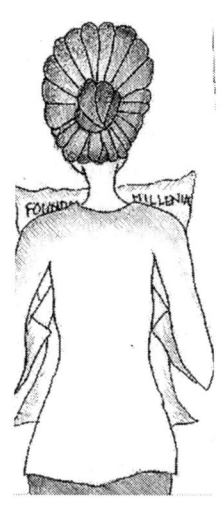

Managing requires, by default, understanding. What isn't understood can't be managed. Understanding in turn requires investigation. Human behaviour must be understood to be managed; therefore, it's imperative that behaviour is investigated to gain understanding. Much of what we encounter as behaviour could be fashioned by environmental conditioning the person in question was subject to. The environment shapes behaviour via the influence of reference groups that populate it. Much of a child's behaviour is learned from the family the child belongs to. With age, there's greater exposure to other reference groups that include informal groups, social class and culture. Contextual influences have a strong bearing on one's behaviour.

It is surmised that millennials' behaviour also follows such norms. Before one manages millennials, one must try and understand the wellspring from which this particular class' behaviour emerged.

My study was aimed at exploring the role of context in shaping millennial mindset and behaviour. To understand the same, it was also important that it be contrasted to the previous generation's behaviour. For the purpose of the study, it was postulated that this behavioural contrast that is 'peripherally' apparent has explanations associated with the context that baby boomers and millennials grew up in the times we believe were different. Baby boomers grew up in a certain context, millennials in another. As part of the conceptualization, segregation within the contexts was investigated. This segregation is based on causative variables that can be clustered under macro and micro variables. The study proposed that the macro variables at play fashion a unique micro context which in turn has a major influence on shaping behaviour.

The study involved exploring five behaviours, namely expenditure, investment, job hopping, technology affinity and socialization, and contrast baby boomers and millennials. The study was done to confirm whether macro and micro environmental factors played a role in shaping the generational behaviour. Such an understanding will have a tremendous impact not only in understanding millennials behaviour but also in managing them as employees, customers, investors, information-seekers, students and individuals.

Several in-depth interactions with scores of X and Y respondents were undertaken and contrasts were drawn across macro and micro variables at play, shaping a context across two different time zones as relevant to baby boomers and millennials. The interaction transcripts were compared and the finding clearly illustrated that when the environmental variables at play alter, they alter contexts, thus altering behaviour.

Savers Versus Spenders

'Think; save some; spend some' has been the mantra when it comes to money for baby boomers. Most baby boomers are careful spenders and have saving habits. Their spending is mostly on essentials and almost has a sense of guilt when it comes to lifestyle expenditures. For baby boomers, the times were different when most of them started their careers. Jobs were hard to come by and compensation was not that attractive. 'Save it for the rainy day' had been deep ingrained in their minds by their baby boomer parents.

Baby boomers had some very interesting things to say:

Those days were different, had to wait for entire lifetime for a home, several years for a car. Today, the scenario is different; few years in industry can help you to get a house loan, few months of salary is equal to the value of a car. At that time, we thought of lifetime employment; today, one year is a lifetime.

We were made to believe that wealth can be built by saving. I carefully spent the income primarily on subsistence. Fact is that neither we had too many things to buy (choice) nor we had too much money to spend.

Millennials on the other hand are more conspicuous spenders. They have grown up in a time that has seen much more global and buoyant economy and higher incomes than their predecessors. Millennials and savings is an oxymoron. Typically, overspending and undersaving is a characteristic feature. They are more like sailors on an annual shore leave than like someone having a financial goal. Most of the expenditure is on lifestyle enhancements or leisure spending such as on cars, bikes, mobile phones, technology products, clothes, electronic gadgets, restaurants, partying with friends, entertainment, holiday and travel. Millennials also outpace their older counterparts in visiting Western or American-themed bars/nightclubs and eating American fast food. On the other hand, home ownership is down among millennials compared to baby boomers. They do plan to have children and buy a home, but just later than their predecessors—in their 30s instead of their 20s.

Stayers Versus Seekers

Jobs were not too many and were hard to come by for baby boomers. The challenge was always to find a job that could last a lifetime. The job security was immense. In the absence of too many jobs available in the market and high security in their current jobs, baby boomers proved to be more of stayers than job hoppers.

A rapid globalization, privatization and liberalization that swept the world in the 1980s and 1990s, muscled by technological advancements, saw the emergence of a global economy and sudden spurt in number and variety of opportunities and jobs for millennials. Job hopping became normal and even considered essential if one wanted to really grow in his/her career.

'One life, one job' theory was defunct. A new theory had started to take its place—'one life, one or multiple careers and definitely multiple jobs'. Most millennials do not mind hopping jobs. They are not very sentimental about their companies and would consider hopping if they get a good opportunity. Millennial workers don't see career paths in the traditional sense and look for companies that are much more flexible. While baby boomers had, on an average, eight jobs over the course of their career, millennials have 29.1 jobs across five industries. Millennials move from one job to the next at a rapid-fire pace. This also does not mean that millennials are not retainable. However, companies have to try harder to retain and engage them. In later chapters, we will see the new rule of engaging millennials.

Defenders Versus Riskers

Baby boomers have seen times when economy was flat, industry was mostly stagnant, jobs were hard to come by and incomes were low. Baby boomers have typically very low risk appetites and they hardly invested in stock markets. Stock markets were considered non-lucrative and risky. After necessary expenditures, baby boomers believed in keeping the rest as savings or invest in secured investments such as post office bonds and fixed deposits.

According to Fidelity Investments, a US-based financial services firm, millennial millionaires are more bullish investors than their older-generation counterparts. In other words, compared to baby boomer millionaires, the millennial millionaires are buying into high-risk asset classes such as venture capital and derivatives. Millennials have grown up at a time that saw a buoyant economy and a sudden explosion in stock markets. Their greater appetite for risk is very clear. In fact when asked, they said that they preferred to pursue more aggressive investment strategies. Wealthy next generations or millennials also had a more diversified investment portfolio than the older generations. They are not only more confident about investing but also consider themselves more knowledgeable. Although millennials may need advice on investing, yet they manage most of their assets themselves.

Millennials have seen 9/11 and 26/11 terrorist attacks and institutions vanishing in a day (the Lehman Brothers crisis). All this while, they have been brought up by parents who have told them that they are capable of doing anything and achieving anything. Their parents have never let their confidence levels to dip. In fact, even the financial crisis that started in 2008 and the great depression that followed could not dampen the spirits of millennials. Five years after the recession set in, millennials remained confident despite suffering financial losses and did not panic or overreact like their parents. Fidelity Investments findings released in a study 'Five Years Later' revealed that millennials have instead taken a more careful approach to their finances and assumed greater control on their spending and investing habits. They are also willing to do things in a different way. As compared to baby boomers, millennials stand out as more upbeat age group even in times of recession.

Technophobes Versus Technophiles

When baby boomers started working, workplaces were largely non-automated. The incidence of technology was very low, almost negligible. Baby boomers have largely been averse to technology or technophobic.

There was no technology so there is no question of being tech-savvy. Even in 1986 in the SBI capital market office there were only 2 desktops which had MS DOS, WordStar & lotus 1,2,3. Each machine could have costed 4–5 lakhs. For lotus 1,2,3 only brief manuals were available, no classes could be taken.

It may come as a surprise to many today that many members of baby boomers actually opposed new technology at workplace. They saw entry of technology as a threat to their jobs!

When computer were introduced after 80s all Indian banks typists went on strike. They were given a guarantee by the bank much on their job security. They were also given assurance of training. Later they became very good computer operators.

Millennials on the contrary have been brought up in an age of technological revolution and automation. They are very comfortable with technology. Most of them use a wide range of apps and download software, movies, music and other content from the Web.

Millennials use their Web-enabled mobile phones more for fun than anything else. They use their smartphones and tablets to download or stream video or music files, send or receive text messages and pictures, play games or get entertainment news and information. And not just that, it was recently found that more than 30 per cent of millennials use their mobile devices daily to search for a job. From texting to podcasting to posting on FB, WhatsApp and Twitter, millennials live in a technology-infused environment that allows them to stay connected 24×7.

One baby boomer respondent made an interesting observation about millennials:

In earlier times, if you would take cigarettes from smokers, you would see withdrawal symptoms in them. Today if you take technology out of people, they will have withdrawal symptoms. If you take mobile from a youngster, he will fall sick; if you ban Facebook for a week, it may be a greater punishment than anything else for that youngster.

That kind of sums it up all. Technology and millennials really go hand in hand, and the mobile phone is their lifeline. They are termed as 'digital natives' who are more interactive online than other age group; they like the simultaneous pairing of information and entertainment. Technology helps them to be flexible and remain connected.

Face to Facebook

For baby boomers, the socialization was limited and mostly real face-to-face than virtual. Socialization was curtailed and moderated by social and family norms. Inter-gender socialization was a taboo in India.

> During my college days, I was secretary of literature and finance club. One day I was talking to another fellow girl-student just to find out whether she would deliver a talk on the occasion of Independence Day celebration. Principal must have seen me talking to her. Later in the day, he summoned me and asked me about my conversation with that girl. I was perplexed.

> Socialization then was more face-to-face. For today's generation, it is more Facebook. However, friendship has no depth these days like we had in those times. My childhood friend now in his 70s was suffering terminal illness. I visited him in Chennai four times last year, before he passed away.

Avenues to socialize for baby boomers were mostly limited to the immediate family, friends and society. They had limited social circle and were at times even reluctant to socialize too much. Millennials, however, live in a networked world with digitized micro networks. They feel good to be connected and are extremely well-networked. Most of their contacts are online and they heavily use social media for networking. They are more mobile and global, and they feel good to get information from anywhere at the click of their finger.

Here's what millennials had to say about their social life:

I have about 950 Facebook friends, 250 connections on Twitter and 160 connections on LinkedIn. I check my Facebook account at least once a day. It helps me to know about the major life events of my friends, but it is more a random activity. On LinkedIn, however, I am consciously building my profile.

Millennials live a high-pace, time-constrained life. For them, face-to-face socialization is difficult and cumbersome.

I am socially lazy. I need social media. Facebook has helped me to stay connected. Friends do not call me often. The best thing about Facebook is that it allows you to know a lot about people without really involving much with them. Facebook also helps to keep a tab on the major life events of my friends and also keep a track of the interests of my friends.

Millennial's need and desire to stay connected on social media is extremely high. They find it hard to imagine a life without having an existence on the virtual world.

A millennial when asked how she will react if she finds herself cut off from FB and WhatsApp, she had to say:

I will not panic if I see a light at the end of the tunnel. But I need to stay connected. Recently, I broke my phone and along with it my connection apps like 'WhatsApp'. I found it quite strange that my phone was not buzzing.

'Kids of the Times'

Too many times, managing millennials has left people both amused and appalled. They are at their wits' end trying to make sense of what and why millennials do, both at and outside work. However, such behaviour doesn't need to be baffling anymore. There's an explanation that is steeped in contextual influences. Millennials are who they are, thanks to the times they live in. Ditto for baby boomers. If baby boomers saved, attribute it to an economic and job scenario. If millennials spend with abandon, that's because the economy is buoyant and so is the job scene, which means that there's more disposable income and greater career security. This causative scenario is true for all behavioural exhibitions. Their job hopping, behaviour, high appetite for risk, tech affinity and preference for virtual socialization, and desire to stay connected have all been fashioned by the contextual influences.

Understanding these causative factors of millennial behaviour won't automatically mean that millennials can be managed better. It will only provide for a mooring to base interventions aimed at managing millennial behaviour. Understanding the source of behaviour goes a long way in understanding behaviour. This in turn builds a strong basis for action that can have greater effectiveness as is designed out of this understanding. For example, the greater freedom with which millennials take to issues only shows that they are children of a freer society. This means that organizational designers have to keep in their mind that the need for freedom and defending bureaucratic structures will be difficult. Tall structures with strong bureaucracy and limited flexibility will surely stifle millennials. This may have an adverse effect on retention. Wanting to keep bureaucracy the way it existed in past by a baby boomer manager will turn more a stumbling block than an initiator when it comes to motivating and managing millennials.

In the context of the workplace, they've often been described as 'overly ambitious dreamers who don't want to pay their dues and are only concerned about higher pay and more time off'. A recent Deloitte's study on the existing millennial workers finds that these characterizations miss the story. The study states and I quote:

Millennials are a hidden powerhouse of employee potential, critical for global business in tough times. Future-oriented, ready to contribute now, opportunity-driven: these are the characteristics of a generation that is already making its mark on the work world. They remain optimistic in the midst of the current economic turmoil. But Millennials are also highly restless. The generation brought up in an era of rapid technological change will seek to earn greater opportunities for rapid advancement and more responsibilities at a younger age, requiring organizations to change the way they attract, develop, promote and retain these talented individuals. In short, they're fundamentally different from other iconic generations. (Deloitte, 2017)

Thus, I reiterate the need to understand contextual and environmental influences which are never static but evolve and change. This means keeping a track of changes on the outside will be important in understanding millennial behaviour that will emerge in such changed scenarios.

PART II

The Life of 'Y'

3
EMOTIONAL AND SOCIAL WELLNESS PARADOX

The concept of wellness was introduced post Second World War. The rapid industrialization and beginning of the industrial era set in motion high physical, emotional and psychological demands from people. As the world progressed towards a modern world and a modern life, these demands only grew and consequently the stressors increased. Well-being of a person ceased to be determined only by the absence of a physical ailment. Curing illness was being replaced by the concept of preserving wellness of a person. Wellness elements include, besides the body, the mind and the spirit as well. There have been many attempts to describe or define wellness. But owing to the subjective nature of wellness, there have been several interpretations of the same. The World Health Organization (WHO) was the first to introduce a holistic description of health of a person as 'a state of complete physical, mental, and social well-being and not merely the absence of disease and infirmity'. Nothing better describes wellness of an individual until date.

A state of complete holistic wellness is a state of happiness. In the second section of the book, as we dive deeper into understanding the life of millennials, we examine their primary four wellness elements—emotional, social, physical and material wellness. We try to gain an understanding as to how the contexts that have shaped them have impacted their wellness aspects, their state of happiness and their life. Such an understanding forms the fundamental basis of understanding how to engage them better. In this chapter, we examine the emotional and social wellness of millennials.

Where Are My Friends?

Mani had over 500 FB friends, some of whom he had met once in a while, mostly his office colleagues, but most of whom he had met only once and became FB friends with. Some of his FB friends he had met only virtually. They sent requests, their profile and photos appeared nice and he accepted their friend requests. Before he knew it, voila, he had hundreds of friends! Every day he was looking at photos of people whom he had never met or will perhaps never meet, pressing likes; sometimes even sharing his comments; looking at their travels, adventures, misadventures, updates about new material possessions, or about a new job, promotion, award, etc.—the list was long and

exhaustive. Few days back, while reflecting on his newly found score of friends, he asked himself how many were for real. He decided to put up an FB post, 'Real friends click likes. I am looking for mine!' He got some 50 likes by the end of the day. He was disappointed—50 out of 500, that's just 10 per cent. But then on the brighter side, it seemed he had at least 50 real friends! But he was not satisfied with his finding. So, he decided to do an experiment. He was really besieged by this concept of real friends and he was determined to know how many he had. Mani had long been overdue for a vacation. So, he took a week's off from office without really telling any of his colleagues. Just a mail to HR and that's it. He left for an undisclosed location for that week. None of his colleagues, neighbours or acquaintances had any idea where he was headed for. No FB updates, no FB check-ins; in fact, he logged out of his FB account for a week and did not use WhatsApp or any other social media app. He just wanted to see if his absence made any difference to the lives of his online 'friends'. He expected some of them to call him, mail him or try to get in touch with him. By the end of the week, he had not been contacted by even one of his FB friends, nothing on WhatsApp as well. His worst fears had come true. None of his FB or WhatsApp connections were real friends. Forget about real, not even friends. They were just connections! He came back from his self-imposed incognito and deleted all his social media accounts.

Mani is not alone in his failed quest to find real friends among his online friends. In all my interactions with millennials, when I asked them that out of their hundreds, sometimes even more than a thousand, online 'friends', how many of them, in their opinion, would stand by them through thick and thin and how many of them would be a part of their major life events, most of them could name only one, very few of them could name about two, while some of them (not surprising anymore) could not name even a single online 'friend'. Millennials seem to be great at making connections but find it really hard to make friends! I call this the *friend paradox*. They have hundreds of online connections, many times called 'friends', but in reality have hardly anyone whom they can call their friend. So, at times, this illusion of having friends, yet being in a friendless situation, can be immensely stressful and a lonely feeling.

Friendless millennials have generally struggled in making friends. Trust seems one of the issues in their being friend famished. D. C. McAllister (2014) wrote a piece on millennials and trust issues for *The Federalist*, citing a report from the Associated Press which shows that millennials trust people less than any generation before them:

> In the mid-1980s, when baby boomers were coming of age, about a third of high school seniors agreed that 'most people can be trusted'. That dropped to 18 percent in the early 1990s for Gen Xers—and then, in 2012, to just 16 percent of Millennials. (McAllister, 2014)

They have grown up at a time of global recession, terrorism, rising corporate greed and insider trading. They have seen institutions crumbling and integrity becoming a rare commodity, and they have been warned by their parents while they were growing up not to trust anyone other than themselves for anything. In short, they have seen a more deceitful side of the world. They do not trust families or marriage that much as divorce rates have climbed up; they do not trust society in general and hence they do not involve themselves in community activities. Overall, there is a huge trust deficit in millennials. The same applies to making friends. For making friends, one has to first trust and understand the other person. Their belief that their friends will stand by them is not very high. Instead, they pretty much know that they will have to fend for themselves and nobody will be there in times of their need.

When Arjun, a 23-year-old student, jumped off the 19th floor of a posh hotel in Mumbai, it looked like yet another suicide case. But as details started tumbling out, the incident appeared even more ghastly and heartbreaking. He checked-in to a premier five-star hotel in the wee hours of morning on the fateful day and posted a video tutorial on FB on how to commit suicide. He then consumed wine, broke the glass of the window apparently with a chair, shared his last post on FB 'see you on the other side' and jumped to his death. The details are enough to send a chill down anyone's spine. But his case should be seen as that of an outlier and ignored. He came to the city four years ago with dreams in his eyes and with aspirations of making a career in this city of dreams. Hailing from a business family, he joined a professional course in a reputed college of the city. Everything appeared good until his academic performance started dwindling. Depression and drug addiction came almost together. The pressure soon became intolerable. What makes the case even more unfortunate and distressing is the fact that an analysis of his FB updates clearly showed his state of mind. It seems that his father had visited him few days back. But after his father left, he again started showing suicidal tendencies. His suicide tutorial became viral on social media but could not bring a friend to save his life.

Brishti has been far more fortunate with friends, although none of the four bosom buddies she has are her FB friends. They are her childhood friends who grew up together and today, although they are thrown apart in terms of distance and time, they remain best of friends. She finds it easy to share all her happiness, worries and pain with these friends. She made friends in college as well but neither they nor her two hundred odd FB friends match her childhood buddies. These were the friends with whom she had loads of fun; they were with her during her difficult years, at a time when her late father suffered a kidney failure; and they are still the ones who are her close confidantes. But with these friends scattered now, and with no real friends online or offline around, she still finds herself craving for genuine buddies.

FB friends are generally not real friends, just connections; professional acquaintances are rarely friends as it is more a competitive environment and since millennials do not socialize much in the real world, they do not have friends there either.

Richard Hoggart in 1957 had written in *The Uses of Literacy* about the 'uprooted and anxious'. These were the talented boys of post-war Britain who were born working class but ameliorated themselves through education. In the process of doing so, they left their communities for good and as a result became sad and solitary figures. For the uprooted and anxious man, there was no direction home. They were too tense and self-conscious to drift into middle-class gatherings with self-confidence, nor could they think of staying friendly with people of their own class. They found themselves not belonging to either of these groups and hence were odd men out! Today, millennials find themselves in a similar situation. Brought up by helicopter parents who always rushed to rescue their child, hardly taught them how to take care of themselves in a world that cannot be trusted easily. Parents became their best friends but as they grew up, they found it difficult to share everything with parents. Technology and social media brought the world to their fingertips and made sure that their online world became a parallel world. Today, they are torn between online and offline world; they learnt how to take care of themselves but do not know as much what caring for a stranger is about. They are close to their parents yet cannot keep calling them their best friends. And, having become used to their own space, they are torn, as Freud had said, between freedom and security. They find it difficult to make friends as too much intimacy limits their freedom and at the same time grapple with loneliness, lack of support and crave for real relationship and security. They find themselves belonging to neither of the 'groups'. Such paradoxical pulls make them 'uprooted and anxious', and constantly trying to balance between freedom and security, online and offline, parents and the society, and friendlessness and at the same time desire to make friends. Their friendships and relationships are more like Bauman's *Liquid Love*. Bauman, a professor of sociology at University of Leeds, wrote this book that is dedicated to what he calls our liquid modern society.

The hero of the book has no affinity connections and has to constantly use his skill, wits and dedication to create provisional bonds that are loose enough to stop suffocation, but tight enough to give a needed sense of security now that the traditional sources of solace are less reliable than ever (Bauman, 2003).

The hero of Bauman's book is constantly babbling into mobile phones, addictively texting, hopping from one chat room to another and dating online. The liquid modern is forever at work, forever replacing quality of relationship with quantity. Millennials today find themselves in a situation where their hundreds of online friends seem to be replacing quality relationships, yet that quantity never seems good enough for that one real friend.

Unable to find real friends, ironically but not surprisingly, many millennials are turning to their trusted and constant companion—technology—to fetch them friends. A whole business model is developing around the concept of finding friends for millennials. These apps are in a way promising 'we will get you friends…'.

For the 20 somethings and 30 somethings of NYC, an app called GoFindFriends offers such a solution. Using the app, one can browse profiles, see the one they like, see pictures, email people and set up events together. The app is designed to help millennials find friends.

Once new users register and set up profiles (including photos and activities and events they will like to do in the city), GoFindFriends uses an algorithm to match them with potential friends. GoFindFriends and similar apps are trying to bring millennials closer to other millennials with similar interests and then encouraging them to meet in real life.

Gathr, a social entertainment app, is organizing gatherings and parties for Internet-weary millennials. Recently, they organized a series of such gatherings in Bengaluru that are becoming popular. One such gathering featured three iconic artists—David Bowie, Prince and Leonard Cohen—and put together a playlist as well as nuanced stories about their lives and how their work came to be. Each gathering is limited to 30 people to keep it intimate yet social. Word on such parties is usually circulated among common groups of friends and social media. Millennials attending such gatherings feel that these occasions provide them meaningful conversations rather than mere social interactions at a pub or faceless interactions over social media.

Similar apps are providing friends for travelling together. Specially targeted towards millennials, their desire to travel with a friend yet being unable to find one has resulted in apps such as backpackr.org, lonelyplanet.com, travbuddy.com and triptogether.com that help millennials find a friend and a companion to travel. One can create a profile and post travel preferences or any recent travel plans. One can also browse through the profiles and can connect with people with similar travel preferences or join people travelling to a similar destination.

If the idea of finding a friend through an app, all for a while, is not weird enough, then it is made even weirder by the idea of renting a friend. Yes, you heard it right! When Clay Kohut, a Texas-born developer and entrepreneur and a millennial himself, pitched for his new app Ameego, he put the idea in what can be probably underlined as search for a friend. 'With Uber, you rent a stranger's car; with Airbnb, you rent a stranger's home; and with Ameego, you rent a stranger!' Rent a friend? Really? So, the new idiom should be 'A friend when I need is a friend I meet!'

Relationship Status: Complicated!

Prerna has always been a very quiet and studious girl. Always the topper in her batch, she never had too many boys as friends. Her female friends were also limited. She had always been serious about her career and she got a job offer on day one of campus place-

ments in one of Indian IT majors (we will call it company A). Even better, she got her posting in her hometown Kolkata. In her first two years at the company, she always got top ratings from her superiors and soon got her first promotion. She was now the team lead. Her parents had long been pursuing her about marriage. Finally, they found her an alliance. The boy Vikram (name

...It's complicated...

changed) worked in another Indian IT major (we will call it company B) but was on an extended-term expat assignment in the USA. Soon their marriage was solemnized. After the marriage, since Vikram's company had no office in Kolkata and Prerna had no present opportunity of going to the USA, they both applied for transfer. With some effort, they both could get transfer to Bhubaneshwar in their respective companies. They stayed together for one year. But after that, Vikram started getting restless. One day, he told Prerna that he could not compromise his career for anything and he will have to go to the USA for another extended assignment. Prerna offered to resign from her company but Vikram did not want her to sacrifice her career.

Vikram left for the USA and Prerna lived alone in Bhubaneshwar. Days rolled into months and months into a year. Vikram's assurances of returning soon kept coming but he kept extending his return date every time. Meanwhile, Prerna faced many difficulties living alone in Bhubaneshwar. Once when she contracted typhoid, she just had the auto driver to take her to the doctor and bring her back to her apartment. Finally, when one of her friends came to know of her state during a chance phone call and informed her parents in Kolkata, they rushed to take care of her. When two years passed and Vikram still did not come back, Prerna applied for a transfer back to Kolkata. Prerna had grown up in Kolkata and was very familiar with the city. Additionally, her parents could at times come and live with her. Her wait for Vikram was becoming long. Prerna never fell short of her duties and during Vikram's absence, when his mother was hospitalized, she took time off her job and took care of her mother-in-law. After three years, Vikram came back to India. He is in Bhubaneshwar and Prerna is in Kolkata. Now even she does not want to leave her job or career. Will they ever get back together? Being so used to living alone, will they be able to live together and make necessary adjustments? Both Prerna and Vikram's parents are anxious. They tried talking to their respective children but to no avail. Prerna's friends had advised her that they both should start focusing on their relationship and having a family together. But career still seemed to be priority. Will Prerna and Vikram's marriage last or is this relationship headed for 'splitsville'?

A 2017 study by the Centre for the Study of Developing Societies (CSDS) in partnership with Konrad-Adenauer-Stiftung (KAS) shows that Indian millennials no longer consider marriage as important (LOKNITI–CSDS–KAS, 2017). The survey conducted among 15–34-year-olds showed that in the last 10 years, the number of youths who believed in marriage had dropped sharply. While in 2007, 80 per cent of the youth believed that marriage was important, 10 years later, in 2017, only about 50 per cent of the youth considered the same. Although acceptance of inter-caste marriages had grown, but marriage as an institution was on the wane. Does this also indicate growing career priorities among both genders and that they were no longer willing to make concessions to the same for relationships or for marriage?

Sona, who is currently in the final semester of her MBA, by her own admission says,

> *I think for us millennials, relationships is a complex entity. We are smart and think we know what we want, but in reality we do not realize what we actually want out of a relationship. Many of us do not realize the value of a relationship when we are in it and appreciate only after the person leaves us or we leave the other person. I do not know why we do that—maybe we have more choices today or maybe we are not planning that much for the future. I sometimes feel that many relationships that I see of my classmates are just for namesake. Not all relationships are frivolous though, but then I don't think either the boy or the girl is ready to make any adjustment today to keep the relationship intact. If career priorities demand or if some concessions need to be made for ensuring social compatibility, relationships do not last.*

Sona herself has gone through the roller-coaster ride of multiple relationships. Her first boyfriend dates back to her school days, when she was still a middle schooler. That lasted nine years. The boy for whom she fell was a wayward and prone to substance abuse. However, he always treated her very well. She was able to transform the boy completely and he came out of his addictions and bad habits. Despite all this, she could not convince her father, who saw no problem with the boy but had reservations with the boy's family who did not particularly have a good reputation. She came from Delhi to Mumbai to complete her MBA and got into a new relationship. This time, just a few months down the line she realized that the boy was not serious and she was just another star on his already 'decorated' ribbon that boasted of more than 30 girlfriends that he had in past. She walked out of this relationship. Her third relationship also ended in a disaster when she found that her boyfriend was actually cheating on her and the other girl was none other than her best friend. This also ended. Three unsuccessful relationships left her distraught and broken. She found a comforting shoulder in Prijosh who helped her come out of the shock. Today, Prijosh is a very good friend and although he has very strong feelings for Sona, she finds it hard to reciprocate the same. She respects Prijosh, likes him too, but she is not sure whether she can have another boyfriend or even look at a long-term future of this relationship. She still has not completely got over her first relationship and is in touch with her first boyfriend. He is now engaged. She knows Prijosh loves her but she does not know whether Prijosh or for that matter anyone will be able to match up to the way her first boyfriend treated her or made her feel. She is very clear about her career and plans to start her entrepreneurial journey soon after completing her business programme but is not sure about future of her relationship. She no longer wants to get married, and she thinks that it is not needed for her to lead her life.

A study by the National Center for Family and Marriage Research (NCFMR, 2017) at Bowling Green State University reveals that fewer and fewer millennials are likely to tie the knot as compared to baby boomers in the 1980s. In 1980, two-thirds of the 25–34-year-olds were already married, while in 2015, just two in five millennials were married. There are clear signs that millennials delay marriage, kids and home owner-ship. This does not mean though that millennials are in any way lazy compared to the previous generation. It is just that marriage is hitting a fatigue level with millennials. They have focused on education (more than the previous generation) and career, and they never had time or perhaps too much inclina-tion to focus on relationships.

Millennials' propensity towards sex also seems to be low. According to a research from the Archives of Sexual Behaviour (Burns, 2016), millennials are significantly less likely to have sex than their Gen X counterparts. Rising teen pregnancy in the 1980s and rapid spread of AIDS during the same time ensured that parents of millennials warned them about sex, put them through scary sex education and continually stressed on the need to focus on professional and academic pursuits. The Internet, mobile and social media ensured that millennials had an access to everything at their fingertips. It is interesting that millennials find it more comfortable to date online using platforms like Tinder than in real life. Tinder, launched by Hatch Labs in 2012, by 2014 was registering about one billion 'swipes' per day. It is also interesting to note that despite a general nonchalance of millennials towards sex, sexting has been very common among them. While it is still not clear whether sexting is preferred by most millennials, the prevalence of sexting among this cohort more than others cannot be denied. The rapid development and adoption of online digital technologies has had a profound effect on the way young people conduct their social relationships. And consequently, the emergence of sexting, or the distribution of sexually explicit photos and videos, has gained widespread attention (Lee, Crofts, McGovern, & Milivojevic, 2015). Some even say that sexting is an invention of millennials. Another study at the Centre of Criminology, University of Cape Town (UCT), reveals that while millennials consider sexting as fun and flirtatious, they are also aware of the risks posed by sexting, including making them more and more self-conscious about their bodies (Meyer, 2016). So, it might be their perplexity with real life and at the same time their cosiness with online life, the conditioning by their parents and teachers during their formative years or maybe it is a combination of all of these factors that has contributed to their changing preference towards relationships and attitude towards sex.

Millennials experience relationship paradox. Their relationship choices have increased. Marriage is not the only option or choice anymore. Choices are plenty—live-in relationships, and even same-sex relationships, are being increasingly accepted in the society. However, at the same time, millennials seem to be wary about entering into relationships or committing too much to any relationship. Their fear of loss of personal space, freedom or even their ability to exercise their own picks whether it is about their career decisions or life decisions seems to be holding them back from a truly fulfilling relationship. Break-ups are common, and sometimes they happen in the ugliest fashion—over WhatsApp or over social media. In September 2011, when an MBA student of IIM Bengaluru ended her life after being dumped by her boyfriend on FB, it was a huge shock for everyone. After they had a fight over the phone, the boy updated his FB status as 'Dumped my new ex-girlfriend. Happy Independence Day'. Unable to swallow this public flagellation and embarrassment, the girl took the extreme step and killed herself. This incident that sent shock waves across the nation revealed the growing mix-up regarding relationship among millennials. Marriage as an institution seems to be crumbling, and relationships seem to be coming with a shelf life. All this makes one thing very clear—relationships are hard for millennials.

I Am Free but so Is the Fall!

Young millennial married couples find it difficult to cope with the demands of modern life; especially among this cohort, both partners are generally working. When the visuals of a 10-month-old baby being brutally beaten by a maid at a day care centre in Navi Mumbai started airing in November 2016 on social media and then on mainstream media, they were so heart rendering that it was difficult to watch. The video captured by the CCTV camera showed a frustrated maid physically abusing the baby while other babies in the day care centre were sleeping quietly, probably under the influence of sedatives. The infant had to be admitted to hospital with several internal injuries. The maid and the owner of the day care centre were arrested.

But this is the common predicament of the millennial parents, young working couples living in nuclear families in cities with no or low support systems. And what happened in that day care centre is not an isolated incident. Several such incidents have been reported. Few years back, a young couple in Bengaluru was traumatized when they found to their horror that the nanny they had hired to take care of their infant baby was actually sedating the baby and renting the baby to the street beggars. Once the couple discovered this, they abandoned the city altogether.

Lack of support system rattles millennials at times and they are completely on their own. But this is also result of a life that they have chosen for themselves. Their desire for greater freedom means that they prefer living alone or in small nuclear families. However, that also means that they have hardly any support system at a family or social level.

I remember Shwetha, a millennial and a spinster, telling me that she wanted her parents to be near her but not with her. When I asked her what she meant by the same, she told me that she wanted her own space that gave her the freedom for late nights, friends of both genders visiting her with no restriction and to be able to live her life without anyone questioning her every other action or she having to justify all her behaviours. Shwetha, an MBA, was living and working alone in the city. However, she wanted her parents to live in a nearby city so that she could reach out to them in times of need. Currently, that was not the case and sometime back when she had a bout of viral fever, she had a tough time for about a week. Simple chores such as cooking and cleaning became difficult. She even struggled to get herself a glass of water or to get medicines from the nearby pharmacy or to visit the neighbourhood doctor. Yet, she was not ready to give up her privilege of the space that she had at that moment, lack of support notwithstanding.

Greater freedom comes with a price and I call this the freedom paradox. They have freedom but they do not have support systems or the security net. If they slip, it is a free fall for them that many a time ends with a thud on the ground!

My Space and I Am the Only One Here!

Progyan is now a homemaker living in Bengaluru with her husband, a techie by profession. Progyan, who is a master of social work, worked with an NGO in the disability sector as a project supervisor and was based out of Kolkata before her marriage. Extremely passionate about her work, she did not give up her job even when her gruelling schedules started to take a toll on her health. However, when after her marriage she had to shift to Bengaluru, she had to give up her job. Her job search in the new city was not all that sweet. She was rejected from a couple of NGOs since she was not conversant with the local language. She was

disheartened by the rejections and finally gave up on her hope of finding a job in Bengaluru, until she learnt the language of the land. And so she had no choice but to don the role of a homemaker. Progyan, who had always been amidst the hustle bustle, suddenly found herself lonely. With her husband having a 12-hour work schedule and away from home, she had no one to talk to or even say a hello! Alien city, with no knowledge of the local language, she was all by herself. Just walls to stare at and no one around, she used to dread the day hours. It was about a year later when one of her college friends shifted to Bengaluru and took up a rented apartment near her place that she had some company. Now she lives in a gated community and has made few more good acquaintances and feels less lonely. Having a supportive husband has also helped her to not get sucked in this loneliness that ails many millennials today. Single millennials or newly married millennials living alone in a big city often feel very lonely. The paradox, however, is that they desperately desire more personal space at the same time. This desire for more space for self has also made them lonelier. While on the one hand they fight loneliness, on the other hand they are not desirous of giving up their space. For Progyan, having her family members or those of her husband living with them is not a choice, although that can reduce her loneliness. Although she has no ill feelings towards either of the family members and neither is she trying to shrug off responsibility of looking after them in times of need, she feels that their living with them will steal away her personal freedom and space that she is enjoying with her husband.

That is exactly what the paradox is! Millennial's desire for their own space makes them lonely at the same time. Space paradox, as I call it, creates a zone where they have no one to talk to or even say a simple hello. Many millennials who work and live alone in cities have no life after office. They live as paying guests or rent up an apartment. They leave for office early in the morning and after they come back late in the evening, they come back to an empty room. No one to talk to about what transpired in the day, all good and bad news are bottled up with no one to share. Weekends are sometimes worse for such people as office at least keeps them busy. Their general state of friendlessness adds to their loneliness. Psychologists say that friendship is like food. We need it to survive. However, lack of close friends and a dearth of broader social contact generally bring emotional discomfort or distress known as loneliness. It starts with an awareness of absence of quality relationships and takes an emotional toll on us. Millennials can easily be said to be the loneliest generation that this planet has ever seen. Many may argue against it and point to the number of parties millennials have or to the crowded pubs, restaurants or malls during weekends. But loneliness is a very funny thing. One can be lonely in a crowd of thousands and yet feel togetherness in wilderness. The number of people or the decibels of cacophony around does not determine whether one is lonely or not. But lack of social interaction and absence of quality relationships can make one extremely lonely.

In his book *Loneliness: Human Nature and the Need for Social Connection*, John Cacioppo had shown how loneliness negatively affects human physiology and emotionally disconnects them from others. Loneliness sets in motion a variety of 'slowly unfolding pathophysiological processes'. Lonely people report higher levels of stress, have disturbed sleep patterns and are hypertensive. Chronic loneliness makes people pessimistic and suicidal. It is not surprising that the latest WHO figures indicate that nearly 0.8 million people die of suicides every year. For every suicide, there are many other who attempt suicide. And yes, suicide is the second leading cause of death among the 15–29-year-olds worldwide.

All Tangled Up!

Emotional wellness is more than just one's capacity of handling stress. It is being aware of one's thoughts, feelings and behaviours. Emotional wellness is related to one's level of depression, anxiety, well-being, self-control and optimism. In other words, experiencing satisfaction, curiosity and enjoyment in life, as well as having an optimistic outlook, defines one's emotional wellness (Renger et al., 2000). Social wellness, on the other hand, means one's ability to communicate with people around and to establish meaningful relationships. Basically, social wellness determines our ability to live in harmony with the society. It is very evident that paradox permeates both emotional and social wellness aspects of millennials. Their quantum of friends does not get them many real friends. They crave for friends yet struggle and even at times shy away from finding good friends. They lack good relationships yet find it hard to commit themselves completely to any relationship. They have more relationship choices and freedom to choose them as well, yet the bonding in those relationships are fragile. Their desire for greater individual freedom and space has also come with a price. Their social support systems are almost non-existent and they are also growing lonelier. Emotionally, such situations are draining and create anxiety in them and make them far more prone to depression. Their general lack of enthusiasm for future and their tendency to live life in present are much a result of their emotional state. They miss real face-to-face conversations a lot, and the communication over FB is often empty and impersonal. They in general find it hard to have meaningful relationships in life. Their predicaments are not understood by the previous-generation members, creating conflicts and a disharmony in their social lives. The paradoxical nature of their emotional and social wellness elements is unique and generates unique pressures on them. How does it impact their state of happiness and being and what does it mean in terms of engaging them—we will see in the later chapters.

4

MATERIAL WELLNESS PARADOX

Is It Not My Job?

Indulekha has now been working in the same company for over 11 years. She works for an Indian IT major and is doing relatively well. But her going has not been that smooth always. During 2012, she was working on a project that was for a US client. The client was a major oil company. Indu was working in that project for over two years. The project had four offshore resources, that included Indu, and two on-site resources. Around the same time, oil prices dropped sharply and this had a direct impact on the project. As a result, although the on-site resources were retained, three out of the four offshore resources were benched. Indu to her  *shock and dismay found herself among those three resources. Ironically, one week before Indu was benched, she had received an appreciation mail from the client for her work. The next three-four months that Indu was on the bench were the most frustrating days for Indu. All of a sudden, she had nothing to do! Added to this, her company had a rule that everyone had to report to the office every day, irrespective of whether the person was on a project or on the bench. This meant that Indu had to travel to office every day. Her seat and system had been taken away from her after she was benched. Indu had to hang around the sprawling campus of the company doing absolutely nothing, sometimes in cafeteria, sometimes just idling around. That was the most exasperating period of Indu's work life. Her ordeal lasted about four months after which she was allocated to a project. After that experience, Indu has realized that good performance is not a guarantee for job security. She could lose her job any day because something in some part of the world changed precipitously. Indu has always harboured a desire to start a restaurant but somehow she has never been able to take the plunge. She says may be it is the change that she is not sure of, but may be one day she will dump her job and pick up another career as a restaurateur.*

Although millennials are upbeat about their career prospects, the job instability continues to haunt them. A survey by ManpowerGroup (2016) shows that nearly two-thirds millennials are optimistic about their immediate job prospects. Sixty-two per cent are confident that if they lose their main source of income tomorrow, they can find equally good or better work within three months. Overall, majority of millennials globally see a promising future and successful careers ahead. However, when it comes to their present job, the lack of stability is a definite worry. Nearly 87 per cent of the millennials expressed job security as their top need, second only to money, in the same survey.

This is once again a paradoxical situation. Their positive outlook towards their careers and a sense of optimism that they will be able to charter alternative career paths, in case they needed to switch careers, is outdone by their growing insecurity about their job. The fact that sudden job loss has not been limited to non-performers but has time and again impacted the good performers has made them believe that job for life is a relic of the past. The present is temporary and they have no choice but to live with this temporariness.

Traditional perception that millennials are job hoppers is actually exaggerated. Various studies show that job mobility of millennials has actually shown a decline. The British think tank Resolution Foundation echoes the fact that millennials are concerned with their job insecurity. Their finding also showed that the generation born 10 years before millennials were twice more likely to change jobs than them. Among the Indian millennials, nearly 94 per cent prioritize job security.

Recently, Snapdeal, the Indian e-commerce retailer, announced its decision to lay off more than 600 employees. Stung by poor strategic decisions, intensifying competition from Amazon and Paytm and huge loss of revenue, the e-retailer finally took the route of lay-offs as a way to release the pressure. The fear of the millennials had been confirmed once again. The last week of February of this year was full of tension for the employees of the third largest e-commerce company in India. The employees summoned by HR were not sure whether the pink slip awaits them or they still have ground under their feet. The magnitude of the latest downsizing exercise can be gauged from the fact that it will leave the company with a permanent workforce of around 1,000 employees. In fact, after these lay-offs, Snapdeal's regional centres in Mumbai and Bengaluru will have an employee count in single digits or low double digits. The handful of employees the company has in cities such as Kolkata, Hyderabad and Chennai are also expected to get the sack. Speaking on anonymity, some industry experts shared that 'Only employees who have relatively low salaries, and those who have been with the company since inception, have some hope of getting retained.' Although the founders of the company admitted to their mistakes that led the company to this state and also took 100 per cent pay cuts, this did not lessen the ordeal of the laid-off employees. Many of them found it difficult to find good job offers owing to the public knowledge of their lay-off. Their negotiation leverage had simply been blunted.

But Snapdeal has not been alone in affecting lay-offs. Cognizant appears set to cut at least 6,000 jobs, which represents 2.3 per cent of its total workforce. The variable payout to employees for 2016, too, is expected to be adversely affected, according to sources familiar with the matter. The lay-offs are likely to be more this year than the routine annual exercise that weeds out the bottom 1 per cent of the workforce for non-performance as determined by the annual appraisal process that ends in March. Last year, the lay-offs were about 1–2 per cent, while two years ago, they were about 1 per cent. However non-performance is not the only reason behind lay-offs. The company is struggling with growth in an IT environment that is fast shifting towards new digital services. Cognizant is said to be looking to cut roles that have become redundant due to the impact of automation on lower-end IT jobs.

Boeing is expected to announce lay-offs anytime. ESPN announced lay-offs. The company expects to save tens of millions of dollars' worth of staff salaries from its payroll by making cuts from among the on-air talent. This would represent the second round of significant lay-offs at ESPN over the past two years, after the company laid off roughly 300 employees in October 2015. The skyrocketing cost of live TV broadcasting and plummeting viewership has contributed in the lay-offs by ESPN. Increased competition from digital services like Netflix has contributed to worsening times for ESPN and for its employees as well.

Disruptive changes such as automation and digitization, failing of previously successful business models, increasing environmental turbulence, intensifying competition and paradigm shift in the way business is conducted are all making business models increasingly redundant. The stress then is managed by cutting down employee size and cost.

Take Sourabh's case for instance. Sourabh Banerjee, a 1980-born millennial, had been hired by a service-based IT company around 2007. He had been performing consistently well but after about 18 months into the project, one fine day he was simply laid off. This was 2009; the recession had hit and the foreign client was facing rough weather. Sourabh was summoned by HR who told him that his contract could not be renewed and he was free to look for other opportunities. The company simply did not have funds to pay him. Sourabh was jobless for about five months. 'It seems all my good work had been wasted', says Sourabh. His savings pulled him through during this period, after which he got a job. In the next three years, Sourabh says that he changed about four jobs.

It seems all my good work had been wasted...

It was in a way a response to the laying-off that I faced. I understood that loyalty had no meaning in today's world. It definitely cannot be a one-sided attribute. The company can ask me to leave any day despite my good performance. Hence I need to strengthen my fortress before the gale hits me. I need to make hay when the sun is shining!

For millennials, job hopping many a times is a response to the kind of instability they face in their jobs. When they know that they can lose their job without any of their fault, the psychological contract simply loses its meaning. Loyalty as Sourabh said cannot be a 'one-sided attribute'. Despite the job insecurity they face, their positive outlook makes them try new frontiers and encash on the opportunities as much as possible when the going is good. All this is to ensure that they can secure and shield themselves, as much as possible, from the high job instability and growing insecurity.

An *India Today* (see Table 4.1) report further adds list of large manufactures, companies and start-ups that have recently either shut their shops or have shrunk their operations, leading to loss of jobs. Some names include Nokia, Goldman Sachs and Nomura, J. P. Morgan Asset Management, TinyOwl and Zomato. Some other companies who are said to be in plans to divest or shrink their operations include cement major Lafarge, Avantha Group (of Crompton Greaves), Larsen & Toubro and Essar Group to name a few.

The *India Exclusion Report 2013–2014* by the Delhi-based Centre for Equity Studies, an autonomous research and social justice advocacy institution, says that only 27 million jobs were

Table 4.1.   Indian Labour Ministry's 27th Quarterly Employment Survey

FY	Jobs Added (Million)	Jobs Lost (Million)
2010	1.1	
2013–2014	0.3	
2014–2015	0.5	
2011–2015		1.5
First half of 2015–2016	0.134	0.043

Source: http://indiatoday.intoday.in/story/employment-scenario-job-crunch-job-less-growth-economy/1/647573.html

Note: Data of eight employment-intensive industries—textiles, leather, metals, automobiles, gems and jewellery, transport, IT/BPO, and handloom/power loom).

added in the supposedly high-growth period of 2004–2010 compared with over 60 million between 1999 and 2004.

Another study by Pew Research Center in the USA showed that millennials are much more concerned about job security than previous generations, both Gen X and baby boomers. Lack or loss of a permanent job impacts their credit worthiness and hence hampers their prestige and chance of getting a loan or mortgage or an apartment for rent. McDonald's, which employs its UK staff on flexible 'zero-hours contracts' that does not guarantee a minimum amount of work per week, recently found that its employees were finding it difficult to secure car loans, mobile phone contracts and mortgages. McDonald's is now contemplating offering workers fixed-hour contracts.

A survey by 'CareerBuilder' some time ago among freshly passed-out college graduates showed that millennials believe that getting a satisfying job and job security both were difficult for them. Job security to millennials means their ability to retain their current jobs, their ability to keep their skills relevant to the contemporary demands and their ability to maintain their quality of life.

Sumit working in a premier watch and lifestyle products company faced an unenviable dilemma not too long back. He was working for the watch division. He was primarily a sales guy. However, when he joined the company more than six years back, he was asked to manage services. He has done really well in his work. Posted in the difficult market of northeast, he created a strong goodwill among the distributors and retailers through his behaviour and promptness in service. His work very well complimented the field sales team. He had received several awards for his work and two years back, he received a service award in a big function. Just months after that, there was a major change at the top leadership level. The new chairman of the conglomerate, of which Sumit's company was a part, had chalked out a new strategy that aimed at building greater efficiency in each of the group companies. As a result, there was a restructuring in Sumit's company as well. The sales and service which were two separate functions in the company were being merged. This also meant merger of roles, and hence sales people would also have to handle service as an aspect in their territories. The service people were either asked to leave or were being redeployed in other jobs in the company. Sumit was among the top performers so he was not asked to leave. But the HR gave him an offer to accept a redeployment in the supply chain department or being ready for a lay-off. He had no choice but to accept his redeployment. He moved into the supply chain department and was transferred to Kolkata. The change of profile meant a loss of incentives that were not associated with his new role, to the tune of about a lakh every year. Relocation to a metro city meant increase in the cost of living. Additionally, he found no interest in his new job. The job was a desk job, something that he was not used to, and was extremely monotonous. His new boss was also very different from his earlier one. He was abrasive and less considerate. Sumit had lost his interest in his work and was slogging in his new role for the sake of his family. He did not deserve such a treatment but then he thought that perhaps he was in a slightly better position than his peers, some of whom had been asked to leave the company.

Lack of job security has affected millennials in many ways. Psychologically, it has made them more distrustful of their companies; they have become sceptical of making life decisions or financial investments, and it has also impacted their credibility. Owing to high job insecurity and disappearance of stable jobs, income and pension concepts, millennials are preparing themselves for a long haul career. Nearly 40 per cent of the millennials expect to work well beyond the age of 65 and at least a quarter of those surveyed expect to keep working past the age of 70 and about 14 per cent expect to work until the day they die.

Despite the gloom, India may be among the few countries in the world that have a reason to be optimistic. A favourable structural growth in the future, presence of a huge demographic dividend and the stability that is provided by democracy may turn things for better for millennials. They are hopeful and positive about their career. They also believe that if they need to switch careers in the future, they will be able to acquire new skill sets and make that transition. This is mostly attributed to their upbringing. Their parents have made them believe that they are good and capable of changing the world. However, their current situation where they experience high job instability makes them jittery at times. The job instability is a big bother for them and it continues to keep them tentative of their present and immediate future. The job–career paradox is a reality that every millennial lives with each and every day.

Where Is the Money, Honey?

But this is not the end of woes for millennials. Pay freezes, pay reductions and other corporate cost-cutting measures have kept many young employees like Sriram in a holding pattern of low earning. A 2009 study of 25,000 millennials conducted by the Futures Company found that nearly 20 per cent of the employees polled between the ages of 21 and 30 had seen at least one pay cut since 2008 and 14 per cent suffered a lay-off. In contrast, only 8 per cent of baby boomers surveyed lost their jobs in the same year. Many who graduated from college find their low incomes combined with crippling levels of student loan debt. This often puts them in a terrible position. The average salary of a millennial today is an estimated 20 per cent lower than the average salary that a baby boomer had at the same age (in real terms). According to US Census Bureau data, the median earnings for full-time workers aged 18–34 were $35,845 in 1980. By 2000, the same cohort was earning $37,355. For the period 2009–2013, however, full-time workers between the age of 18 and 34 had median earnings of just $33,883. According to a research from the Equality of Opportunity Project, led by Stanford economist Raj Chetty, 91.5 per cent of the 30-year-olds in 1970 earned more than their parents did at the same age, adjusted for inflation. By 2014, just 50.3 per cent of the 30-year-olds in the USA were in a similar position. The figures are consistent in different parts of the world. The finding contained in a study 'Stagnation Generation' by the Resolution Foundation, UK, shows that millennials typically earn around £8,000 less in their 20s than a person from the previous generation, thanks to weaker economic prospects.

Sriram Bapat, a fresh out of college, joined an auto-manufacturing company as a management trainee. A commerce graduate with an MBA in marketing, he was able to secure the job offer in his first attempt. He was happy with the company and his profile. However, the compensation package was not that attractive. He was in two minds whether to join the company or not. However, left with no other good offers, he decided to accept the offer. That was 2010. He worked hard and in less than a year he was able to prove his worth. He expected good variable pay out. However, by 2011, the passenger vehicle market was slowing down and he did not really receive his first set of variable pay as expected. He was expecting a good appraisal at least and a pay hike. However, by mid of 2011, the company announced a salary freeze. His hopes of a good salary hike were dashed. Seven years later, Sriram is still working in the same company with a compensation that is still not at par with the projections that had been made when he was still in his college. Not that he has done poorly. He has consistently been among the top performers in the company and has been give more responsibilities to shoulder. These enhanced responsibilities have not necessarily been matched by the rate at which his compensations have increased. Last year, he finished paying back his education loan that he had taken for doing his MBA. As a result, he has not been able to save a lot. He expects to use his earnings more for himself now onwards.

It is said that one's final pay cheque is dependent on the initial salary that one commands. Low initial salaries, occasional pay cuts, at times irregular incomes and fear of loss of jobs have no doubt filled millennials with a feeling that they need to work until the day they die. They have become the first generation to earn lesser than their parents.

What's more, today's millennials are deeper in debt than their parents were at their age. Paradoxically, lower incomes and fluctuating earnings have not desisted millennials from spending on luxury goods, cars, luxury hotels and lifestyle products. And, hence, the maintenance cost of this generation is quite high.

A look into the spending patterns of Indian youth provides a very interesting insight into how millennials spend their money.

Money, Well! Spent...

Indian millennials are spending big time on beauty services.

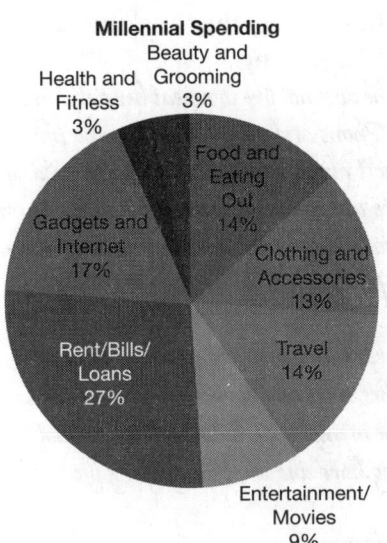

Millennial Spending

Beauty and Grooming 3%
Health and Fitness 3%
Food and Eating Out 14%
Gadgets and Internet 17%
Clothing and Accessories 13%
Rent/Bills/Loans 27%
Travel 14%
Entertainment/Movies 9%

Take Sara and Sujoy, both millennials and working in very successful careers. Sara is an ad professional and Sujoy works in an event management company. Both say that personal grooming is very important and they need to take care of their appearance and presentability. Their grooming and beauty spend ranges between ₹7,000 and ₹10,000 per month. They do not find anything wrong with the same and consider this as an investment in their life and career.

A recent Associated Chambers of Commerce and Industry of India (ASSOCHAM) report revealed that cosmetic, apparel and mobile are other areas where millennial spends have shown a sharp increase. About 75 per cent of India's youth spends on cosmetics, apparel and mobile have surpassed ₹6,000 per month, against their average expenditure of less than ₹1,500 in year 2003, an increase of over 300 per cent.

Rising beauty consciousness due to changing demographics and lifestyles, rising media and social media exposure, greater product choice, growth in retail segment and wider availability have contributed in the demand spike.

The results of a dipstick survey that I conducted among millennials, with a sample size of about 650 millennials, were not too different. Besides the expenditure on rent/bills and loan EMIs (27%) that constituted the biggest spending head for millennials, the rest was spent on food, lifestyle gadgets and travel. Food and eating out (14%), clothing and accessories (13%), travel (14%) and gadgets and Internet (17%) constituted the major expenditure heads, together making up to nearly 60 per cent of millennials' spending.

Misha parties every weekend and she does not like to repeat her outfit in the next party. She has two phones—an iPhone and a top-end Samsung phone. She recently bought a footwear that cost about ₹6,500. She has ordered an AC for her apartment as summers are approaching. Misha, working as an admission counsellor in an upmarket college in Noida for the last three years, has recently applied for a car loan. She plans to buy a Polo or an i20. She adds,

After paying my rent, EMIs and credit card bill, I set aside a bit for my savings. The rest I spend on my clothes, shoes and parties. Why shouldn't I do that? After all I have no one else in my life, no liabilities and I do not know about tomorrow. I am working hard and want to enjoy my life.

Misha is not apologetic about her indulgence.

Food also forms a major part of millennial spending. On an average, a typical millennial spends anywhere between ₹1,000 and ₹15,000 for cosmetics (see Figure 4.1), ₹3,000–25,000 for apparel and ₹5,000–35,000 for mobile on yearly basis. Travel, clothing, food, movie and personal grooming are all top spend areas of millennials. Mobile expenses are also high. Spending on gym memberships and expenditure in malls and coffee shops are on the rise too. Millennials are far too much fashion conscious and prefer brands over non-brands. A survey of credit card spending by MasterCard indicates that members of the generation known as millennials are increasing their spending on 'luxury' items—designer clothing and accessories, tech gadgets, jewellery, etc.—faster than any other age cohort.

Millennials are also pushing brands to act digitally. Today, 70 per cent of luxury purchases are influenced by online interactions. The online presence of millennials is huge, and they do a lot of their shopping online as well. This also means that they are leading spending on the Internet more than any other generation. Millennials are leading the Internet growth in India. The avenue for online transaction growth is phenomenal, averaging 60 per cent based on compound aggregate growth rate during 2014 and 2020. The growth for overall Internet market is seen at 45 per cent compound annual growth rate (CAGR) during the same period.

Luxury and high-end bikes are making great inroads in India. Take Triumph bikes, for instance, priced at premium, 16 per cent of their current sales come from millennials, that is expected to go up to 30 per cent in the next two–three years.

Millennials consider themselves as globe trotters, but they like to travel in style. A study in America by Chase Card Services reveals that millennials are more likely than older travellers to seek out hotels with luxury services such as dry cleaning (32%),

Figure 4.1.   Beauty Infographics (India)

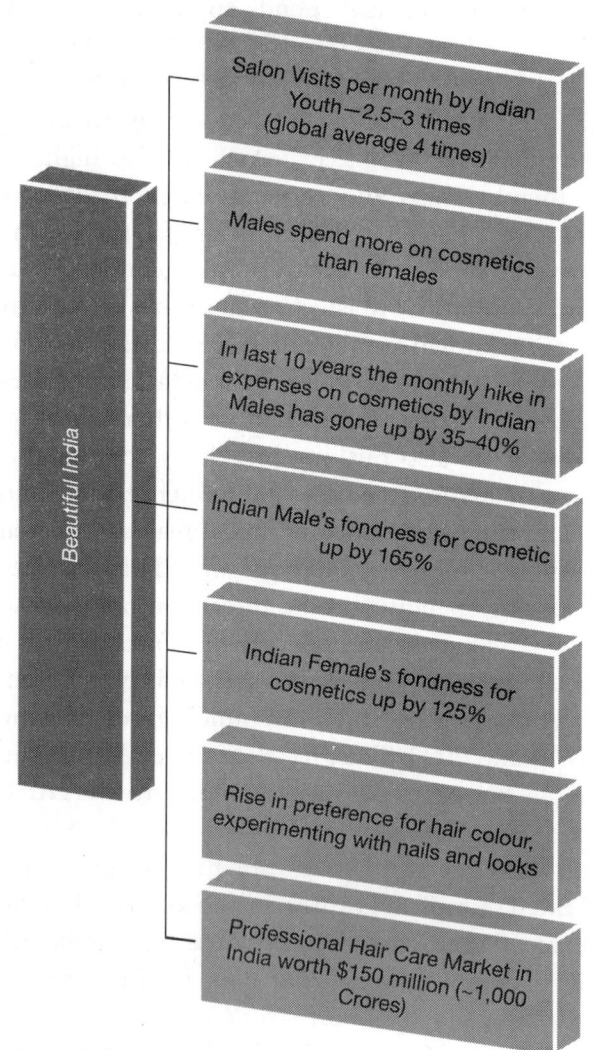

Sources: N. Singh (2015) and R. Singh (2013).

massage or spa services (30%) and pet-friendliness (23%). The survey also reveals that millennials want to make connections in person and via social networks while travelling. Millennials will represent 40 per cent of the global market for personal luxury goods by 2025, revealed a new research by Bain & Company and Farfetch.

Some data also suggest that millennials might be spending more than they earn. Armed with a credit card, millennials have generally spent more than their earnings, hoping to repay their credit card bills sooner or later. The resultant credit card debt has been on the rise.

But then it would not be fair to blame millennials in any way for the way they spend their money. Their spending behaviour and high maintenance cost is not without reason. The high cost of maintenance that millennials incur is due to three main reasons. The first reason relates to a sub-conscious belief of millennials. They have grown up at a time of uncertainty, and hence they believe in living their life in today and not tomorrow. They do not even know whether tomorrow is going to come because of the large-scale uncertainty and risk due to various political reasons. Hence, they wish to enjoy their present and not postpone things for the future. Secondly, millennials are a very aspirational generation. They are exposed to the world now and do not settle for less than the best brands. 'They can and they will have it' is the attitude. And thirdly, nothing of this generation is private, thanks to social media. The resulting partly conscious and mostly sub-conscious pressure that builds up is huge. One ex-college friend poses with an Audi and captions it—'the new beast'. Or another friend uploads photos of a holiday trip to a foreign exotic location. These are enough to trigger a big lash of inequity among millennials. The competition to which their parents had introduced them and their aspirations accentuate the same and trigger spending. Not that previous generations did not have such comparisons and feeling of inequity, but lack of privacy in the life of millennials makes it worse and exposes them to a world where one's worth is measured by externally visible frills and decorations.

Pocket Full of Dreams!

Millennials have grown up with high career aspirations and a desire to make a mark in their careers. However, they have come to the corporate scene at a time when the economy has seen a recession, the volatility is too high and the job market is not really expanding at a rate that was expected. As a result, job instability has risen. Their incomes have naturally not matched the aspirations that they grew up with and have generally taken a hit on their earnings. High exposure in their lives has meant higher peer pressure for them. The uncertainty in the world that we live in today has meant that their trust in future is very less. They do not know whether they will be able to sustain their incomes or the world order will be stable enough or they will survive amidst all the violence and terrorism in the world. Hence, they wish to live their life in the moment 'now and today' and fulfil their dreams and desires. These factors spike up their maintenance cost. Overall, it has meant that paradox has dotted their entre material wellness zone as well. Their optimism for a good career is not matched by job stability on the one hand and their aspirations for a good life are not matched by their incomes on the other.

5
PHYSIOLOGICAL WELLNESS PARADOX

Kites Don't Fly Any More

Makar Sankranti was approaching and Vishal was reminiscing his childhood days, when he with his gang of boys would have fun and frolic, running
down the narrow lanes of his village in Etawa. Makar Sankranti is a Hindu
festival, observed in reverence of 'Surya' or Sun. Traditionally, it marks the
first day of movement of Sun in to 'Makara' or the Capricorn, end of winter
solstices and beginning of a period of the year when days are longer. Makar
Sankranti is marked by festivities, fairs, celebrations and food fiestas. Vishal
remembered how he with his friends would fly kites whole day long, also one of
the traditions of the festival. They would have kite-flying competition as to
whose kite could dislodge rival's kite by cutting its thread with one's own. The
one whose kite prevailed would scream 'Wo kaata' or 'Got you'! Vishal like his
friends would save money for months so that they could each have at least a
dozen kites and good-quality 'manjha' or thread seasoned with glue and cut
glass that would make it sharp. All would be in good fun. The bare roofs of the
houses would be crowded with boys, girls, men and women, all taking part in
kite flying. In between their kite-flying sessions, Vishal would run down the
stairs and grab some sweetmeats that his grandmother would make at home

and gobble up to his delight. Those were the days. Vishal missed those days. Now living in Bengaluru, working in a multinational publishing house, he longed for those days in Etawa, his friends, sweets, his family and the colourful kites. Vishal decided that this time he will find some kites and fly them on the day of Makar Sankranti. Getting kites in Bengaluru was not so easy. He googled and finally found a kite maker and seller in old city of Bengaluru. He called the person using the contact mentioned on the online yellow pages site and confirmed his address. When Vishal reached the kite maker's place, the latter, a middle-aged person named Yousuf, seemed a bit surprised at the effort that Vishal had made in locating and purchasing the kites. Vishal bought four good-sized kites and a generous roll of manjha. Next day was the festival. He bought some sweets too. They could not match the taste of the sweets made by his grandmother, but then they would do for the time being! Vishal woke up early next morning, took a bath and left for his office. He wanted to start his day early so that he could wrap up his work by afternoon and enjoy the evening flying kites. He had even invited some of his team members for the kite session. Around lunch, Vishal got a call from one of the large universities that they wanted to have a meeting with him regarding the new curriculum revision and the new set of prescribed books. The meeting was important. Vishal and his team had been making efforts towards this for a long time. If the meeting was successful, it could mean a big sales order for the company and incentives for his team. However, the meeting was in the other part of the city and he was likely to get delayed in the evening if he attended the same. Then what would happen to his kite plan? Vishal had little choice. He left for the meeting. The meeting went on well but by the time he finished, it was already past evening. A long drive back and it was 10 p.m. by the time he reached home. He was tired and his body was aching. Kites were lying in his living room. He glanced at them and smiled unto himself,

opened the box of sweets, ate a piece and then retired for the night. The kites and manjha are still there in Vishal's attic, the ones that never flew.

Millennials have million reasons to celebrate, but they hardly have time to celebrate. Earlier, there were only a few festivals. Now thanks to social media and globalization, we have become a part of the global community and we have countless special days and occasions to celebrate. Traditional festivals notwithstanding, the whole Valentine week is there that has rose day, hug day, kiss day, propose day, teddy bear day, chocolate day and of course the Valentine day; then there are friendship day, birthdays, anniversaries and so on. With the increase in breakups, there are even break-up parties! But where is the time to celebrate? Birthday parties do not happen on that particular day but are rather pushed to weekend; anniversary dinners are also on weekend; promotion parties, girls' night outs, the weekly bash, all are pushed to the crowded weekend. Birthday cakes, anniversary flowers, emojis, all come via FB or WhatsApp! There are some likes on that post. Those who have forgotten your special day are suddenly reminded, thanks to these posts and FB notification alerts. They wish you by writing a 'comment', you thank them, they again like your 'thank you' and it is done! Birthday celebrated! The likes and wishes on FB by those who had almost forgotten you, and you had forgotten them as well, give you some dopamine shots. These are your birthday gifts! Use the smiley emoji to show you are happy!

The crisis of a millennial's life and that of the modern world is that there is no time to enjoy the fruits of one's labour. Everyone is busy and everyone is rushing. Millennials work hard to become prosperous and even harder to remain prosperous. They are told right from their school days that they live in a competitive world where they have to always put that 'extra' effort to outdo the competitor sitting next to them. They learn that being busy is equal to being successful and once they become successful, they become busier; they get more responsibilities and promotions, become busier and get handsome pay, but they keep on becoming busier and busier. After all, business of business is busyness! They keep postponing holidays, breaks, time with family and so many more precious moments in hope that someday they will get time for themselves, time to enjoy the money they have made, but that elusive 'break' keeps eluding them. 'One last time' and then we will have a break! They keep on saying this to themselves, but the only thing that lasts is last!

A 2009 *Harvard Business Review* survey revealed that 94 per cent of the American professionals worked about 50 hours per week, out of which 50 per cent of them worked more than 65 hours a week. This was excluding the 20–25 hours per week that they spent on their smartphones outside of workplace, doing job-related work. The Organisation for Economic Co-operation and Development (OECD, 2015) survey shows that Mexico is the busiest country, with highest number of average work hours per worker. Indians work 8.1 hours per day, more than the average of the developed nations such as the USA, Australia, UK, Italy and Germany.

The high working hours are often rationalized under the garb of increasing complexity and the global expansion of trade. Yet, research proves this claim to be untrue. A work by Leslie A. Perlow and Jessica L. Porter (2009) published in *Harvard Business Review* states that 'it is perfectly possible for consultants and other professionals to meet the highest standards of service and still have planned, uninterrupted time off'.

The mad race, a culture of cut-throat competition and an incessant desire for more often drive millennials who form major part of the workforce to the edge. It starts impacting people, giving them an impression that they are running against the time and somehow their legs must move faster than the two hands of the clock. So, it is as much lack of time; it is also a psychological state that makes people feel good about themselves when they call themselves busy, though it does not allow them to really focus on things that they should!

Business of Business is Busyness!

Being busy is being important, being valuable and being worthy. Busyness is our defence to our vulnerability that millennials experience living in a hypercompetitive world. Hsee et al. (2010) in a work titled 'Idleness Aversion and the Need for Justifiable Busyness' found that many professed goals that people pursue may be merely rationalizations to keep themselves busy. They conducted an experiment where they asked a group of participants to fill a survey form and submit the same. They could submit the completed forms to a nearby location or to a distant location about 15 minutes away. If they submitted the form at the nearby location (idle option), they would have to wait for the rest of the experiment session. The distant location would, however, take more time (busy option). They were also told that for their effort, they would get a milk chocolate or a dark chocolate. In the first case, where they got the same chocolate irrespective of whether they chose the near or far-away location, only about one-third of the participants chose the distant location; whereas, when the kind of chocolate that they would get varied milk chocolate for the near and dark chocolate for the distant location, the number of participants who chose the distant location almost doubled. Reward or the kind of reward that one gets was used as a justification for busyness.

Millennials are caught in this quagmire of busyness. There is always a justification for being busy, and being busy is a kind of security. That does them little good as it keeps them away from many things that are worth their life and happiness.

Sarah is guilty of missing her parents' 50th wedding anniversary party; Pulkit is guilty of missing the first annual-day performance of his little daughter studying in nursery; Kundan can only lament the little time he could give to his ailing mother before she passed away; Subbalaxmi, working in night shift catering to US clients, cannot remember the last time she had dinner with her family—there are many and enough instances where the busyness of millennials have only made them miss out on things that they later lament.

'It feels like a race', says Hansika, who works as a team lead in an IT-services company. Millennials work at a stupendous pace. That should actually leave them with more time, but on the contrary, it actually leaves them hardly with any time. The paradox of pace versus time could not be stated any more. Speed is the undoing of the millennial generation. They are on a high-speed 'ride' or at least feel like they are on one; however, instead of being a smooth 'one', it is a roller-coaster ride with 'crests and troughs'. It thrills them for some time but then on a prolonged haul, it is enough to make them dizzy and nauseated. What's more, they find it difficult to get off this 'ride' as well!

Hansika tells me that she feels she has running shoes on.

Right from my school days, once I moved to higher classes, my father got me several tutors. He never believed that I could cope up on my own, although I very well could! After school, I had to rush from one tuition to another. Then get back home and complete my school work, do my studies, eat my dinner and crash to bed. I had to score more than 90 per cent, a target set by my father, so that I could secure admission in the best colleges. I gave up my music classes, dance classes and my hobby for clay sculpturing during that time. I am now working with a large MNC and am still giving up things that I like or love most so that I can have more time to work. I have to get promotions, hikes, incentives, bonuses. I feel like I am running on a treadmill, running faster and faster, yet really getting nowhere!

All Work and No Play Makes Jack Unhealthy!

There is no dearth of opportunities for people like Hansika, but then living in a world that is on a perpetual run mode, health takes a back seat. The physical, emotional and psychological well-being of millennials have taken a major hit. It would not be incorrect to say that millennials are perhaps the unhealthiest generation that the world has ever had. This is what I call as the opportunity paradox. Despite having opportunities to work with the best brands, global travel and work opportunities and work on the best technologies, the health has not kept pace with the same.

Timir blames the recent gastrointestinal problem that he suffered on his poor schedule, eating habits and sleep patterns. Working in a global bearing and mechanical power transmission components company, Timir looks after a very critical function within the IT support team. He and his team provide information security globally.

We hardly work for the India location offices. Majority of our time is spent on working for US and European locations. Hence, my workday starts from 1 p.m., between 1 and 4 p.m. I work for China clients and from 4 p.m. onwards, I work for US and

European clients. I usually have light breakfast and finish lunch at home by 11 a.m. Once I reach office, I hardly have time to breathe, forget about eating. I often carry my dinner from home. On a few lean days, I get time to eat my dinner by 8 or 9 p.m. But on most days, I carry my dinner box back home. By the time I reach home it is 11:30 p.m. and I end up having my dinner past midnight. I also do not get good sound sleep. Usually, by the time I go to bed it is 1 p.m. and at times the work stress just keeps me awake. I get up early in the morning to catch some time with my daughter before she goes off to school. My entire system went for a toss due to my irregular eating times and sleep. Also, at times, there is a long gap between my two meals. At times, I feel hungry when working in office but hardly have time to eat.

Timir had a severe bout of gastric and acidity-related attack recently. Severe stomach ache and digestion issues grounded him for about a week. But health is not the only issue bothering him. He laments the fact that he hardly gets time for his family and friends. He hardly gets 15–20 minutes every day, out of the 24 hours, with his little daughter. His wife often complains of his absence during evening hours and their inability to socialize or have outings. His friends have stopped calling him and he is never available. His health, family and social life, all appear to be in a state of flux.

The number of cases of colon and rectal cancer has surged among millennials according to a research by American Cancer Society, published in the *Journal of the National Cancer Institute* (Siegel et al., 2017). Even though exact causes have not yet been found, the prime suspects include obesity, a sedentary lifestyle and poor diet.

Sleep disorders are very common among millennials today, faced with a severe shortage of time. Sleep is not only therapeutic, but lack of sleep triggers health disorders. Sleep is classified under rapid eye movement (REM) and non-REM phases. During the night, sleep alternates between REM and non-REM phases four to five times. The non-REM phase, the initial part of our sleep, helps in physical repair of our body. During the non-REM phase, the pituitary gland is activated that helps in the repair of our body. The REM phase helps in mental consolidation and hence a good sleep helps us in remaining mentally alert. Lack of good sleep not only robs us of our alertness but also triggers many types of ailments that include hypertension, high blood pressure, diabetes, immune malfunction, digestion problems and obesity, and it even reduces life expectancy of a person. Poor concentration levels, mood swings and anxiety are generally associated with sleep disorders. Poor sleep also aggravates our stress levels (Buxton et al., 2012). Dr Christine Swanson and her co-workers found out that lack of sleep increases the risk of bone loss that can have long-term impact on the health of the entire body (The Endocrine Society, 2017).

Dikjyoti Phukan is doing her professional studies in business management. Her father is retired and is not keeping well. There is a lot of pressure and expectation from her parents that she will get a job soon after completing her studies and then she should get married. The pressure and stress of performance to fulfil the expectations of her parents coupled with the deadlines of studies and projects make Dikjyoti feel like she is living in a pressure cooker. She hardly has time to eat or sleep properly. She often skips her breakfast, substitutes lunch with a glass of juice and the only proper meal she has is her dinner that she gets delivered from a tiffin service. She always has a fear that she might not be able to perform good enough to secure good grades and finally a job. Hence, she often ends up putting extra effort. That keeps her awake late in the nights. With irregular sleep patterns, often resulting in lack of sleep and poor eating habits owing to time pressure, Dikjyoti could not escape impact on her health. She recently suffered from severe gastric and digestive problems. She had to consult a doctor and was on medication for close to two weeks. She still suffers from occasional stomach aches and dizziness.

No Recession of Depression

Neuroscientists (Goldstein et al., 2013) working at University of California, Berkeley, have found in their research that deprivation of sleep can amplify anticipatory anxiety. In other words, it makes people more anxious and makes them hyperreactive to situations, people and events. The already anxious people (those who are anxious by nature) can, therefore, face the greatest harm as a result of sleep deficiency. Millennials, who generally experience sleep deprivation, no doubt suffer more from anxiety and stress.

Kritika lost close to 20 kg and became anaemic after she shifted to a new city to pursue her dreams. Constant pressure of work, poor sleep and eating mostly junk food took a toll on her health. Her prolonged use of computers especially during night hours has also worsened her eyesight. Kritika also feels that her generation is not too organized and suffers from such time anxiety because they fail to plan and prioritize their work. Kritika says, 'We are so focused on results that as long as that comes, we don't care for anything else. But luckily, I have support of my parents. My cousin was not so lucky'. Naveen was a brilliant student but his parents had very high expectations from him. He used to often come to our place and break down. He felt that he was never able to make his parents happy who always compared him to his elder brother. In between, Naveen's best friend died in a train accident. That affected him even more. He used to go to railway stations and search for his friend. He could never accept that his friend was no more. One day, all of a sudden, Naveen just disappeared. He was untraceable. All searches, police complaints and newspaper adverts did not yield any result. Kritika says,

My father was always very supportive towards Naveen. After his disappearance, once he could get Naveen on the other side of the phone. Despite my father's assurances that he would stand by him, Naveen refused to return. He just said that if his parents did not support him, why anyone else should do the same. After that day, we have not heard anything from Naveen.

According to a white paper from Bensinger, DuPont & Associates (BDA, n.d.), millennials experience greater levels of depression compared to baby boomers and Gen X. Besides causing headaches, sleep disturbances, anorexia, irritability, mood swings, diminished levels of concentration and heightened levels of anxiety, depression was found to negatively impact performance at work. Performance pressure was also behind rising levels of depression. Depression can often push people to the edge and make them take extreme measures.

Hemant says, 'Half of the people of our generation do not know what we are doing. We are pursuing so because of peer pressure, societal expectation,

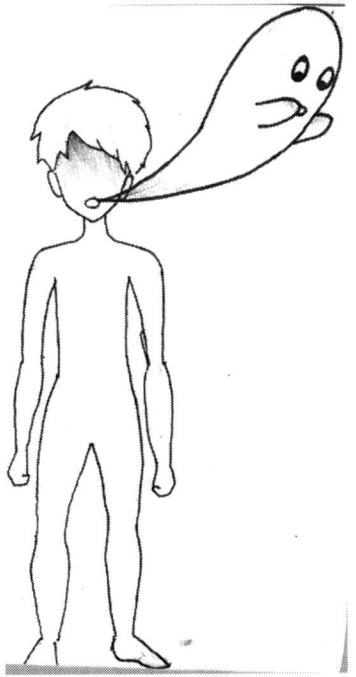

parental expectations and it often feels overwhelming'. To substantiate his comments, he narrates an anecdote involving one of his ex-colleagues, Sean, who was a brilliant student of law, studying in one of the top law colleges in the NCR region. He excelled at most of his subjects but international law was his forte. For his accomplishments, he was awarded by the International Law Students Association as the best 'student of the year'. He got an opportunity to pursue his internship with one of the topmost law firms of the country. Hemant recalls that six months later, when Sean came back to submit his dissertation report, he and his friends were shocked to see Sean. He had lost good amount of weight and looked frail. His voice was bleak. On quizzing Sean, Hemant came to know that Sean had been under a very demanding schedule. He liked the work he was doing but he was working on a 19-hour work schedule, on a daily basis, with no weekends or holidays. But Sean was reluctant to give up the internship as he liked the nature of his work and was also concerned about the impact of such a decision on his career. Fast forward to another six months. Hemant had graduated and was proceeding for his internship under a Supreme Court advocate. He wanted to meet Sean but learnt that Sean had gone back to his home. He had left his internship and was under severe clinical depression. He recognized only a few people, hardly talked to anybody and had lost interest in whatever he was doing. He used to be a big movie buff and also used to have an excellent collection of music. All those were things of the past for him. He was only a poor replica of his former self. His career was perhaps over even before it could really bloom. Hemant himself juggling through many roles from professional to personal has felt burnout many a time and fears that he too might end up like Sean one day.

Researchers and mental health professionals at Stanford University had coined a term 'Duck Syndrome'. Depression often goes unnoticed. People seem to be fine on the surface, akin to a duck gliding effortlessly on water. But deep within, a storm rages that flares up suddenly one day and ravages the person. Anything could trigger this sudden explosion, but the fact that the fire of depression seethes quietly within unnoticed makes it lethal.

Neha supposedly had two boyfriends! Yes, you heard it right! Whether Neha was confused or was two-timing the boys was not clear, but Srishti recalls that she had some relationship issues and some bully girls living in the PG accommodation got a whiff of the same. They started blackmailing Neha for the same, threatening her to spill the beans to her boyfriends or shame her publicly. Srishti recalls the day Neha committed suicide,

[S]he appeared fine. Neha was my roommate. On that fateful day, I had just come out of the bath when I heard the commotion. Someone said that Neha had jumped from the terrace. I ran up to the terrace and when I looked down, I could see the lifeless body of Neha lying on the ground. She was not moving at all. I rushed downstairs, but by the time I came down, she had been shifted to the ambulance. Later in the evening, I came to know that she had died of brain haemorrhage caused by the fall. I was so traumatized by the incident that I had to be actually taken to a psychiatrist by my mother. I received counselling session for about a fortnight before I could learn to cope with the tragedy. No one knew what Neha was going through. She seemed like a normal girl like us but it turned out that she was going through a lot. The scary image of Neha's lifeless body still floats in front of my eyes at times.

When a celebrated Bollywood and Hollywood actor Deepika Padukone publicly confessed to suffering from depression, everyone was surprised. How could someone so successful, so attractive and so sought-after become depressed? After all, didn't she have everything that millions aspire for? That's exactly the problem. Appearances are deceptive. On the surface, everything seems to be fine, when it is actually not. Deepika, a millennial herself, told in an interview to NDTV that she often felt empty, directionless and felt like breaking down at the drop of the hat. She had to not only seek professional medical help but also undergo medication. Deepika's confession before a nation that treats mental health as a taboo was indeed brave. It goes on to show the price that millennials often have to pay for a successful career or for the pulls and pressures they face in their personal life. Deepika has gone a step ahead and created the Live Love Laugh Foundation to help people dealing with depression and mental health, often fighting a quiet lonely battle.

India, by the way, is the most depressed country in the world. According to a latest WHO (2017) report, India has nearly 50 million people suffering from depression and another 30 million suffering from anxiety-related disorders. A nation that has perhaps the largest millennial population in the world, where a major proportion of the population is below 35 years of age, the numbers indicates very clearly the poor state of millennial mental health. The world figures are not too good either. Suicides were stated as the leading cause of death among 15–29-year-olds, globally, with India being the suicide capital of the world. The enormity of the problem can be inferred from the fact that this year's World Health Day theme was on depression and mental health. Depression and poor mental health up the chances of physical ailments and diseases as well.

Sourabh, a techie, working incessantly for the last 10 years in a desk job, often with high work stress and pressure to deliver, has developed a chronic back pain. He consulted a doctor who has told him that one of his vertebrae has developed a problem and surgery could be one option. Sourabh still considers himself lucky. One of his ex-colleagues, younger to Sourabh, fit and fine, suddenly collapsed one day after lunch. He died of cardiac arrest. He had no previous history of hypertension. Sourabh says that another colleague suddenly blacked out for close to 90 minutes when he went to restroom. After he came back to consciousness, he found himself lying on the wet floor. He was diagnosed with sudden obstruction of blood flow to his brain. It was supposedly stress-induced.

Is this the cost of modernity, a cyclone that is creating a vortex of stress, depression, anxiety and physical maladies? The health of millennials has become a victim of the world where opportunities are galore but the spin of the wheel is so furious that it often creates a high centrifugal force that throws them away from the centre.

Time Ain't My Mate, Health Ain't My Wealth

Paradox dots the physiological wellness of millennials as well. They have more reasons to celebrate, yet find no time to celebrate. They work at a lightening pace, yet they are always short of time. Their pace fails them like failed brakes of a car that loses control. They have a plethora of opportunities, but their health has taken a severe beating. Both their physical and mental health have denigrated to a stage where it has become worrisome. What will be a world like that is full of people who have access to almost everything but are crawling and out of steam? The physiological wellness of millennials is not only poor but worse than any other generation that has come before them. Audrey H. H. Tsui (2008) called wellness to be a casualty of rising prosperity. Can then an unhealthy generation bear the weight of the world in the future? Do the world and the organizations need to do something urgently? What can alleviate their physiological stress? We will attempt to explore this in the later chapters.

6
PARADOXICAL LIFE AND HAPPINESS REVERSAL

Millennials' story is not about exasperation and struggle. They live a life that is bridled with unchosen and unforeseen challenges. Yet they put up a brave, resilient face and cope with the paradoxes that cloud their life. Millennials should not also be seen as a burden. They are the most advanced generation in terms of technology, and more importantly they are the youth force who have immense potential and power. They are trying their best to cope with the subterranean risks and uncertainties of life. Most of them have faced such adversities putting up a brave face towards the world that burdens them with weight stacks, with a smile plastered on the face.

Their life is definitely neither simple nor easy. Paradox encompasses all the wellness elements—emotional and social wellness, material wellness and physiological wellness. Worse even is that they have no choice but to live with these paradoxes. Most of the paradoxes affect most of the millennials, something that they may not be consciously aware of, yet they continue to be impacted by the same. In this chapter, we take one final look at these paradoxes and see how this phenomenon has led to a reversal of happiness for the millennials. The attempt, therefore, is to create a sense of genuine deep empathy for millennials that in turn helps understanding them and their life better. Understanding is the foundation of a new design and leadership approach to better engage millennials at workplace, marketplace and the third place (social context).

Emotional and Social Paradox

Millennials are emotionally more vulnerable than the previous generation. Their vulnerability comes from absence of real friends and real relationships in their lives.

Friends Paradox

They have virtual connections in the name of 'friends', hundreds of them, yet find it difficult to have one real friend. True friends were classified as those one turns to in emergencies (Kirkova, 2014). The difference seems to be that between reel and real. On the one hand, the 'screen' shows friends, so many people who want to be their friends (friend requests) and some other FB suggestions about people whom they could befriend. This notwithstanding, they cannot rely on any of them. A survey of British women showed that most millennials on an average have 338 FB friends but researchers found that the average number of true friends came out at just five, with some women admitting they have only one.

Relationship Paradox

The relationship choices have increased in both type and number. The kinds of relationships that millennials can get into have also increased, thanks to a more liberal world. The number of people open to have a relationship has also grown in number. Yet, the readiness to make adjustments, let go their insecurities and wholeheartedly commit to a relationship seem to be diminishing. The result—obviously more relationship haemorrhages and casualties. Millennials are shying away from marriage and even from having their own kids, more than ever before. And those who enter into a relationship find it hard to sustain it.

Riya's story is so symbolic of the situation that many millennials find themselves in when it comes to relationships.

Riya met a guy on a social networking site, before her marriage. Later, Riya and Rahul met in person. Both of them liked each other's company and got along really well. The relationship continued for few years. She wanted to move ahead in the relationship, but he was hesitant. Over a period of time, she realized that although she cared a lot for him, the response was not similar from the other side. She realized that he was afraid of making a commitment. He loved travelling, going around places and doing his own stuff. Somehow, he felt that marriage would inhibit his freedom. He was not prepared for the same. She tried for some time, but he did not change his mind. Finally, she saw their relationship going nowhere and one day told him that they cannot continue in this way. She relocated to Bengaluru, where she took up a job. Time passed and both of them

moved on in their lives. She got married to another person she met through a family arrangement. Riya was no longer in touch with Rahul.

After about a year, she got a message from Rahul that he had come to Bengaluru and wanted to meet her. She decided to meet him as they had parted amicably and there were no hard feelings. They met in a café and she came to know that he was seeing someone in his city. He, however, had a confession to make. He admitted that not committing to her was the biggest mistake of his life and he really felt a sense of loss only after she left. She believed him, but they both had moved on in their lives and there was no room for anything else. He left. She came to know after a couple of months that he got married to the girl he was dating. Riya was happy for him. She will always remember him as a good friend and she was sure that he too will never recall his time with her with any bitterness.

During my meeting with Riya, I asked her that when Rahul had come back and confessed his mistake, had she been not committed at that time, would she have accepted Rahul back in her life? Riya answered in negation. She never found any reason to go back to things or people from whom she had moved on. Rahul was definitely very late and there was no way to turn the clock back!

I do not know whether Rahul was still shying away from commitments or not in his new relationship, but Rudra, Riya's husband, was shying away from something else.

Riya loves kids but she has none of her own. She told me that few years after her marriage with Rudra, she found out that he did not want to have kids. She was shocked and couldn't come to terms with this for some time. Added to this was the peer pressure. Most of her friends had been married like her and were having kids. The regular status updates by her friends on FB about their newborn kids, their birthdays and their photos was making her feel even more deprived. This created even more stress on her. She longed for her own child but her partner was not willing to have kids at all, and seeing her friends happily making babies, she felt a strange kind of void. They had several arguments over this issue that often turned into fights. For about a week, they did not talk with each other. She was going through a tumultuous time. He had some childhood *trauma about which he never spoke openly. But all in all, he was not ready to commit for kids. Their married life started to get affected. After some time, she saw no point in pursuing this any further with him. He was otherwise a good person and a very caring husband. She decided to live with this reality that she will never have kids. She told me that she is now at peace with not having kids in her life and they were in a way happy in their lives.*

Was Riya a bit unlucky in finding people who have been affectionate towards her but have found it difficult to commit completely themselves in the relationships? But then hasn't this been the millennial paradox who have struggled with friends, relationship, freedom and space. If their craving for friends and meaningful relationships is true on the one hand, then their inability to find ones or finding one but having difficulty in committing themselves to the relationship is also true on the other hand. Their fear of losing their freedom or desire for individual space has often meant that they lose relationships or friends, realizing their value only after losing them forever. They have freedom and space, but they also have become incredibly lonely.

Rise of the DINK Couples and Single Parents

DINK couples or double income, no kids couples are on the rise. Married couples, who are both working, mutually agree not to have kids. The number of such couples has shown a gradual increase among millennials. Various reasons contribute to such a decision. Millennials spend their early years mostly repaying their education debt. Having children may mean spending their prime years in bringing up children and educating them. Knowing well that what they have today may not last tomorrow, some millennials are unwilling to lose the best time of their life. Not having a kid means less responsibilities, more disposable income and more time for themselves. As selfish it may sound, it actually is not. Millennials do not have an assured income like the previous generation. With low job stability, their income may shrink suddenly and it might put severe financial strain on them. They are not even sure whether they are ready for such a responsibility or whether all this physical, emotional and psychological strain that they undertake in raising kids would be worth or not. But not even for a moment should one assume that this is an easy decision for millennials. Many DINK couples actually yearn to have kids at some point of time. Their life situations many a time create a sort of fear in them. The growing career centricity of both males and females and work pressure also make them apprehensive whether they will be able to provide enough time and attention to their kids. And contrary to popular perception, DINK couples are not restricted to urban areas. The 2011 population census in India actually showed that DINK couples were more in rural areas, owing to economic constraints and low incomes. Having kids is a big commitment and though most millennial couples yearn for kids, they find it difficult to commit themselves to such a huge responsibility. Delaying of parenthood is often related to their desire to be good parents.

While there is rise of DINK couples on the one hand, in parallel, another trend has shown a spike. The number of millennials choosing to be single parents also seems to be increasing. A research by researchers at Johns Hopkins University reveals that 'only about a third of all mothers in their late twenties were married when all their kids were born. And two thirds of them were single when at least one of their kids were born' (Cherlin, Talbert, & Yasutake, 2014). The number of American millennials choosing to be single parents is on the rise. While in India there may not be a specific study on millennials, however, another study done in the context of metro cities in India shows that the number of single-parent households is increasing in the country (Sundar, Mookharjee, Babar, & Ravikumar, 2011). In Chapter 3, I had cited a study done by CSDS (2017) that showed a sharp drop in the percentage of Indian youth who shun the idea of marriage (LOKNITI–CSDS–KAS, 2017). The statistics are no different in other parts of the world. A research published by Bowling Green State University, USA, shows that the majority of today's 25–34-year-olds have never married. Contrastingly, in 1980, 68 per cent of this age group were married (*Daily Mail*, 2017). In another research done by Pew Research Center, marriage propensity amongst millennials compared to that in baby boomers in the 1960s. It found that the proportion of white millennials older than 25 who had never married had doubled compared to the similar age group in the 1960s. The proportion of black millennials in the USA who had never married and had always been single had increased fourfold since the 1960s (*Time*, 2014). Another statistical study done by Allen Downey, a professor of computer science at Olin College of Engineering, also confirmed the fact that most millennials are either avoiding marriage or delaying it. The number of males and females among millennials who were likely to remain unmarried was substantially higher than previous generations. While marriage is not completely dead, there is a definite slowdown. More and more millennials are choosing to remain single.

Freedom Paradox

A 2013 study by Millennial Branding and oDesk found that over half of the working Gen Ys surveyed had quit their jobs to pursue independence and work for themselves (oDesk, 2013). Research has also indicated that millennials have more freedom and job options than any other group in history (PrincetonOne, n.d.). However, social support that has been described by Lin, Simeone, Ensel and Kuo (1979) as 'support accessible to an individual through social ties to other individuals, groups, and the larger community' has disappeared to a large extent. In the absence of real friends and meaningful relationships and because of delayed marriages and small nuclear families, millennials have poor social support system. Social isolation and low levels of social support have a big negative impact on the mental and physical health of millennials.

Space Paradox

Similarly, millennials' desire for individual space has brought them more loneliness. 'Relationships Indicators Survey 2011' showed that most of the Gen Y felt extremely lonely, much more frequently as compared to other generation members. Despite being heavily networked over social media, they were lonely. Social networking did not reduce their lonesomeness.

Saji confesses that she grew up as a lonely child. Having both her parents as working, she experienced long spells of loneliness staying alone in the house. She had no one to talk to or have a conversation. The lonesomeness grew so much at times that she feared losing her power of speech. Finding no one to talk to, she says that she used to talk to herself. She talked to birds, plants many a time, just so that she can hear her voice. Although she has very loving parents and they tried to make up for their long hours of absence by giving her a lot of attention when they were around, that did not completely alleviate her loneliness. At that age, when she was growing up, she had so many stories and secrets to share. But she found hardly anyone who would have patient ears! She is now married and is a mother to a 10-year-old boy but she still has not been able to forget that time of her life. As a result, she is very conscious of not letting her son go through the same experience. She works as a teacher in an international school and has always made a conscious effort to work in the same school where her son is studying. That keeps their timings synchronized and she can give adequate time to her child when at home. She tells further that she goes through immense stress at times, maybe because of her previous experience and consequently her fear that she might not be able to do enough for her child. Nevertheless, having a supportive and understanding husband relieves her stress to a large extent.

Saji does not have too many friends. She does not place her maximum trust on her online friends. She still considers the two friends that she made during her college days as her best friends. She is married to one of them and the other friend is Arpita; although they live in different cities and do not meet very often, Saji shares a special bond with her, like with no one else. When her husband had proposed to her when they were still in college, initially she had turned down the proposal as she thought that there will be compatibility issues. But then when her present husband suggested that if they get married they will be able to treasure this friendship for life, she could not resist the offer. She still holds this friendship dear to her heart! As a couple, they have seen both good and bad times in their 13 years of marriage, but their friendship has helped them sail past the adversaries. Her relationship with her husband has also assuaged her loneliness.

Soumi, married to a corporate hotshot, finds her time at home extremely boring and feels lonesome. Her husband leaves home by 11 a.m. and is back only close to midnight. Long hours of doing nothing and no one to talk to makes her feel tired and depressed. Soumi, who also has a small daughter, says,

I know that maybe he is trying to fend for us or maybe I am overreacting. But the fact of the matter is that from Monday to Friday, he does not have time to even talk to us. Even when he is at home, he is working on his laptop and that continues on most weekends too. Sometimes after coming back late in the night, my husband continues to work until 2 a.m. on his laptop. I am also concerned about the impact all this is having on his health. But my loneliness is huge.

Soumi is worried about the impact that long hours of her husband's unavail-ability is having on her young child. Of late, she feels that her daughter is growing irritable and is having mood swings as she misses her dad's presence. What makes it worse is that other kids of her age enjoy the company of their father, especially during evening hours. Soumi also complains of depression. Even though she tries to catch up with her friends in the evening, but then that does not still alleviate her loneliness. She also tries to engage in her pastime activities. But then she feels so depressed at times that she does not feel like doing anything or talking to anyone. She loves music and is also a very good singer herself, but these days she does not like to listen to music or to sing. Their mar-riage has not been short of a fairy tale. They met through common friends at a wedding and liked each other. They met more often and the liking only grew as the days passed. Even when he moved to another city as he took a new job, they never lost contact. Interestingly, she made the first move and proposed to him. The families were very supportive; small hiccups notwithstanding, their marriage was solemnized. She has until now shared a very healthy relation-ship with her husband but she finds it very difficult to deal with the current situation. Being surrounded by people is not really an answer to loneliness.

Material Wellness Paradox

The perceived material prosperity of millennials is both true and false in their own ways. Although standard of living has gener-ally improved, but in real terms their prosperity has not kept up with the expectation compared to the previous generations.

Income Paradox

In terms of face value of money, although the income of mil-lennials shows an increase over the previous generation's income, however adjusted to inflation and extrapolated over time in terms of expectations, they are actually earning less than their parents. Their desire to make most of the present in light of an uncertain future, their aspirational nature and the high peer pressure in the absence of privacy in their lives have shot up their maintenance expenses. A study by the American Institute of Certified Public Accountants shows that

> over three quarters of millennials want to have the same clothes, cars and technological gadgets as their friends, and that around half of them have to use a credit card to pay for basic daily necessities such as food and utilities (Investopedia, 2016).

They spend more on luxury goods than baby boomers. However, they continue to struggle with financial stability with their credit cards bills spiralling at times out of control and many of them struggling to pay their bills. Most of them do not save or invest for the future.

Career Paradox

Millennials are extremely optimistic and aspirational about their careers. Most of them are even willing to take risk, if this is what it takes to pursue the career of their dreams. Yet, the instability in the job market continues to keep them on tenterhooks.

Sandeep came on promotion to Bengaluru, working in Office Depot. In partnership with Reliance Industries, Office Depot was operating in India and was in the business of office stationaries, housekeeping supplies and corporate gifting supplies. Sandeep's happiness did not last long as he came to know that Office Depot was planning to close operations in India stung by low margins. They offered their partner Reliance to continue the business solo, which was not accepted. Hence, all employees were given some time to search for a new job. Sandeep had never been in such a situation. However, he found his next job very soon. After his successful stint in the next company for a couple of years, he got an offer from Uniconnect, a company that offered mobile sim cards to international travellers. They were setting up the Bengaluru office and were looking for someone for sales head position. The position was attractive and so was the remuneration. Sandeep decided to take the plunge. He resigned from his company and accepted the Uniconnect offer. While still on notice period in his old company, he was requested to conduct interviews on weekends so that he could put together his new team for the Bengaluru branch. He agreed for the same and conducted close to about 100 interviews, out of which he shortlisted close to 20 profiles. All this while, things were smooth and fine. But a surprise waited for Sandeep. On the day of his joining, when Sandeep called the company's HR team to enquire where he should report for completing joining formalities as the branch was not yet up and running, he was asked to wait for the CEO's call. After two days, he got a call from the CEO who told him that their Bengaluru branch plan had run into rough waters due to some unexpected challenges and they had shelved the plan for some time. He was given two choices—one to come and join in Mumbai where he would be given similar position and the other to look for a new job and take two months' salary as severance pay. He was shocked. He felt cheated. On receiving the offer from Uniconnect, he had left his previous company where he was well-entrenched, and now he was suddenly left with no job! Sandeep chose the second option as he was not in a position to shift from Bengaluru. That would cause a lot of disturbance to his working wife and child. Sandeep tells me,

> I did not face any monetary problem in the next two months, but the period was full of stress. On the one hand I had to search for a new job with nothing in my hand, and on the other hand I felt really wasted sitting in the house alone doing nothing. Morning my wife would leave for her work and my son for his school and I would just be left in the house. That was a very frustrating feeling. But I really got to know my real friends during that time and my close friends helped me wholeheartedly.

Sandeep eventually got a job and a good one too. But he recalls his Office Depot and Uniconnect experience as a learning that he will have to be ready for uncertainty and any sort of eventuality in his job context any time.

Take Abhishek's experience for instance! He was working as a campus programme manager at SlicePay, a digital payment start-up that offers micro-credits to students to meet their everyday cash needs. The company works on a band of interns who work on a part-time basis, promoting the company's offering in various campuses and getting new enrolments. Abhishek as a campus programme manager was in charge of managing all the interns—hiring them, then conducting product as well as process training for the interns and then deploying them on the field under a specific zonal manager. He was also responsible for collecting their performance reports from the zonal managers, guiding those who were falling short of expectations and also managing their compensation. He would also conduct occasional activities to entertain the interns and keep them motivated. Team outings, team lunches, etc. formed part of such activities. He had to ensure that the interns whom he had hired were retained in the company for at least three months. He liked the culture and the kind of autonomy that he was given to do his job. He was able to automate a large part of operations with a direct approval from the CEO. The company was also very happy with his performance and the regions that he was managing was recording 50 per cent growth on month-to-month basis. But then this was not enough to keep his job secure. The company failed to get the second round of funding on time and it being a start-up found it difficult to retain a large part of its workforce. Close to 33 per cent of the workforce was laid off. Abhishek also lost his job. Although the company has offered severance pay and is also offering outplacement services to help him find a new job, it is now more than a month that he is jobless. As he restlessly searches for a new job, he tells me that he is looking for job security more than the compensation that he gets in his new job. Will his desire for job security be ever fulfilled or will it remain a mere dream?

Kyra Joshi, currently on a sabbatical, preparing for the 'mains' exam of the state judiciary, has decided to risk it before the 'storm' hits her. She has already cleared the 'prelims' and is bullish about the 'mains' as well. If she successfully clears the 'mains', then she would be eligible to be appointed as a junior judge in the high court. The seed of her dreams was sowed about 18 months back when she was asked to take care of the legal and compliance team *of her company. Kyra, a business graduate, secured her job about five years back in one of the top technology companies in India, in the HR function. As an HR professional, she handled several responsibilities. Impressed with her stellar performance and owing to the law degree, she was asked to join the legal and compliance team. She enjoyed her new responsibility. As she started revisiting her law books, one day she felt that she needed to give her law career one more shot! But that would mean that she would have to take a break from her job and prepare for the coveted judiciary services in the country. It was a risky decision, considering that she was well-entrenched in her company. She tells,*

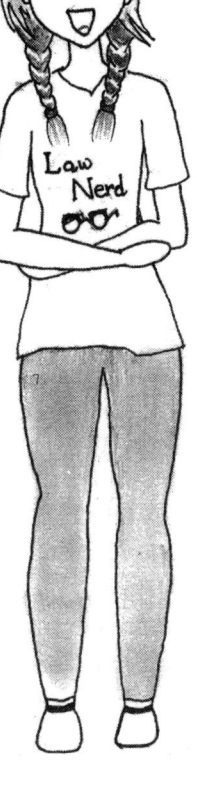

But then I thought, though I was doing well in my company, still some day my job might simply vanish if the economy or market takes a major hit. I told myself, I have done a lot for the company, now it is time to do something for myself! And I took the plunge.

The material wellness of millennials has also suffered. Their career aspirations have been dulled by unsteady jobs, and their generous spending on lifestyle and luxury goods have been dampened by dwindling incomes and rising debt.

Physiological Wellness Paradox

Physiological wellness determines our health. Mental and physical health of a person is generally a function of the kind of food that he/she eats, the soundness of the rest/sleep and a generous dose of relaxation and fun. In all these areas, millennials have taken a huge blow.

Pace Paradox

Millennials live in a world that moves and operates at a breakneck speed. In keeping pace with the affairs of this world, they often find themselves in a 'race' that hardly leaves any time for them. They do not have time to eat, sleep and relax or to entertain themselves. Result is that it leaves them harried, tired and unhealthy. The number of millennials suffering from physical ailments and mental health issue is overwhelming.

Opportunity Paradox

Millennials have a multitude of opportunities in a globalized world, but the demands of this world have been so high that the cost for the same has come in the form of erosion of health. Time is surely under strain, but the growing stress in lives of millennials, as they deal with a ruthless professional life and uncertainties that grasp them, has not left them being particularly proud of their health. It will not be exaggeration to say that millennials wear the crown of thorns that thrills and kills at the same time!

Celebration Paradox

'Work hard, party harder'—this theory has been ground in the system of millennials since beginning. However, ironically, while they have found the work demands unto the brim, somehow 'party' has sunk somewhere deep! So many reasons and occasions to celebrate, but the question is when? Even weekends are under threat as far as the demand of their work goes. If it is not work, then it is a company outing or an outbound team building/leadership training programme where attendance is not a matter of choice. And if they refuse weekend assignments, they are immediately branded as unprofessional.

The haste in the life of millennials has made time a rare commodity for millennials. Consequently, their poor eating habits, sleeping habits, exercising habits, a continued stress of missing deadlines and a fun-less life have led to the deterioration of their mental and physical health. The paradox could not be greater.

Reversal of Millennial Happiness

The net result of these paradoxes in the life of millennials has been a reversal of their happiness. When we compare them to the baby boomers, who are the parents of millennials and also their senior bosses, the picture that emerges is very interesting. Factors that were the cause of happiness for baby boomers have reversed and have brought unhappiness to millennials. Likewise, whatever baby boomers lacked in their life has come to millennials with ease. Essentially, it represents a depth deficit. The reversal of happiness has meant that millennials' emotional, social, material and physiological wellness have all hit rock bottom. Baby boomers on the other hand did quite well when it came to their emotional, social and physiological wellness. Even in terms of material wellness, they did not fare too bad.

THE LIFE OF Y

	Boomers	Millennials	
😊	Less but real friends	More connection	😊
	Strong bonds	More relationship choices	
	High social support	Greater freedom	
	More time for active socializing	More space	
	High job stability	Greater career optimism	
	Relaxed time to celebrate	More occasions to celebrate	
	Slow pace of life and work	More and varied opportunities	
	More time for self		
	Good mental and physical health		
	Good income		
	Lower maintenance cost		
😞	Less connections	Less real friends	😞
	Less relationship choices	Weak bonds, relationship fractures	
	Lesser freedom	Low social support	
	Restrained individual space	Heightened levels of loneliness	
	Low career optimism	Low job stability	
	Counted occasions to celebrate	Less time to celebrate	
	Less and limited opportunities	High pace of life and work	
		Hardly any time for self	
		Poor mental and physical health	
		Lower income	
		Higher maintenance cost	

This paradox has pinched life and consequent reversal of happiness has deep and far-ranging implications. Millennials lead a life very different compared to the previous generation and they have no choice but to lead the same. Considering that their realities are different, their needs and aspirations are also different that is often expressed in their difference in behaviour and mindset. Hence, the manner in which an organization engages with them and engages them cannot be the same. This applies in all contexts—engaging them as employees at workplace, engaging them as customers at marketplace and engaging them as valuable contributing members of society in the 'third' place. In the third and final section of the book, we will see how this understanding and deep empathy about the life of millennials can be used to engage them and create an effective sustainable organization.

PART III

Engaging the Millennial Generation

7
THE NEW RULE OF
ENGAGEMENT

———⊷◉⊶———

When the HR director at SAS was asked about the logic behind the vast array of benefits and services that SAS provides to its employee, he famously replied, 'There is nothing altruistic about all this. This is a for-profit business. We do all this because it all makes good business sense'. SAS CEO Jim Goodnight went on to add, 'I keep my employees happy and they keep my customers happy'.

So, do happy and engaged people help a company make more profits? Research definitely shows that it does—Thomas Wright, a professor at Fordham University, claims that employee happiness accounts for as much as 10–15 per cent of the variance in performance between different employees.

Happy and engaged people are more productive, more likely to receive a promotion (people like happy people), absent themselves less from work, show fewer fatigue symptoms and are more committed to work.

VUCA World

Engagement is ensuring that people are cognitively and emotionally connected to the company so as to elicit voluntary behaviour that is both productive and effective. Study after study have proved that engagement is positively linked with better financial performance of the firm, better idea generation and innovation ability of a company and better ability to withstand the challenges thrown by a volatile, uncertain, complex and ambiguous (VUCA) world.

The concept of VUCA was presented by the US Army War College to describe the more VUCA multilateral world which resulted from the end of the Cold War. It was not until the late 1990s that this acronym took shape, but this term really took roots after the 9/11 attacks on the USA. VUCA was subsequently adopted by strategic business leaders to describe the chaotic, turbulent and rapidly changing business environment that has become the 'new normal'. The economic crisis of 2008–2009 rendered most existing business models ineffective, and thereafter the explosion of social media and millennial generation on the global scene altered many existing business beliefs and notions.

While volatility has to do with the nature, speed and magnitude of change, uncertainty relates to the unpredictability of issues and events, complexity denotes the multiple and difficult-to-understand causes of a problem and ambiguity adds to the other three factors. Ambiguity makes it difficult-to-understand the meaning of fast-moving, unclear and complex events. VUCA model identifies the internal and external conditions affecting organizations today.

VUCA presents stiff challenges to business leaders all over the world to continuously assess their strategies to gain and sustain the competitive edge of their companies. In the face of ever-increasing stakeholder expectations, changing customer demographic profile and expectations, changing ways in which talent is managed, and rapid pace and direction of technological change, business leaders need to continuously innovate and find better ways of managing. VUCA has altered the business scene in a manner that can be best understood from this analogy. Earlier, business scene was like a chess board. The playing field was known; the players knew their pawns, bishop, knights, and rooks, besides the king and the queen. The only element of surprise was the strategy and 'moves'. However, VUCA has ensured that today business scene looks like an interactive video game where the surprises are at every corner, the context changes fast and even the ground appears to be shifting. The challenges are manifold and the surprise is not restricted to the strategy and the 'moves', but even the ground realities might alter suddenly and new opponents might appear who were never ever in the scene before. Few years back, the offline retailers could have hardly imagined that online retailers such as Amazon and Flipkart would pull the rug under their feet.

VUCA is the new reality, and business professionals need skill sets to deal with the contextual challenges more swiftly and in a more adept manner. Organizations on the other hand need a strongly engaged millennial workforce and highly engaged millennial customers to survive and thrive both in the workplace and in the marketplace.

Abysmal Levels of Engagement

Despite such strong correlation of engagement with individual happiness, creativity and organizational success, engagement levels have dipped across the world. Peter Drucker had once said, 'So much of what we call management consists in making it difficult for people to work'. Often organizations manage their most precious asset, their people, in the most clumsy and dysfunctional way. No wonder only 13 per cent of employees worldwide are engaged at work, according to Gallup's new 142-country study on the State of the Global Workplace. The bulk of employees worldwide are 'not engaged' or even worse rest are 'actively disengaged'. While the 'not-engaged' employees lack motivation and are less likely to invest discretionary efforts towards achieving organizational goals or outcomes, the 'actively-disengaged' ones are not only unhappy and unproductive but also likely to spread pessimism among other co-workers. This could be potentially damaging for the company. The middle segment or the 'disengaged' lot (where the maximum population resides currently) represents both an opportunity and a threat for the companies. The opportunity is to convert them to the 'engaged' set, and since they have not drifted too far away, it may not be too difficult to bring them back in the fold. The question remains who acts first—the companies or the actively disengaged ones?

With the new generation entering the workforce in large numbers and with clear indications of their growing conflicts with the older generation, poor engagement levels are indicative that most companies around the world have not been able to manage the new-generation workers in a manner so as to elicit motivation and discretionary efforts from employees towards achieving organizational goals or outcomes. Disengagement remains a common problem and engagement remains a common challenge around the world. Only companies need to take the wake-up call and realize that engagement is a business solution and an engaged workforce represents a business opportunity in helping them create greater value in their firms for their customers and meeting the companies' and shareholders' objectives.

Carpet-bombing or Drone Strategy?

Engaging millennials is not about carpet-bombing people with loads of events and information. Instead, it is about planning specific interventions that may ask for their contributions and involving them, so as to create an engagement not only with the event or the initiative but also with their families and friends. It must be something that they would like to tell their families and friends about, something that really excites them about a company. Also, it must not attempt generalization. Specific interventions for different sets of people should be designed. That creates deeper engagement.

For years, advertising agencies have beaten up the concept of 360 degree communications—of tracking consumers wherever they are and inundating them with (hopefully relevant) messages. Chuck Brymer, president and CEO of one of the world's most consistently awarded creative agencies DDB, was one of the first to move his agency away from the carpet-bombing of consumers with ad messages via a thousand different media. In the words of Brymer himself, 'I want to get to your connections. I want to engage you in a way that inspires you to communicate with your 6 degree (friends of friends, family and acquaintances)'. When DDB under Brymer's leadership designed Volkswagen's multiple-award-winning 'The Fun Theory' campaign, it showed that it was possible to extract fun from mundane activities like taking the stairs instead of an escalator or recycling. This was done by transforming the stairs into a gigantic playable piano, and the act of recycling bottles being turned into a game with points. The idea was built on the concept that the message connects one not only to the brand but also to one's friends; a message one could can pass on, participate in and play with. This created much deeper engagement.

A few years back, a very interesting corporate social responsibility (CSR) effort was undertaken by a reputed and popular finance brand Sundaram Finance in Chennai. The brand over a period of time has been  part of many families in South India by truly demonstrating to its customers its correct brand values corporate vision. The company hardly advertises, and it has positioned itself in the minds of the customers mainly through strong word of mouth marketing and well-networked distribution of their products with strong focus on service across South India. However, the key to their ascent has been a much-focused promotional campaign. As a part of their CSR push, the company along with Ogilvy PR came out with the novel idea of promoting Carnatic music among kids in Chennai, since it was found that more kids in that part of the world were getting hooked to computers, chats and TV shows. The company saw a great opportunity here and branded this CSR programme as 'Sundaram Finance Sunday Kutcheri' (music concert). The programme was held in a park and the concept was developed to provide young kids aged under 15 to showcase their musical talent. The audience for this programme were the young and aspiring musical talent, music connoisseurs and morning walkers in the park. The programme was held every first Sunday between 6.30 and 7.30 a.m. Kids with good flair in music were selected through audition tests. After the first half-a-dozen kutcheri, the concept caught on newspapers, and channels came forward to cover it. High on recall and low on cost, this focused CSR effort of the company not only struck a strong chord with the people but also engaged them with the brand.

Both DDB and Sundaram Finance moved away from carpet-bombing promotional strategy; instead, they came out with campaigns that were specifically directed towards engaging their target audience and achieved phenomenal success.

The poor engagement levels around the world show beyond doubt that with millennials slowly making up largest percentage of working population, the traditional engagement methods and models have yielded very little. The new rule of engagement is having a very focused and customized engagement strategy for millennials, instead of carpet-bombing them with models that have not been designed keeping them in mind. Whether it is about engaging millennial employees or customers, it is no more about carpet-bombing; instead, it is about directed drones that cost less and do more!

The New Rule of Engagement: Drone Strategy

The attempt of the previous chapters has been to provide a deep insight and understanding about the life of millennials. It clearly shows that their life challenges, priorities and contexts are significantly different from those of previous generations. Millennials are racially and ethnically diverse, and much less homogeneous than the boomers. It is a group born in the age of the Internet (as opposed to TV), which drives both diversity and connectedness. In addition, hiring millennial employees has often been considered to be as difficult as attracting millennial customers. Millennial employees are smart and opinionated, and have grown up with a multitude of choices. They are not afraid to challenge management and are willing to confront the status quo. The managerial implications to millennials' entry into the workplace are complex and have to be investigated within the multi-generational context that contemporary managers experience.

The new rule of engagement of millennials is built on the foundation of deep empathy and has two core beliefs—first that before we engage them, we need to have a real understanding of their life goal, aspirations, the kind of pulls and pressures they experience, the kind of paradoxical life they lead, the kind of behaviours they exhibit and the reason behind those mindsets and behaviours; and second that we need an engagement strategy for millennials that is built on such understanding. The new rule of engagement hence moves away from the traditional models, akin to carpet-bombing and is replaced by one that has been specially designed to engage this unique and powerful cohort.

So, what are the new drones, or say drivers for engaging millennials? Based on years of study and countless interactions with millennials, I very firmly believe that these 13 attitudinal drivers of millennials are key to engaging them. These drivers are further classified as cognitive drivers (prompt logical thinking and rational processing) and affective drivers (evoke emotional response and are connected to feelings) or are hybrid between the above two. These drivers are generic drivers and hence can be applied in various engagement contexts—engaging millennial workers, customers, volunteers, learners and community leaders.

We will call these drivers as drones, for the customization done in their design and specificity of their application in being solely directed towards engaging the millennials.

Drone 1: Freedom

Freedom to millennials means having the right to their own space and own time. They call it 'my space, my time'. They do not want anyone to encroach on their space, as much they are ready to give that space to others. Freedom also means to them a choice to live life for themselves and not to impress anyone. They want to have a choice of doing things and making their own decisions. They do not want anyone compelling them for anything; therefore, words such as mandatory and compulsory repel them, and they feel an immediate infringement to their individual freedom. They want to experience new things and hate to be tied to anything that pulls them back. They want to have their choice when it comes to selecting the field of their education, career or marriage.

Freedom is a hybrid between cognition and affective. It is as much cognitively processed as it evokes emotional responses from the cohort. Millennials are also reflective and wish to give more freedom to their children when they have them.

Region, religion and income have no effect in the way this generation looks at freedom. However, gender differences seem to exist in at least the way they value freedom. Females react with stronger emotions at any suggestion of compromising their freedom. At one point of time during the focus group, a male participant suggested that one should try to adapt and adjust if at times freedom is curtailed. This was vehemently opposed by all other female participants. Two things became very clear—one that freedom was a very 'me' thing and the participants did not like to be told that they should not complain too much when their freedom was curtailed; second that any suggestion about adapting and making adjustments if freedom was ever curtailed offended the females more than the male millennials. Recently, when two hostels of Delhi University barred female students from stepping out of the hostel premises during Holi festival, the female students cried 'injustice' and forced the hostel authorities to relook at their decision. Millennial women are far more confident and assertive than the previous-generation counterparts. Study shows that they not only have been able to close the educational gaps in most parts of the world but are also extremely confident of closing gender gaps that exist today (Jacobs, 2017). Despite this, they are less bitter and do not identify themselves with traditional feminists. There is a general feeling among millennial women that 'the term "feminism" has been hijacked by a minority of vocal extremists who have redefined it as "gender feminism," claiming that gender is a patriarchal social construct created in order to oppress women (Nielsen, 2017)'. They are more aware about their rights and they are far more forthright when it comes to protecting their freedom.

Drone 2: Feeling Valued

Millennials like to feel valued. They like to be accepted and given due credit and recognition for their work and contributions. They seek an individual identity and are not averse to making uncommon choices related to their career or otherwise that helps them stand out in the crowd or garner attention. They like to be valued in their families, among their friends, in their work groups and in the workplaces. It gives them a sense of satisfaction and also acts like a motivator. Even small recognition goes a long way in making millennials feel valued. They like a sense of challenge in what they do at their educational institutions or at their workplaces. A sense of challenge in their assignment provides them an opportunity to display their capabilities and become more competitive. This in turn gives them a sense of accomplishment that once again makes them feel valued.

'Feeling valued' is more an affective driver than cognitive. Lack of recognition and respect for their work and contributions elicits strong emotions from millennials. They feel that their productivity is lowered when they are not given due credit for their work as it fills them with negativity, irritation and resentment, and they tend to lose interest, ignore or quit and move away.

Drone 3: Growth

Millennials believe a lot in personal growth and self-improvement. Contrary to popular belief, they also have a philosophical approach to personal growth. They feel that such growth as a person must help them to keep a check on their desires and be happier in their lives. They believe that their constant boredom with the status quo pushes them towards growth. They also believe that growth is a function of their deficiencies. Hence, they qualify personal growth in terms of both emotional and cognitive growth, both at a personal and a professional front. They believe that new learning, experiences and education lead to growth. They do not discount the importance of social learning and think that it plays a major part in their growth. They find an environment filled with a sense of challenge and opportunities to be much more conducive for growth. They also appreciate the need for continuous learning for they feel that one's growth equates to one's success. Growth is processed cognitively. Faced with a situation where they find it difficult to learn new things and grow, they seem to take a careful and consultative approach to change or to get out of such situations. They are not averse to quitting or moving away from environments or organization that stunt their growth, but generally they do not try that as a first resort. They will generally adjust to adverse situations, reassess and make a better choice. In other words, they take a logical reasoning path to prevail over their families or organizations and make choices that allow them to grow. They also wish to discuss and seek guidance as to how they can grow better.

Drone 4: Connected

Personally as well as professionally, this generation feels that it is very important for them to stay connected. However, since they are constrained with time and even as they call themselves a bit 'socially lazy', they prefer social media to stay connected. Millennials are heavily connected on social media, for personal, social and professional reasons.

Millennials also use their mobiles and messaging apps like WhatsApp to stay connected. They have a strong desire to stay connected and become restless if their phones are not buzzing. The exhibit alongside is a real feed from a social media site and is a status update of a millennial that goes on like 'Phone broke down. No WhatsApp, no Facebook. No news updates. Life's tough man'.

While most of the desire to remain connected appears to be for emotional reasons, there are certain practical reasons as well for which millennials wants to remain connected. Millennials are dominating the online shopping revolution around the world. The traditional 'shop till you drop' has been replaced with 'shop wherever you drop'; from 'mortar-and-brick' formats to more of 'tap-and-click' format. The marketing mix element of 'place' has been completely transformed by millennials with shopping becoming location independent. According to the research released recently by Goldman Sachs, older millennials (aged 25–34) are more likely than any other generation to spend most of their clothing budget online. Separate data collected by the firm over time have found that the online spending habits of 35–44-year-olds have lagged this group by about one–two years, with those aged between 45 and 54 straggling another two or three years (Gustafson, 2016).

Few years back, when an Indian IT major tried to gag the voices of its employees on FB, it boomeranged on them big time. The story goes back to 2009–2010 when Infosys introduced a new role and career enhancement policy that changed the way vertical mobility would occur in the company. Dubbed as 'iRACE', the policy developed due to growing concern from its clients on the capability of the company's resources in client-facing roles, many of whom had been promoted due to retention pressures, rather than on their competencies. Faced with flak from its clients, the company hired a consultant who in turn developed this new role and career enhancement policy that would scrutinize all vertical mobility cases within the company meticulously focusing on competencies. What made this policy controversial was the fact that it was implemented with retrospective effect which meant that the employees promoted in the recent past would also be re-evaluated. This resulted in over 5,000 demotions across the company. Furious employees spilled their anger and dissatisfaction on social media. Instead of addressing the concerns of the employees, the company soon came out with a social media policy that was largely seen as a way to restrict employees from sharing their ire on social media. This resulted in even more disconcert among employees and bad publicity. In the age of ubiquitination of social media, can such restrictions really make a difference? Should companies try to gag such voices or should they make an attempt at finding out the reasons behind such disenchantment? Around the same time, Kimberley Swann, a 16-year-old was fired from Ivell Marketing & Logistics, a product development and sourcing company, for describing her job as 'boring' on FB. Miss Swann working as an office administrator found her job of filing, stapling, shredding hole punches and scanning paper as wasteful and monotonous, and so she let out steam by sharing the same with her friends on FB. She was given marching orders from the Ivell premises.

Will such a measure help? According to a survey by global Internet content security provider Trend Micro, the percentage of employees visiting social networking sites at the workplace is on the rise globally.

If a video on YouTube has made a local taxi driver of Varanasi a celebrity, and if an engaging FB account has made some popular foreign (Starbucks, Coca-Cola, Skittles) and Indian (Vodafone Zoozoos, Fastrack, Tata Docomo) brands garner a huge following, then there must be more to social media than being a negative publicity tool.

So, it's time that companies start identifying how they can leverage social media to connect and better engage with their own employees. Also, companies must try to address 'real' problems by doing a root cause analysis, rather than quell dissent on the social media. Additionally, they must also provide for internal communicable platforms that allow for a dialogue between the firm and its employee constituents and use them as a tool to better internal processes.

Finally, a sense prevailed over the company when it announced two new initiatives 'Infy Bubble' and 'Infy Radio'. 'Infy Bubble' was an FB version for the employees where they could air their opinion and criticize or praise new policies or announcements by the company, whereas 'Infy Radio' was an infotainment initiative. Along with entertainment of the employees, it would also ensure that employees are communicated on new developments of the company. A separate study had found that employees felt a growing sense of communication gap as the company grew bigger in size.

Drone 5: Support

Millennials lack support system as most of them live alone in cities with no one except themselves to fall back upon. Hence, support from family is very important for millennials. They owe it to their parents and trust their parents to stand by, no matter what comes by. They like to consult their family at times for decision-making. They also feel the need of a guide or a mentor. At different stages of their life, they feel the need of a different mentor—parents, then teachers and then mentors in professional life.

However, there are two very interesting things about millennials when it comes to the support that they seek:

1. As much as millennials yearn for a support system, they are not dependants. Confronted with a challenge, most of them want to face it on their own. However, if things go beyond their control, they turn for help to those whom they trust.
2. Millennials who have not received the kind of support they have expected from their parents or friends have become slightly bitter about the same.

Support is again a hybrid. It is partly a cognitive driver and partly affective. Millennials need a support system and its absence makes them restless, worried and even stressed and depressed. Having said this, they also want to believe that they can face such situations and cope up. They anticipate extreme unpleasant situations like losing their parents or their jobs and believe that with their abilities, they will be able to tide over such adversaries.

Drone 6: Novelty

Novelty or newness for millennials means realistic new experiences. By their own confession, they find it difficult to do repetitive things and cannot live a monotonous life. They find it almost compelling to explore possibilities, new places, new people, relationships and even new abilities in themselves. They love adventure and may engage at times in even crazy things for the sake of novelty. They like spontaneity and unconventionality and look for newness and change constantly.

Novelty is a cognitive driver. In an environment with hardly any opportunity to learn new things and new experiences and to adopt unconventional approaches, millennials believe in quietly working on a new idea and then bringing out the results for everyone to see.

Drone 7: Collaboration

Millennials believe in collaboration as it leads to learning and complimentary skilling within teams. Collaboration, according to millennials, leads to idea generation and knowledge creation. The benefits of collaborating is central to their decision whether they wish to collaborate or not. They are careful about collaborating and lay emphasis on the importance of right collaboration, right reasons to collaborate, right people to collaborate with, right time to collaborate and right stage of the project when collaboration should be undertaken. They generally follow a measured path to collaboration:

1. Introspection (why and when to collaborate)
2. Clarifying the idea (collaborating for idea generation or collaborating to refine idea)
3. Deciding the nature of collaboration
4. Choosing the collaborator
5. Freezing the opinions
6. Collaborating

Collaboration is definitely a cognitive driver. Millennials are also open to informal and virtual collaboration routes.

Drone 8: Care

Millennials place importance on emotional security more than any other form of security, something that they miss so much. They like to be cared. They expect love, affection, care and personal touch. Although they are hesitant to ask for care, yet they like it when they receive attention. They also find sharing as a way of caring. Some of them even suggested that they look for emotional connect with the companies they engage with.

Care is an affective driver. Care motivates them and lack of it upsets them and sometimes even makes them feel lost. They, however, find it difficult to express lack of care. They may find life meaningless when they do not get enough care but will not show it to others.

Drone 9: Accountability

Millennials contrary to popular belief are responsible but at the same time expect others to be responsible. They believe that responsibility and accountability go hand in hand. Words that they associate with accountability are fairness and honesty.

When they are working with others in a group, they expect the other group members also to be responsible since everyone in the end enjoys the same benefits and rewards. However, millennials like responsibility to be a matter of personal choice and forced upon. They also want due credit and recognition for being responsible.

Accountability is a cognitive driver. When they find others not responsible enough, they mostly voice their opinions without any fear of conflict. They believe in straight talk and cautioning the person, even conveying one's displeasure. They also think that collectivist cultures breed more irresponsibility, since in these cultures responsibility is often thrust on the individual but at the same time it is easy to avoid the same.

Drone 10: Flexibility

Millennials think that their generation is more flexible than the previous generations. They understand flexibility in terms of lack of rigidity in rules, regulations and provisions that allows them to make more choices. They expect flexibility in their families as well as in their organizations. Rigidity actually puts them off and might even turn rebellious.

Flexibility is a hybrid but more of an affective driver than cognitive. Millennials believe that flexibility is a basic human right. They feel that lack of flexibility is taking a toll on their productivity, work–life balance and health. Faced with lack of flexibility, they first try to adjust but if nothing works and they cannot cope with the stress, then they are likely to quit.

In the case of flexibility, some gender differences are observed between males and females that could be even culture specific. While both of them expect flexibility and consider rigidity as a spoiler, men expect women to show greater degree of flexibility when it comes to taking care of home and kids. They seem to believe that home and children are primarily the responsibility of the women, who on the other hand feel that both partners need to be equally flexible and consider home front as a joint responsibility.

Drone 11: Sense of Balance

Millennials think that they live an unbalanced life. Situation plays an important role in whether they can attain the balance that they are seeking between professional, social and family life. They try to prioritize at times, yet that fails on more occasions than not. They emphasize on the importance of good planning in ensuring balance in their lives. They also try to balance between different relationships. Despite all this, a sense of balance eludes them and causes stress in their lives.

Sense of balance is more an affective driver. Lack of balance leaves them frustrated and tensed, many a time even depressed and at other times hopeful that the balance will swing back on its own.

Drone 12: Fun

Fun is an important element of millennials' life. They like to do serious stuff too in an environment that is light, informal and fun. Fun means pleasure, excitement and even at times freedom to do try crazy ideas. Spending time with family, hanging out and chatting with friends top the list of fun engagement for millennials.

Millennials like a workplace that has a fun and relaxed environment, a place where they get enough opportunities to challenge the present and experiment the future. Flexibility to try something new, a sense of accomplishment and encouragement from seniors equal to fun at workplace for millennial workers.

Fun undoubtedly is an affective driver. Without an element of fun, millennials find life boring and see no excitement in their pursuits. Brands that are associated with fun element engage better with millennials. Mahindra, one of the revered Indian automobile brands, has always tapped the fun element in its marketing campaigns and has been largely successful in engaging the millennials. The 'Live Young, Live Free' campaign, which underlines Mahindra's leadership in the utility vehicles segment, has been quite a rage.

Another campaign of Mahindra that is creating ripples is a film for the launch of its 'Young SUV', the recently launched KUV100. The campaign again conceptualized by Interface Communications stars film star brand ambassador Varun Dhawan and is set to the Hindi song *'Tere mere saath jo hota hai'* by Lucky Ali. The 'Weekend Life' campaign around their offering Quanto was also a superhit.

Drone 13: Instancy

Millennials believe in 'today', 'now' and this 'instant'. They believe in living in the present. They neither think too much about the future nor plan too much in advance. Their prime attention remains in living their life in the present.

Instancy is a hybrid between cognitive and affective. They like pragmatic people who believe in taking quick decisions. They also like instant feedback for their work. They believe that instant feedback helps them correct their mistakes, keeps them interested and makes them more confident. They expect continuous real-time feedback. Nitin Nagaich, managing director of Convate, a global recruitment consultancy firm adds,

Satish Chandrasekaran
7 hrs · @

I am super glad that I quit working for any company. I mainly saw wicked wolves, super wolves and majestic wolves. Nevertheless, they were all wolves. But there were few great human beings too!! They were not VPs, GMs and senior managers but were just trainees and executives. After 5 months of quitting, I found only Human around me. The wolves are gone with their own kind. Politics, power, prestige is gone. Designations dint matter anymore. I am no longer stuck with utilitarian idiots who judges the usefulness of my being through CTC, I found a deeper love for life that needs no judge. When I quit, all of the wolves died. Sum it up, higher the power, lesser the human you become... If this hurts your ego, it only shows how right I am.

👍 Like   💬 Comment   ↗ Share

The feedback needs not only to be instant but it also needs to be right feedback given in the right manner. The feedback should not only state the problem but the manager must be able to lead the employee towards solution. Hand-holding during difficult times is important. That creates longer engagement and inspires the millennial workers.

This update on a social networking site by Satish Chandrasekaran got me intrigued. Satish, a millennial, quit his job to start his own venture. He seemed completely disillusioned by his previous employer. What would have made him so bitter about his employer? He had been my student and I have known him to be a pleasing person with lots of friends. His jibe at his past employer was not only surprising but also very intriguing. I spoke to him and what came to my knowledge calls for a lot of attention from employers and leaders managing millennials.

We will have to wait until the next chapter to find out causes behind his disengagement with his employer.

At a time when most companies are scrambling and struggling to engage millennials, the drone model of millennial engagement offers a unique design that can be applied in various scenarios—engaging millennial workers, customers and valuable contributing members of the society. The coming chapters are more solutions and less discussion in terms of engaging this unique cohort.

8
ENGAGING MILLENNIALS
AT THE WORKPLACE

Millennials have piqued the curiosity of many a researcher in the recent times. Despite this generation demonstrating different behaviour and mindsets, the change was not clear and managers were not able to see the huge impact that this generation would make on this world. All sort of researches have been conducted and we know a huge output came out of those, but still there is much to learn and process in order to understand what might be their long-term objectives. We have seen them growing up with a tech affinity that surpasses any of our better guesses; they largely contributed on technology development, not only stimulating the market with demand but also actively walking the extra mile to give a concrete contribution in terms of research and development while working for companies. It is still hard for people coming from the Gen X or baby boomers to understand how to hire and engage millennials, most probably because they are using the parameters that worked well in their time to attract millennials, a process that clearly doesn't work most of the times.

We also had a close and deep look at the lives of millennials. They lack what they need most—wellness. Their state of wellness is not particularly good. That makes it even more necessary for the organizations to design an engagement strategy that addresses the wellness deficit and aims to raise the same. This will mean a more win-win outcome for both companies and millennial workers. Companies need to rethink their strategy when it comes to hiring and engaging millennials. The old designs are hardly working. In other words, what worked for the older generations do not appear to be clicking for the millennials.

Organizational design has three primary elements—structure, culture and control systems. While structure represents the hierarchy and reporting mechanisms in a company, culture refers to a system of shared assumptions, values and beliefs, which governs how people behave in organizations. Control systems, also referred to as reward systems, ensure the manner in which rewards and benefits are distributed in an organization and the extent and manner to which they are used to control people. The reasons behind their different mindsets and behaviour make it amply clear that there is a need for a new organizational design when it comes to engaging them. They abhor hierarchy and bureaucracy; they do not like rigid mechanized culture with too many rules. A control system that is based on command, infiltratory supervision, hire and fire, carrot and stick, and coercion-based disciplining does not work when it comes to millennial workers.

Millennial employees' work-related characteristics and attitudes are radically different from all previous generations at work. They are also incongruent with conventional thinking in terms of how new entrants in workforce should think and act. They are independent, confident and self-reliant. They are uncomfortable with too many rules. They do not accept authority of their seniors by virtue of their position; they rather accept authority of one who sets examples. They have higher expectations of equality and diversity at their workplace than their previous generations and seek an encouraging and supportive management style that allows them to perform well in a dynamic environment. They want clear directions at workplace; however, they despise micromanagement and become irritated with laziness and abhor slowness. Reason for millennials' low acceptance of authority is embedded in their upbringing. Gen X views boss as an expert—someone whose hard-earned experience and skill demand consideration and deference. Access to authority is limited and must be earned. In contrast, millennials think that they can go in on the first day and talk to the CEO about what's on their mind. But this is how their baby boomer parents raised them to believe that their voice matters. And hence, while Gen X will take orders and follow them, a millennial will always want to know the reason why they must do what they have been asked to do.

Sociologist and philosopher Max Weber had classified authority as charismatic authority, traditional authority and legal authority. Charismatic authority refers to a leader who has desirable traits and competencies that adorn him/her with a magnetic pull that he/she has on people. They put their highest level of trust on such a leader. While traditional authority refers to a dominant leader, legal authority refers to a legitimacy of the leader by virtue of the positional power that the society or organization has bestowed upon him/her. Millennials do not easily accept traditional and legal authority and do so just to be compliant at times. In real terms, they accept charismatic authority, a leader who is a role model for them and one who can establish a strong faith in his/her followers through his/her unbiased action, objective behaviour and superior skills.

Millennial Lens: What Do They Expect from Their Employers?

What would a millennial look for when choosing a company to work? What are the factors that will bear more weightage than others? If companies wants to attract millennials, then they must take into consideration what they really expect from their workplace. By understanding the values and motivations of this cohort, businesses and organizations can redesign the strategy to build attractive workplaces that appeal to these young workers.

The results of a research-based survey undertaken by me, comprising millennials of both genders, of different nationalities and ones with and without job experience, are very interesting and provide good insight into millennial expectations.

When asked what they would look for in an employer of choice, many of them showed preferences for a friendly environment: this may mean that working is often stressful and a friendly working environment might help them to fulfil the job responsibilities.

Interviews distinctly showed how well aware they are of the economic crisis, and it was possible to extrapolate a particular focus on salary, especially among those who had some work experience. It is significant to know about their focus on career opportunities combined with a desire for a stimulating job; they clearly stated an interest in redefining tasks so as not to deal with boredom.

When asked to rank the factors in order of preference in terms of what they expect from their employers, a slight difference was observed between those with and without job experience. The millennials passing out of college with hardly any job experience ranked 'opportunities for growth', 'flexible work environment' and 'openness to ideas and diverse thoughts' as top three factors they value in an employer.

A slightly different result was observed in the case of experienced millennials who had given highest priority to 'quality of life/life balance', followed by good 'benefits, perks and compensation' and 'empowerment and freedom for decision-making'.

Factor Ranking	Millennial Fresh Out of College
1	Opportunities for growth
2	Flexible work environment
3	Openness to ideas and diverse thoughts
4	Meaningful job
5	Empowered workplace
6	Rewards and recognition
7	Good quality of life
8	Exciting career opportunities
9	Attractive compensation, benefits and perks
10	Continuous real-time feedback
11	Value for individual goals and aspirations
12	Socially responsible company
13	Fun place to work, casual environment
14	Collaboration opportunities
15	BYOD and use of social media at workplace

Factor Ranking	Millennial with Work Experience
1	Quality of life
2	Attractive compensation, benefits and perks
3	Openness to ideas and flexible work environment
4	Career opportunities and collaboration
5	Opportunities for growth
6	Socially responsible company
7	Value for individual goals and aspirations
8	Meaningful job
9	Continuous real-time feedback
10	Rewards and recognition
11	Fun place to work and casual environment

As a tech-friendly generation, they eagerly mine data through media and they are daily exposed to loads of information, data and trends. As foreseen, a wide number of different companies were named; among them, Google still ranked number one among the dream companies to work for among the millennials, with 12.5 per cent of the sample voting for the company. An engaging environment and a passion-led workplace were cited as the reasons for choosing Google over other companies. This further underlines the fact that despite the not-so-conducive economic environment in which they live, they still look for a job in which they can make use of what they are passionate about and do something meaningful that is not constraining.

Hiring Millennials and Opportunity for Early Engagement

Hiring is an opportunity for any company not only to find right hires but also to establish early engagement with new recruits. Many companies ignore the importance of this phase and the kind of impact that hiring experiences have on engagement. It has been seen that early work experiences have a formative effect on millennial employees. Hence, if these experiences are good, then the motivation levels are high. Conversely, if they are poor, then it not only lowers the motivation levels but also makes them more cynical of employer's decisions and initiatives. CEOs of leading corporations have bet their money on hiring and spending considerable time involving themselves in the process. According to LinkedIn co-founder Reid Hoffman in his new book *The Start-up of You*, FB founder Mark Zuckerberg spends close to half of his time in hiring new recruits for his company. Not so long back, Marissa Mayer, an ex-Google employee and the present president of Yahoo, had decided to review every new hire that the company makes. Arianna Huffington takes out time to interview each and every hire at *The Huffington Post* (Business Insider, 2017). LinkedIn, Facebook, Yahoo and *The Huffington Post* are iconic brands and have been leaders in their own ways. The kind of focus that topmost leaders in these companies have on hiring underlines the point made earlier very well.

Poorly conceptualized and conducted selection processes by companies not only result in poor hires but also dent early opportunities to engage new hires and also result in poor publicity. Companies should not forget that word of mouth today has become digital and millennials are not averse to openly airing their criticisms about poor experiences. The converse is also true. At times, even though a millennial candidate may not have made the cut but is impressed by the smooth selection process, and the professional manner in which he/she is treated can make him/her to talk well about the company. A good hiring process can significantly bolster the goodwill of a company.

Good listening, interpretation, and analytical and communication skills are the top expectations of companies when they
look for people to hire. Companies also value their learnings
from their previous jobs. Millennials are expected to exhibit
empathy. Loyalty is also an expectation to some extent. Mr
Siddharth S. N., head, business HR in a large retail group based
out of India, echoes what most companies perhaps want to
ensure while hiring millennials that how long are they going to
stay in their companies.

> We are not expecting them to stay forever in our companies.
> However, when I ask them how long do they plan to stay in
> the company and they say I don't know, then that is a red flag
> for me. Even if they plan to stay for two years and they tell it
> assertively, I am fine.

Hire for Competence

Subhra Banerjee, Bengaluru branch head at Aahaa Stores Pvt.
Ltd, says,

> Millennials come dear and any mistake in hiring is an undesir-
> able cost to company. We rely on competency-based hiring
> when it comes to hiring the sales force.

The Chennai-based company, which is a one-stop solution for
office supplies servicing corporate clients and raised $1 million
funding recently, distinguishes its sales force into two distinct
types—'hunters' and 'farmers'. The 'hunters' are the ones who
acquire new clients and hence when hiring them, stress is laid
on aptitude for sales, communication, negotiation and persua-
sion skills. Besides, it is important for them to have a hunger

for sales. Once the client is acquired, they are handed over to the 'farmer' who has to build relation with the client, fulfil all their needs, attend to escalations and increase volume of business through client satisfaction. While hiring 'farmers', emphasis is on the ability of the candidate to build and maintain relationships and their level of empathy.

Hire for Ability

One of Britain's biggest graduate recruiters EY, the global accountancy firm, recently announced that it was scrapping the requirement for applicants to have a minimum 2:1 degree pass or UCAS point score of 300 (the equivalent of three B grades at A level). The company made the decision to change the application rules for its graduate, undergraduate and school-leaver programmes after an independent study that rated its in-house assessment programme and numeracy tests as 'a robust and reliable indicator of a candidate's potential to succeed'. This is part of the company's effort to attract millennial talent and hence open up opportunities for talented individuals regardless of their educational background and provide greater access to the profession. Educational qualifications, although important, need to be discounted a bit with respect to millennials. The increasing employability gap and at the same time company's need for talent need them to be flexible in terms of educational backgrounds. Instead, having highly validated selection tools that help in identifying real talent is more important.

Previous job experience is more a measure of what a person has done and may be not so much of what a person can do. In other words, just because a millennial has been in a poor job before that does not mean that he/she is not worthy enough. Millennials are not afraid of even switching careers. Interviewing millennials is more an opportunity to measure their potential or what they can do and less of taking a stock of their previous performance.

Set Wet: What to Expect!

Subhra Banerjee goes on to add that once the resumes are forwarded by HR, he usually does cold-calling to the candidates. He says,

> That saves company both time and money. Millennials are found to be more open-minded and if they love their job they are ready to give more than 100 per cent to the same. Cold-calling helps in three ways—one I can understand whether they understand the job content really well and whether that excites them; second whether as a company we will be able to meet their expectations; and, finally, whether they have a career objective, some kind of plan for their future. Usually the ones who have a clear path envisioned for themselves stay longer and perform better.

Millennials do not like ambiguity and are comfortable if the company has a clear set of expectations from them. They get frustrated when certain expectations are made evident to them post hiring that were not known to them beforehand. They perceive such cases to be unprofessional and exploitative. Hence, it is important to clarify what is expected out of a particular role right at the time of selection. For millennials, the utility of departure is greater than utility of dependence. In other words, if they feel that the contract between them and their employer has been breached in some way, they like to leave rather than negotiate further.

Hiring Can Also Be Innovative

Research clearly indicates that millennials know how to solve problems and shorten their learning curve by using technology collaboration tools such as mobiles, Bluetooth, laptops, handhelds, electronic mails and text messages. In fact, they are the first generation whose Internet consumption exceeds TV consumption.

At L'Oreal India, the cosmetics and beauty products company, graduates and postgraduates being considered for a job have to play a game called 'Reveal'. It simulates the work environment; players move through various challenges across departments—finance, sales, marketing, operations and research and innovation.

Another interesting research on millennials showed that their learning is positively impacted by incorporation of visual elements, and hence graphic novels provide a more attractive medium of learning to communicate business concepts than traditional textbooks. The 'Reveal' game that candidates get to play at L'Oreal India seems to be built on the same principle. Candidates pick an avatar and interact with graphical characters in different departments. They start with product development and then navigate their way through three rooms and answer over 500 questions. Meanwhile, a computer program keeps a tab on time spent to complete each task and assesses logical reasoning and analytical skills.

Tell 'n' Sell

Millennials have been brought up by parents who have always told them that they can do anything and achieve anything they set their eyes on. They have been educated in schools where everyone has been given a participation certificate irrespective of who won and who lost. Hence, they have grown up with a feeling that their ideas have a power to change the world. They are eager to share their ideas and work on what they feel passionately about. They like to associate with companies that give them an opportunity to contribute their ideas.

Selection process is also an excellent opportunity for telling the good candidates as to what are the exciting future plans of the company and what is in store for them should they become a part of the company. Millennials are career focused and wish to know whether they have a good future in the company that they are about to consider. Siddharth S. N. heading business HR of one of the largest retail group in India says that their company has a 'Sponsored Career Mobility' programme targeted especially towards millennials, under which 5 per cent of the top performers in the company get career passports. The passport entails them to a guaranteed vertical mobility every year and monetary incentives. Such efforts have brought down the attrition from 10 per cent a month to about 4 per cent a month and retention of high potentials has gone up to 97 per cent in the company.

Flexibility Helps!

Millennials love flexibility in terms of work arrangements and use of social media at workplace and want their offices to be a fun place to work. Giving them an impression of lack of flexibility is like turning them away after inviting them for a party. Making millennial candidates to fill in lengthy forms that often make them fill unnecessary and repetitive information about themselves and putting them through too many formalities during selection process or later are again turn-offs. Millennials prefer less process-centric and less formal organizations. Again, turning onboarding to be a boring event of lectures and form-filling exercise does not really gel with millennials. Rather onboarding should be a fun event, an opportunity to let new recruits interact with senior leaders, making them feel welcomed and giving them wings to fly.

Overall, the idea of the selection process should be to create an opportunity for millennials to showcase their talent, their passion and abilities and at the same time to make this process a rich experience for them, making them genuinely feel welcomed and excited about their future career prospects in the company.

Deep Engagement

The expectation created during the hiring phase needs to be sustained post their onboarding. This requires deeper engagement interventions that are design-based and focused on stimulating both cognitive and affective connect of millennials. If one thought that millennial employee engagement is only about taking them for picnics or making them do team-building activities on Fridays, think again! Millennial engagement isn't about episodic interventions. It's about designing an organization that engages. In the discussion to follow, we will look at the realities of engaging millennial workers and corresponding design elements for the organization.

Career, No Barrier

Millennials see growth in its totality perspective. They see emotional and cognitive growth, financial growth and growth in wellness terms together. New learning and experiences are a way to grow—millennials recognize this fact. They live in a time where the only constant is change. Hence, they know that continuous learning and self-improvement is the only way to grow. Their strong aspirations to grow and succeed in their jobs come across as the biggest reasons of their attrition. Their belief that one must hop jobs to achieve such growth and success is the fuel to their decision to switch loyalties. They want lifelong learning, expect on-the-job training to stay marketable and proactively plan their own careers and professional development. They expect not only career development opportunities but also clear demonstrable career support from their organizations as well as from their immediate managers. At workplace, they seek match between their personal interests and aspirations and the career development initiatives taken up by the company. They expect to change jobs often during their lifetime, especially if their talents are underutilized.

Organizations have a big role to play in ensuring that career and learning needs of millennial employees are fulfilled, but managers have an even bigger role in facilitating career growth and transition. Managers can make or break the career of an employee. As they say, people leave managers, not organizations.

Manager, Not Damager!

Rana Pratap Mukherjee recounts his first job experience. He got this job from his engineering college campus. He joined as facility management engineer responsible for networking and improving basic infrastructure for core banking solution of his client—an Indian MNC bank. Rana cannot forget the humiliation he faced on his first day from his manager. On being introduced to the manager, the latter ridiculed him by asking the HR in front of him that why such a novice had been assigned to his team. Rana says,

I felt very bad. It was my first day and I was so excited. All my enthusiasm died after being introduced to my manager. He did not even ask me a question, nor did he test my technical skills. Without knowing anything about me, he passed a judgement on my abilities.

As days passed by, the bad behaviour only grew. Rana came to know from his peers that the concerned manager was doing this to other members of his team as well. Apparently, the reason behind such behaviour was his frustration for not being transferred to his home state and city despite repeated requests that he had put up to the management. His technical expertise was also behind him not getting the transfer as the management of the current location did not want to lose an expert like him. However, that was filling him with frustration and anger, that he would often vent on his team members for no rhyme or reason. Rana did well in the project despite the odds and got appreciation from his peers, although his manager never acknowledged his contributions. After a while, Rana could not take the bad behaviour anymore and requested for a change of project. He adds,

I had contemplated even leaving the organization had they not changed my project. I just could not tolerate the daily dose of bad language and behaviour of my manager. However, luckily I got a new project and that ended my misery.

But as he added more years to his experience, he understood that such mangers were not a rare commodity. Working in another company, he experienced a different kind of problem. He was working in a UK-based project. He was a part of the Bengaluru team. Another team from Gurgaon was collaboratively working with them on the same project. Both teams were of equal strength and *importance. However, since the operational head was based out of Gurgaon, the Bengaluru team was often ignored when it came to accolades and appreciation. Most of such recognition went to the Gurgaon team, despite the fact that Bengaluru team was doing equally good work. There was largely a discontent among the Bengaluru location team members. They tried to take up the matter with the global delivery head but he expressed his inability to help them as he was not involved in the day-to-day running of the project. Rana says,*

> *It felt like out of sight is out of mind! And not only me, all my Bengaluru team members felt the same.*

Finally, most of the Bengaluru team members left the organization, including Rana. In his current organization, Rana found his manager going out of the way not only to recruit him but send him to on-site foreign assignment recognizing his talent.

Supportive and fair managers can build high degree of morale in their team members and lead them towards higher performance. Zeemer has been luckier than Rana in finding managers who have stood by him and have helped him deliver and grow. There are some good managers after all. Zeemer's experience below shows and proves how good supportive managers can have a cascading effect on the performance and morale of millennial employees.

Zeemer had a direct reporting to his Indian manager and a dotted line reporting to his US manager Mike. While the Indian manager took care of administrative issues, Zeemer reported day-to-day activities and issues to Mike. Meanwhile, his company acquired a new company and some integration was going on between Zeemer's company and the newly acquired company. Zeemer's team received a request from the integration team regarding an assignment that his information security was asked to do. The request came to Zeemer directly. He was not sure whether his information security and compliance team could handle that request or if they were supposed to handle such a request in the first place. Hence, he asked for some time to review the project.

He had neither turned down the request nor committed anything to the integration team. He discussed the same with Mike, who asked him to turn down the request received from the integration team since he felt that the task should be done by the latter and not by Zeemer's team. Zeemer was a bit tentative to do the same on his own as few of the integration team members were very senior in the organization. He was concerned about the impact of his refusal on the perception of his seniors who might take an offence. Additionally, the task was critical and if not done, it could potentially stop the entire integration process itself. Finding himself on a sticky wicket, he requested Mike to join the conference call with the integration team to resolve the conflict. Mike could have easily avoided the meeting and could have asked Zeemer to handle on his own. However, he understood Zeemer's position and his predicament. Mike not only joined the meeting but managed the situation so tactfully that not only were there no heartburns, but he also ensured that the integration team did the job. Zeemer felt relieved. He has been particularly lucky with his managers. Even his Indian manager is very supportive. Zeemer tells me,

> If I ever feel that there can be some problem in the project and there can be an escalation and I go to him, he tells me just one thing, 'Zeemer don't worry I am with you. You fearlessly do the needful. If anything goes wrong, you will find me standing with you'. That is such a confidence booster. Believe me that no challenge has been unsurmountable after that kind of support.

Zeemer recalls one such incident when there was a peculiar problem with the SAP PCo system that their company was using. There were random downtimes because of this problem. There was a pressure on Zeemer from the top management to resolve the same. Zeemer with his team tried their best but could not diagnose very assertively the cause of downtimes. Anyway, they came up with a possible solution. But the implementation was very risky as if the implementation went wrong, it could cripple the entire system. When Zeemer went to his manager with the plan of action, although there was a huge risk involved in the change that was proposed to be implemented, his manager gave him a 'go-ahead'. The solution was decided for early morning *implementation. In the wee hours of morning when at 3 a.m. Zeemer reached with his team to their office, he found his manager already there waiting for them. Zeemer had not asked for his manager's presence. In fact, other than monitoring, he had no role to play in the implementation. But the presence of his manager gave such strength to Zeemer that all his apprehension faded away. The implementation was successful. After they finished the work, Zeemer and his entire team were taken for a breakfast treat by his manager.*

DESIGN ELEMENT

PMS Overhaul

In the last two years, the number of leading companies who have scrapped the bell curves and/or the annual performance appraisal process altogether has raised a big question in the manner performance has been managed and measured in the organizations. In 2015, Accenture announced scrapping of bell curves. Bell curves system of managing performance of people forcing managers to compulsorily rank a particular percentage of people in various rating categories to overcome the tendency of managers to be less objective in rating, thereby not being able to discriminate between real good performers and poor performers, has lost its meaning. M. P. Sriram, a partner at Aventus Partners, an HR consultancy and talent acquisition firm (*ET*, 2015), says,

> Today, goals are no longer pushed from the top level to the bottom, but emerge through collaboration and are the result of a dynamic interplay between levels and various parts of the organization. To follow the typical bell curve, team leaders had to re-categorize employees. Often good performers

were labelled as average to fit the curve. This unseen hand of moderation resulted in disgruntled and disengaged employees.

Besides Accenture, few other companies such as Cisco and Infosys have scrapped the bell curves. What is even more stunning is the brave decision of some companies to withdraw the much touted and revered annual performance appraisal system. Accenture is one of them who led the pack. But others such as Adobe, Deloitte, National Australia Bank, KPMG, HCL, GE, Microsoft and Cognizant followed the suit. Annual performance reviews do not work more often than they do since the vast amount of time that this process consumes does not leave managers with any time for doing real evaluation of employee performance. Besides, managerial bias at times, the subjective metrics, poor feedback and poor follow-up on post-appraisal action plans render the system ineffective.

These companies have realized that with the millennial cohort populating their spaces at an increasing rate, such annual measurement methods consume a lot and produce very little, often becoming counterproductive in the process. The ways in which companies manage and measure performance of their employees need a systemic overhaul. The new system needs to be quick, objective and one that makes feedback real-time, giving employees an opportunity to work on them. It is like parallel testing in software engineering where debugging happens during the testing phase itself. Such a system allows for managers to provide more real feedback rather than depending on memory at the end of the year. Real-time feedback also allows for feedback from other stakeholders to be better taken in cognizance. For example, feedback received from clients or from other teams who are impacted by the work of the recipient of the feedback. This should not be confused with 360 degree feedback. I am talking of real-time assessments and feedback, one that eliminates loads of unproductive work and managerial bias, offers instant feedback (something that millennials crave for) and provides ample time for development on the go! The current feedback at the end of the year is nothing but crying over spilled milk, no chance of setting right what ought to have been long back. Looking at the past to work in the future does not give present a chance at all! Ongoing feedback does, however, allows a person to receive and act on the feedback at the same time. As Nitin Nagaich, managing director, Convate—a global recruitment consultancy—puts it,

> The feedback needs not only to be instant but it also needs to be right feedback given in the right manner. The feedback should not only state the problem but the manager must be able to lead the employee towards solution. Hand-holding during difficult times is important. That creates longer engagement and inspires the millennial workers.

The process-centric system, one that is focused on finding weaknesses, needs to be replaced with a development-centric system, one that is focused on leveraging on strengths. The new system would depend less on tools and framework and more on people-to-people conversations that would solve real problems that the organization is confronted with. Learning then must become a corporate goal and company must be able to craft variable career paths for people, depending upon their interest and strengths.

GE uses an app called 'PD@GE', which means 'performance development at GE'. Through this app, managers give frequent feedbacks on short-term goals assigned to employees, who will be improving their skills instead of only being evaluated. Workers can also give or demand input anytime through a function called 'insights', which isn't restricted to their direct supervisor, or even to their division. Cognizant's solution consists of gamifying the method, which is a digital platform with the shape of a game to create a collaborative workplace where progress and achievements are monitored in real time and celebrated without the burden of writing long and tedious performance appraisal forms. Gamification is about integrating game elements to existing processes to create employee engagement and create effective feedback loops. A confluence of factors is facilitating gamification of employee engagement at Cognizant—social and mobile technologies allowing collaboration, the growing millennial population who are accustomed with such technologies and advanced data analytics that allows real-time behavioural assessment. Gamification transforms mundane tasks into interesting ones, generates ongoing feedback and facilitates development.

Grooming Managers

Most managers belong to the previous generation and they are often led by myths that have been in prevalence about millennials. A poor understanding of their mindsets, behaviour and their life results in low empathy among managers for their millennial team members. This results in rough edges that often erode engagement. In several opportunities that I had to talk to and/or train corporate managers, I understood that there was a tremendous difference in the outlook and managing styles of managers with respect to millennials, before and after such training programmes. After one such session at Tata Consultancy Services way back in 2012, a manager came up to me and told me that now he knew why he was having problem in getting registrations for the weekend marathon from their millennial employees. Another manager of the same company told me that it is never easy to keep millennials on 'bench' even when the company provides training to them during their unassigned period. He always wondered what made them so restless but after the session he was able to relate to their career-centrism and their desire for instant gratification accompanied by a sense of pragmatism.

Move Beyond Conventionality

Millennials like unconventionality and exploring the unexplored. They are generally bored by traditional way of doing things and want to try new things and experiment with new technologies.

Pulkit working as senior IT manager states,

I have two kind of millennial members in my team. Real talents who are top performers, difficult to retain. When they come to me and tell me that they want to work on a new technology or implement a new technology in the company, if I refuse they will get very demotivated. For them, working on new and exciting technologies and assignments is more important than pay and promotion. I encourage them and try to fulfil their aspirations as much as possible. At times I buy a little time from them if the technology they are demanding is costly and involves more decision-makers. The other lot of millennial workers in my team are work horses. You need them as well in the team. For them, a good work environment, regular pay hikes and incentives work well in keeping them happy. However, the talent outnumbers the work horses. Hence, keeping them engaged is not an easy job.

Organizations need to be extremely innovative in their approach of managing millennials. An organizational culture that supports innovation and creativity, allows experimentation, has a high tolerance for failure and celebrates failures as a way for learning new lessons that help one to succeed in the long run does well in engaging millennials. Others risk losing them.

Sumer is working as an information security expert. He is well-recognized for his expertise in his present company. He is getting a handsome pay and perks. He has a very understanding manager. The work culture is good. Yet, he is contemplating changing his job. Sumer presents the curious case of millennials. What would make him stick with his present company? A bit of spade work reveals that the new offer that Sumer has received is from another multinational company that wants him to join as the head of cloud information security. Sumer considers the opportunity to work on cloud security very exciting and also a very promising career move. He predicts cloud and mobility as the future. Hence, an opportunity to work on cloud security in an expert role is too irresistible!

DESIGN ELEMENT

Idea Junctions and Innovation Labs

A systematic mechanism of encouraging idea generation from millennial employees, capturing the same, providing them an opportunity of working on the same while providing them resource and morale support and once the idea comes to development stage letting them manage and take it to the next level needs to be institutionalized. Stung by missed innovation opportunities, Microsoft sometime back launched the 'Garage' initiative. 'Garage' is a worldwide community and resource for all Microsoft employees that encourage problem-solving. The initiative allows interested employees to work on their idea, with resource support from Microsoft during their weekends or free time. The company has created Garage spaces across various locations of the world where it has offices. The initiatives of Garage participants across these locations are also influenced by the resident needs by engaging with local community. Every year, as a part of the Garage initiative, hackathon mojos are conducted that allow a fast-paced 48-hour window to all Microsoft employees to hack an idea and the winning teams get an opportunity to pitch the same to the company leaders. The successful ones get to work on these projects for the next year. The experimental lab allows the team working on Garage projects to get early feedback from clients and take their projects to the next level. The Garage initiative even runs internship programmes for bright, talented students.

You Need Two Hands to Clap!

The commitment of millennial employees is directly proportional to their perception of how much their organization is committed towards them. Their perception of a supportive supervisor determines their job satisfaction. Their loyalty is a function of the ability of the organization to help them develop their competencies and appreciate them for their efforts. They would rather leave their firm than be dependent. Siddharth S. N., head, business HR, says,

> For the first time, millennial workers have made the company sit up and take notice that commitment is a two-way traffic. Commitments made during hiring phase if they are not sustained later, millennial workers see that as a breach of

commitment. They will not even come to renegotiate that with their employers. They will simply leave!

Veer had been working in a company for three years. An engineer by profession, he was doing well in the company but he believed that whatever he was doing as a part of his job was adding little value to his career. Hence, he decided to have a discussion with his manager. He told her clearly about his expectation in terms of the work that he wanted to do and that he will be forced to look for opportunities outside if he did not get his desired work profile. His manager assured him that she would do the needful and asked Veer not to think about leaving the company. But then after few months, the manager left the company and a new manager took her place. When Veer spoke to the new manager about the discussion that he had with his previous manager and the assurance that she had given him, the new manager was not positive about the same.

You know when a new manager comes, everything changes, the goal, the direction, the approach…. When I broached the discussion that I had with my previous manager, he told me that he was not aware about the same. The old manager it seems had not told him anything about the discussion and the promise she had made. My request was turned down. I felt fooled and cheated.

Veer felt that the company had failed to keep the commitment that was made to him. It was the responsibility of the outgoing manager and the new manager to ensure that proper knowledge transfer occurs not only about the technical aspects of the project but also about the aspirations of the people who work in the team. However, that had definitely not happened and Veer had been left in the lurch like most of his team mates. Veer adds,

This is when I decided that this place is not for me and I left the company soon after this incident. I think most companies are busy making their clients happy so that they can make more money, but in the process they forget their people. However, the fact is if they take care of their people, the clients will automatically be looked after well.

Veer is right but then more companies need to realize the fact that they are as good as their employees. Millennials being in the thick of action will hold their employers accountable as much they are held accountable for their jobs and responsibilities.

Accountability also means fair and just treatment for them. A broken trust is a broken relationship. The manner in which their managers and leaders treat them makes a lot of difference to the way they look at their future prospects with the company. Many of them actually think that they can do a better job than their managers when it comes to building trust and managing a team.

Nishi alleges that her previous manager accepted bribe from her colleagues to promote them and delay her promotion unfairly. She recounts an incident where one of her colleagues who was also the team leader actually gave the manager a costly LCD TV just before the appraisals. Nishi was due for promotion, but when the appraisal results were announced, she was not promoted citing performance issues, while the team leader who had obliged the manager got his promotion. She missed her first promotion opportunity in the company because of her manager. She tells me,

> *When I become a manager, I will ensure that nothing like this happens. The truly deserving get their due in the organization. It is not as if I have not found any good manager. But in my career till now, out of the five managers that I have worked with, I found only one manager who was very supportive, fair and objective.*

Nishi tells that in the past due to the absence of her manager, even though she was just the lead, she got to handle a project independently. The project was so successful that she got an appreciation mail directly from the client.

DESIGN ELEMENT

Culture, Culture, Culture

A successful company has three ingredients—culture, culture and culture. Leaders of such corporations spend less time in meetings and more time in building cultures. Samsung's transformation from low-cost original equipment manufacturer to a global electronics giant owes a lot of credit to the chairman of the company Lee Kun-hee. The difficult cultural change that Lee was able to bring in the company created an innovative climate that made Samsung Electronics Co. Ltd a global name to reckon with! Culture is the basic fabric on which engagement is woven. Alan Mulally's successful effort in getting an iconic but loss-making brand Ford back into business has been no mean effort. But more than anything, Alan's efforts were directed at changing Ford's culture and creating a sense of ownership among Ford workers. Most corporations have a culture that is incompatible with the millennial generation's expectations, aspirations, mindsets and behaviours. Putting millennials in such cultures is like transfusing blood of a wrong group into a person's veins. You can't expect a miracle. Cultural transformation is at the heart of millennial engagement.

Meaning, Not Menial

Millennials have low tolerance for boredom; they do not like menial jobs. They like new challenges and early responsibilities at work. Millennial employees are eager to contribute in the organization that is worthwhile. They seek challenge and excitement in their jobs that they wish to be flexible. If the job fails to enthuse them, then they are usually misfits. The message is very clear—hire only those who are enthused by the job and are aligned to organizational goals. Millennials want to do meaningful jobs and make an impact by showcasing their skills. Sushmita, a computer science engineer, working for the last 10 years in an IT company, finds her job monotonous. She says,

> After working for so many years, I find my job boring. The work is almost same in most projects. I am actually tired of this! I will like to work on something more challenging, some new technology, something that pushes me to think more creatively.

Identity Is More than a Card

Millennials want to climb up the corporate ladder faster, not necessarily at the same pace as their previous generations have risen or have been recognized. They want and seek constant feedback and look for instant gratification when it comes to rewards. They are habituated for being praised for their efforts and not the results that they achieve. They are looking for a 'remixed' set of rewards; they look for high-quality peers, flexible work arrangements, prospects for advancement, recognition from company and boss, a steady rate of advancement and growth, and access to new experiences and challenges, over monetary rewards. Millennial employees have more practical expectations from their employers such as salary, health care and retirement benefits, job stability and career satisfaction.

Don't Treat Voice as Noise

Millennial employees are more demanding and can fearlessly express their opinions. They feel included if their opinions are taken into consideration. They are highly opinionated and view themselves as consumers to the organization where they work. Millennial graduates entering the workforce give top priority to their employers treating them as individuals, providing them variety in their daily work, investing in their competency development and giving them enough freedom at workplace to enable initiative-taking and decision-making. A constant nagging and a directive manager may be a turn-off for millennial employees.

DESIGN ELEMENT

Job Design

Millennials want their jobs to be meaningful and make an impact on the company and its future. Designing jobs have never been as important as they are now, considering the preference of the new generation at work. Companies need to focus their attention on re-conceptualizing traditional job roles and redesigning them in a way that they are made more meaningful, offering greater opportunity for millennials to contribute.

Reverse Mentoring

Millennials have a different outlook of the world and of the organizations. They are brimming with ideas and are eager to share them. They are also extremely good with technology. Reverse mentoring is a great way to tap into these ideas and millennial's knowledge of technology. Hence, leaders become mentees and their team members (millennials) become mentors. The concept and practice of reverse mentoring started by GE's Jack Welch in the late 1990s has become the need of every organizational design to engage millennials. It costs nothing and produces a lot. On the one hand it makes millennials feel genuinely valued, on the other hand it helps leaders (belonging to older generation) leverage on new knowledge, digital technologies and new ideas, helping them in turn to create competitive advantage for their companies. As good as it sounds, reverse mentoring programme needs to be not only incorporated in the organizational design, but it also needs to be designed and structured properly with accountabilities in place for the programme to do well. Only then it will make a real impact.

Company	Reverse Mentoring Programme
Pepsi-Co India	Ycom
Microsoft	Elevate
Vodafone India	Digital Ninja
AXA	Digital Reverse Mentoring
US Bank	Dynamic Dozen
PwC	Mentoring Connections
Cisco	Reverse Mentoring

Total Rewards

Competitive salaries, career track, flexible schedules, challenging environment and appreciation for good work are some of the factors deemed important to attract millennials. However, they are pushing the envelope a step further and are asking employers to go beyond traditional compensation and benefits to create an environment that is creative, challenging, team-oriented, fun and financially rewarding. This generation is vocal about their job expectations. Leaders must conduct regular town hall meetings or open houses with millennial employees in a slightly informal set-up to ensure that their voice is heard. However, equally important is the need for providing a thorough follow-up on the feedback the leaders receive from millennials in such open forums to establish credibility of these forums and instil a belief that the voice of millennials matters and their views make an impact on how the company functions and on the decisions.

Remember, millennials lack social support and are emotionally vulnerable. An organization that genuinely cares and supports its workers does a whole lot of good in improving the social and emotional wellness of the millennials.

Care, Not Scare

Abhishek was one of the top project managers in his company. He had been in the company for only about 36 months but had rose in prominence for his deft handling of projects. The company had a client in Mumbai and based on his superlative performance, Abhishek was asked to take up an assignment to establish the new project at the client location. The assignment would last for just over a year after which Abhishek would come back to his hometown. When he landed in Mumbai, to his utter shock, he found that his lodging arrangements had been done in a shared three-bedroom flat. Upon entering the flat, he found couple of other strangers, one spread over in the living room and the other lazing in another bedroom. They were not even employees of his company. The idea of sharing accommodation with complete strangers in an alien city did not appeal to him. Such accommodation was unacceptable based on the benefits that he was entitled by the virtue of his rank; but more than anything else, there were security issues. He lodged a protest with the company headquarters and only after he threatened to return without working on the assignment did the company provide him with an alternate accommodation. Clearly, the company was only interested in getting the assignment done, but cared little for him. Abhishek compares this experience with his present company and says that the latter is heaven compared to his former company. In his present company, whenever someone is scheduled to travel, they just have to raise a travel request online. The rest is taken care of by the HR and the travel desk—from tickets, to bookings, accommodation, food, local transfers, daily allowances, etc., everything works like clockwork. The process is simple and efficient, and the arrangements are always better than one's expectation.

An organization that functions bureaucratically and has cumbersome people processes frustrates millennial workers who are bewildered by long meaningless processes and delays.

People Primary, Process Secondary

Even after spending 11 years in the same company, Farah has a grudge towards the HR department of her company. Although she finds her work good and is generally satisfied with things in her company, she holds HR responsible for lowering her seniority in the company for no fault of hers. When she joined the company, she was asked to upload her educational and experience-related documents. She did the same. According to her, no one told her to submit a copy of the passport as well. A year later, when she did not get the confirmation letter, upon enquiring from HR she was told that since she had not submitted a copy of her passport, her probation period could not be terminated. She was taken by surprise as she had not been told or reminded even once during the last one year since her joining about passport being a mandatory document for conformation. Getting a passport was not easy for her. She was living in a paying guest accommodation and arranging an *address proof was difficult for her. However, after going through all the hassles, finally after three months she got her passport. Even after submitting a copy of the passport, she did not get confirmation immediately. It took another four months for HR to issue her a confirmation letter. Worse still, her confirmation had not been done from retrospective effect. In effect, it meant that her confirmation got delayed by seven months and hence she lost her seniority in the company by an equal period. Despite her follow-ups, this anomaly has not been corrected until date and she continues to be behind her peers, who joined along with her, in terms of seniority and compensation.*

Design Element

Communicate Where They Listen

Proactive communication to employees before a void for the same is felt is essential. It also needs to be done through a medium that millennials access. Using company's internal social media network is one of the best ways to communicate to these new-generation workers.

Institutionalizing Care

Millennials miss social and emotional support systems in their lives. Taking care of small social and family needs of millennial employees does not cost too much but goes a long way in allaying their worries and anxieties. Care can take various forms—a buddy system where an older employee acts like a buddy to a new employee and helps them in familiarization process and settling down, or various facilities created at workplace to provide support to new mothers or medical needs of employees and their families. However, the ground rule remains only one—the care-giving approach has to be genuine and must emanate from the culture of the organization.

Keep It Simple

Bureaucracy, loads of paper work, and cumbersome and long processes not only make millennials feel frustrated but they also get an impression that the company has not caught up with the times. Keep it simple is the bottom-line mantra for all such admin and HR processes.

Hello! Get (ME) a Life!

Millennial employees give higher priority to maintaining their work–life balance, parenting and contributing to the society over income. They want to achieve professional satisfaction and at the same time do not want to forego personal freedom. Personal time is more important for them. They believe that they should have the best of their personal as well as professional lives. Millennials do not wish to trade off their lives for work. Companies that forget to focus on the life of millennials and do not offer them opportunities to socialize and celebrate small occasions often find millennials more as passengers rather than residents in their companies. An HR head speaking strictly from a personal viewpoint remarks, 'No matter how rich their job is, you do not give them the weekend off and they might simply walk out'.

DESIGN ELEMENT

Flexible Workspace

Workplace concept has long been replaced with the workspace concept, leveraged by technology. The workspace does not necessarily need a brick-and-mortar office always. Flexibility on where to work from and when to work cannot be similar for all companies; however, it can be a common rule. The organizations which still insist that employees come to office every day and stay for a fixed number of hours compulsorily are simply living with an outdated design that does little to enthuse millennials who live in a world where they are expected to be on the job 24×7, 365 days a year. When in the evening they log out of office, they do not necessarily log out of work. They are expected to log in from home and attend late evening meetings or calls that go up to sometime late in the night. In such a situation, expecting them to work in the traditional 9–5 office schedule and report to the physical office even if they do not need is like mixing hot sauce with chilli pepper. Bring flexibility in and throw rigidity out!

Dial a Technophile

Millennials are a technology-savvy generation and also the first generation to have used electronic mail and mobile phones since their childhood. Their Internet consumption exceeds TV consumption and they are also more comfortable with technology and value connectivity.

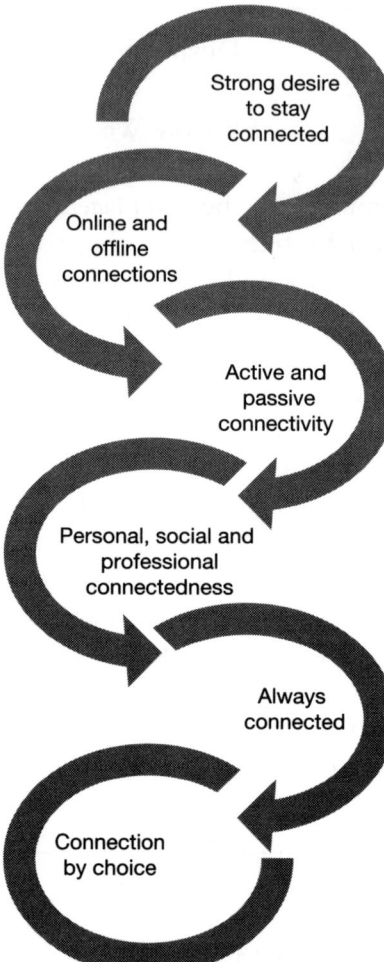

Most millennials have learnt to multitask as a result of their childhood conditioning wherein their parents enrolled them in sports, music lessons, along with school activities, all at the same time. Millennials take to multitasking with technology at their disposal as if it is an extension of their being and have the ability to transform a task creating a more appealing outcome. Along with this, they even manage to find time for social interests. Millennials' multitasking habit and ability to quickly switch from one task to the other is often mistaken as their impatience. They know how to solve problems and shorten their learning curve by using technology collaboration tools such as mobiles, Bluetooth, laptops, WindowsCE handhelds, electronic mails and text messages.

DESIGN ELEMENT

Tech-enabled Workspace

In my last two customer experiences, millennial personnel impressed me with the power of technology. At the Airtel office, the customer care executive used tech-enabled handheld devices to log in my porting request for a mobile number, validated by citizen card details and completed the process in less than 15 minutes. For a medical insurance product that I recently purchased, the insurance agent processed my request at my location using a handheld tech device. A tech-enabled workspace that offers faster operations and seamless connections to complete business processes has an empowering effect on millennial employees.

Building Social Wide Area Network (SWAN)

By this time, we know a lot of realities about millennials; among them, two that are relevant to mention here are as follows: one is their constant desire to say connected and second is their being very vocal about their opinions. Companies have faced backlash from millennials irked by the policies of the companies who went ballistic on social media pouring out their discontent openly. Recently, Indian techies took on to social media to vent their ire on single-digit salary hikes and lay-offs. The FB employee groups were overflowing with comments and remarks that were very critical of their companies. The negative publicity and the damage to the employer is huge in such cases. Some companies try to gag the voices of their employees using social media policy. Frankly, that does not work. In an age of ubiquitous social media and digital technologies, no amount of policy-making would restrain spread of employee voices. Infosys is one such company that has burnt its fingers in the past. But it was smart enough to come up with à la FB version for Infosys employees called 'Infy Bubble'. Hartford came up with a similar version for their company called 'WEConnect'. Few other companies have also done the same. However, with millennial employees making a beeline at the workplace, this is less a matter of choice, lest the company wants to risk ignoring their employee voices and listening to them along with the rest of the world on social media.

SWAN allows social networking among employees within a company. It promotes real-time two-way communication, opportunity to employees to voice their opinions, discontent or appreciation and also facilitates collaboration.

Leader as Mentor

Millennial employees prefer and expect guidance, flexibility and support from their supervisors. They expect their supervisors to be their mentors. They also wish to receive feedback on a daily basis from their managers. They will be willing to accept supervisory or managerial roles in companies if they receive more support in their new roles.

Manaswati recalls her experience as a teacher at Indira Gandhi Memorial High school in Barasat, West Bengal. She had just finished her masters in arts and was on a lookout for a job. She had casually dropped her resume at this school; however, she got an immediate call for interview. She was initially appointed as a day-scholar teacher for four months. She was required to teach hostel students after the school hours. Dedicated as she was, she used to turn up in the school during morning hours like other teachers. She used to spend her time reading in the library and preparing for the classes. Her dedication did not go in vain and after four months, she was appointed as a full-time teacher in the school. She was allotted to senior classes and considering that she herself was very young at the time and had just finished college, it was not easy for her to manage grown-up kids. Some unruly boys in her class also tried to create some disturbances while she was teaching. She told me that she used to get angry and disturbed and felt like quitting at times. However, during such testing times, the person who helped her was her principal Mayuri Dutt, who was

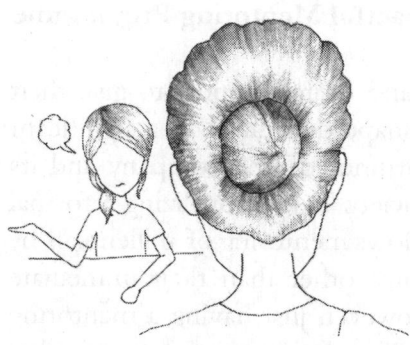

known to be very strict and students as well as teachers used to tremble at the mention of her name. But Manaswati found Mayuri Dutt to be extremely understanding. She empathized with Manaswati's situation and regularly guided her on how to deal with such problems and mentored her on other aspects of teaching. Gradually, Manaswati emerged as one of the best teachers in the school and she was often quoted as an example to other teachers. Manaswati says,

I am still in touch with her. She still sends me WhatsApp messages. What I have learnt from her is helping me in my teaching career even today. Had it not been for Mayuri Dutt, I do not know whether I would have been groomed the way I have been as a teacher. I really owe it to her!

Manaswati has always been a sought-after teacher wherever she has worked in her career spanning more than a decade.

Millennials also expect their leaders to have more spine in dealing with the client demands if they are unjustified. The teams are often working on shoestring resources and do not find adequate support from their management to request clients for extra resource support. Many millennials complain about working on non-critical processes during weekends, even though working on holidays was supposedly reserved for critical processes.

DESIGN ELEMENT

CALM: The Impactful Mentoring Programme

Millennials need intellectual and moral support to give their career wings and their ideas shape that can have a significant impact on the future and fortunes of the company and its stakeholders, including the society. Institutionalizing a formal mentoring programme that allows mentoring of millennials by senior leaders of the company, other than their immediate supervisors, is imperative. However, just having a mentoring programme is not enough. The design must be such that makes the mentoring programme an impactful one. I suggest a design CALM—create, attract, link and measure. The mentoring programme needs to be created and formalized in the company. The programme then needs to be marketed to the millennial employees. They must find it attractive and gainful. Then a match-making process needs to be undertaken where mentees and mentors need to be connected. The mentoring programme must be measured for its effectiveness on a continuous basis.

Millennials must see their leaders as someone they can trust and who will support them in the right manner with unflappable commitment for integrity and being assertive at times of crisis. We must remember that they refuse to follow leaders by position, and they do more so by the leaders who set an example through their behaviours and actions.

Redesign the Organization, Shape Attitudes, Create Engagement

Organizations are crafted not by chance but by design. As much a good design inspires and creates systems, structures, culture and leadership processes and shapes right engaging behaviours, a wrong design can create pitfalls and organizations that actively disengage. Understanding of life, mindsets and behaviours of millennials should create a basis for a right design that can impress and impact right attitudes that create strong engagement for the millennial workforce.

9

ENGAGING MILLENNIALS AT THE MARKETPLACE

Two incidents contrasted by every measure—one my own personal experience and the other that shocked not only the USA but also the world, the one that may not have made national headline but created a deep positive impact. The only thing that is perhaps similar in both these incidents is that both companies in question are well-known American consumer brands.

It was my son's 11th birthday and we were hosting a party for his friends in the evening. We had decided to treat the kids with Domino's Pizza. The nearest Domino's Pizza outlet was about 12 km away from our house. The road leading to the same was under metro rail construction and hence was dug up and replete with narrow diversions. The traffic squeezing through those diversions made movement irritatingly slow at times. The party was in the evening. We reached the Domino's outlet at Yelachenahalli and ordered for the pizzas and sides. When it was time to collect the order and pay, I discovered that I had forgotten my wallet at home. My wife was not carrying hers as well. We had left all our money at home and had nothing to pay to collect the order. Our home being away, the store did not have any provision for home delivery. Going back to home and coming back again to collect the order would consume a lot of time and effort considering the poor condition of the road. I was in a fix. There was no way I could leave back the order, there was no way I could collect the order as well, at least for the time being! Considering all options, I decided to take the arduous journey back home and come back with money to collect my order. We communicated our situation to the store manager and told her that we will come back in some time to collect the order. When we were about to leave the store, the store manager called us back and asked us to take our order and pay later. I was surprised. The bill was more than a thousand grands and she was just letting me take that without paying a penny. She told us that she understood that it was our son's birthday and the order was important. She also understood that the delay that will be caused by our journey to fetch the money will put the party in the evening under some pressure. We thanked her profusely and left the store with smile on our face. Next day, when I went to pay on my way back from my office, I asked the store manager that didn't she have any apprehension in letting me go without paying? She smiled and told me, 'Sir, we trust our customers and want them to be happy'. The kind of empathy and trust that the Domino's store manager had shown had really touched us. From then for us if it is pizza, it is Domino's!

While Domino's was making customers for life, United Airlines was busy losing them in hordes. Dr David Dao, a 69-year-old Vietnamese-American grandfather, had settled down with his physician wife Teresa on United Airlines flight 3411 readying to depart to Louisville, Kentucky, from Chicago's O'Hare Airport on Sunday, 9 April 2017, little knowing that in a matter of few minutes his life will be turned upside down for none of his fault!

It turned out that United Airlines had overbooked the flight and needed to bump off four passengers to make way for their staff who were urgently needed in Louisville. Three passengers who were offered $1,000 compensation agreed to take the next scheduled flight. For the fourth seat, United apparently settled on a seldom-used policy of simply picking a passenger at random, something the airline's ticketing fine print apparently allows. The randomly identified passenger turned out to be Dr Dao who refused to deplane the flight on finding that the next scheduled flight was not until the next day. Dr Dao reportedly told the crew that he was a doctor and he had to be at work the next morning because he had scheduled patients to see.

What transpired next was something no one ever expected! Heavy-handed airport police officers pulled off the 69-year-old father of five from his seat, dragging, kicking and screaming him down the aisle. His lawyer later said that he lost teeth and suffered a broken nose and a concussion.

The cell phone footages taken by other passengers of Dr Dao's torturous removal went viral on social media and United Airlines received scathing criticism from the world community. The brutality and insensitivity with which United removed Dr Dao and the initial defence of the actions and decisions of the United staff by its CEO Munoz made people around the globe furious. #BoycottUnited started trending on social media and even those who had never flown United swore never to fly with the US carrier.

Under heavy public outcry and pressure, and faced with the prospect of a lawsuit from Dr Dao, the United CEO retracted his earlier comments and issued a public apology for the incident. The lawsuit would have been costly and caused even more public relations damage to the company and hence United went for an out-of-the-court settlement with the victim for an undisclosed amount.

Despite the apology and settlement, United Airlines will never be forgotten for what it did to its passenger. The infamous video clips will stay as digital footprints and the company cannot completely salvage the loss in reputation and image that it has suffered.

If the first incident is an epitome of customer service, the second one is an abyss of the same. While any-generation customer will react in the same way like you and I will, millennial customers are hardly likely to forget or forgive this crass corporate heartlessness and indifference. The evidence of this comes from the digital outrage that broke out after the news and the video clips went public. Within the first 48 hours of the news breaking out, United Airlines was mentioned close to three million times on FB, Twitter and LinkedIn. Hashtags like #BoycottUnited, #NewUnitedAirlinesMottos and #FlyTheFriendlySkies, sarcastic of United's advertising slogan, began trending on social media. One such mocking tweet was retweeted 93,000 times on Twitter! That is one bad publicity that United could ill afford and more so the anger it experienced from the millennial community active on social media.

The New Breed of Millennial Customers

Companies need to rethink and reset their assumptions about millennial customers. They are a new breed of emerging customer segment that is growing at an increasing rate and will comprise major percentage of the customer segment that companies cater to in the coming years. What's more, they are different and they think differently, behave differently and buy differently. The current state of engagement of millennial customers worldwide is not showing a bright picture. Only about a quarter of millennial customers are engaged. This is lower than engagement levels of customers of any previous generation. Even more disturbing is the fact that more millennial customers are actively disengaged and are likely to spread negative remarks about brands that have spoiled their experience or treated them shabbily. This is bad news and goes on to further underline the fact that companies are not winning millennial customers with their current engagement strategies. The dismal levels of engagement both inside the organization (millennial workers as we have seen before) and outside the organization (millennial customers) should cause companies more headache than political tensions and economic uncertainty. Two major stakeholders in business belonging to millennial generation do not connect with the brands.

At the heart of such disengagement of millennial customers could be poor understanding about them in the first place that gives rise to wrong strategies or a belief that old strategies will work on this new breed of customers. Right and good understanding is a precursor to engagement. This has been the belief of my research and of this book.

Before we attempt to set out the new rules of engagement of millennial customers, let us have a good understanding of these new-generation customers.

Online Has a Huge Buy-in

Globally, the preference for shopping online is growing. However, millennials are leading this pack. What is even more intriguing about millennials is that their preference for shopping online has only been growing in the recent years.

Year	Percentage of Millennials Who Prefer Shopping Online
2017	67
2016	54
2015	51
2014	51

Source: UPS, Big Commerce.

Millennials also do a lot of their pre-purchase research online that has a huge bearing on their purchase decisions.

Smart APPeal

Nearly 63 per cent of the millennials who shop online use their smartphones and apps to complete their purchases. The overwhelming use of mobiles and apps shows that mobility- and apps-based marketing is the future. Smartphone adoption rates are among the highest among millennials and their ability and desire to leverage on technology to complete their purchases are very high. Some of them use multiple channels for their shopping; however, a whopping majority use single channel (online for their purchases). Research also shows that the shopping satisfaction using smartphones has increased over the years with better applications, payment options and increased security of digital transactions.

Millennial Mobile App Survey

To further understand the millennial intimacy with smartphones and apps, I conducted a millennial mobile app survey. Nearly 750 respondents participated in the survey that consisted of millennials who are still in college and millennials working in corporate, both males and females and hailing from different ethnic backgrounds. All of them who were surveyed use smartphones and mobile apps.

Top Five Apps: Easy Recall		
Rank	**Mobile App**	**Percentage**
1	WhatsApp	76
2	Facebook	57
3	Instagram	27
3	YouTube	27
4	Paytm	22

Top Five Apps: Used Daily		
Rank	**Mobile App**	**Percentage**
1	WhatsApp	89
2	Facebook	50
3	Instagram	31
3	YouTube	24
4	Gmail	10

Top Five Apps: Used More than Once a Day		
Rank	**Mobile App**	**Percentage**
1	WhatsApp	80
2	Facebook	33
3	YouTube	24
3	Instagram	18
4	Gmail	10

Top Four Most Liked Apps		
Rank	Mobile App	Percentage
1	WhatsApp	55
2	YouTube	20
3	Instagram	16
4	Facebook	13

Social networking apps are the clear favourites when it comes to recall, usage frequency or likeability of the apps. WhatsApp is a clear number one, even ahead of FB. However, FB is still maintaining quite a healthy presence among millennials; YouTube and Instagram, both visual social mediums, attract a lot of millennials.

In another study done by VoucherBin (2015), the findings showed that nearly 46 per cent of the millennials relied on social media for their purchase decisions. However, more than 80 per cent depended on user-generated data for their purchases.

Put these two pieces of findings together and it becomes very clear that social media have not only a great presence in terms of app preference among millennials but also a big impact on how they shop and what they purchase.

The millennial app survey threw some other interesting insights.

Top Apps Used Once a Week	
Rank	Mobile App
1	Amazon
2	Ola Cabs
3	Zomato
4	BookMyShow
4	Paytm
4	Uber

Top Apps Used Once a Fortnight/Month	
Rank	Mobile App
1	Flipkart
2	LinkedIn
2	Uber
2	Google Maps

Top Apps Used Only for Special Purpose/Occasion	
Rank	Mobile App
1	Ola Cabs
2	Uber
3	Amazon
4	Myntra
5	BookMyShow
5	Google Maps

The apps used less frequently are the transaction apps that are used when one needs them. Social networking apps are the engagement apps that have greater connect with millennials. Once a week or once a fortnight/month apps or the apps used only for special purpose/occasion for millennials are mostly shopping apps (Amazon/Flipkart/Myntra), entertainment apps (BookMyShow), transportation apps (Ola Cabs, Uber, Google Maps) or e-wallet app (Paytm). LinkedIn's presence in this list shows that professional networking is less frequent among millennials than personal networking.

But then there are some apps that are either not used at all or were used once but are no longer used. The pre-loaded apps are hardly used by millennials. The list is long and includes all such apps that have been pre-loaded by the smartphone manufacturer. It is such a waste of memory space. Millennials would rather exercise their choice in choosing apps, downloading them and using them. Worse still, pre-loaded apps are difficult to uninstall and stay as vestigial portions on screen and phone memory.

A bit of shock awaits when it comes to apps that were once used but are losing out in terms of millennial favour.

Apps Not Used Any More	
Rank	Mobile App
1	Snapchat
2	Snapdeal

The ground beneath the feet for Snapchat and Snapdeal seems to be slipping away fast. These two, although getting majority thumbs down from millennial respondents, were not the only one to be abandoned. Once popular gaming apps seem to be fading as well. Temple Run, Clash of Clans, Subway Surfers and Pokemon Go were named by the respondents. It is very clear that if apps are not reinventing themselves and do not offer something of value to millennials, after a period of time they become redundant. The list also has apps that are faced with the exit route even before they could start their summit ascent. Voonik, Hotstar, Imo, WeChat, Limeroad, Retrica, Ajio, Gaana and Saavn do not seem to be doing too well when it came to millennial users.

Attention Is Toughest Retention

Millennial customers have one of the lowest attention spans that any generation ever had. It is hard to hold on to their attention and more so to gain it back again and again. A research carried out in Canada showed that the average attention span had fallen from 12 seconds in the year 2000 to 8 seconds by the year 2015, which is less than that of a goldfish that has an average attention span of 9 seconds. (Low attention span is no good news for marketers who try to gain the same on shoestring marketing budgets.) To put the difficulty of the marketers in numbers, average cost per thousand impressions (CPMs) of prime-time ads has risen over 15 times since 1966.

BAd Is What I Do!

Millennials do not trust traditional marketing or advertisements. A study by a US marketing and strategy firm, the McCarthy Group, showed that close to 84 per cent of millennials do not trust traditional advertisements. Further, Fractl and Moz study titled 'Inbound vs. Outbound: Consumer Perspectives on Marketing Effectiveness' suggested that millennials find ads disruptive and close to 63 per cent of millennials block advertisements (BAd). The ads that they find irrelevant are blocked for sure. The relevant ads have slightly better chance. Paid ad searches were found better than mobile ads that did not do particularly well. Clearly, advertisements are not the best way to reach or appeal to millennial customers.

Dear or Peer, Did They Find Anything Peculiar?

Millennials refer to peer reviews extensively before making a purchase decision. They would even refer to reviews done by their friends or even those whom they do not know personally, rather than believing completely on an advertisement. A study by the Center for Generational Kinetics, Bazaarvoice and Kelton Research revealed that close to 84 per cent of the millennials report on user-generated content having some influence on their purchase decision. American Lifestyles report from global marketing firm Mintel also suggested that nearly 70 per cent of millennial consumers rely on online reviews before making a purchase. Millennials seek reviews from family and friends and are equally open to anonymous peer reviews. They trust people more than companies and paid advertisements. There are couple of reasons for the same, much of which are connected to their life and the way they have grown up. They have grown up at a time when they have seen corporate greed getting better of ethics in many instances. It has inherently made them sceptical about companies and the claims that they make. Overzealous marketing, hidden pricing, fine prints, all have not gone down well with this generation particularly. They have also seen their parents fall prey to such clever marketing many a time and are on their guard. Besides, they do not have both time and inclination for doing an extensive offline search or research about a product or service they are buying. Reading online reviews is an easy and fast way of making a decision regarding a purchase. And lastly, millennials do not have much disposable income and they want to put their money to good use. Reviews are their way of mitigating the risk element in a purchase, particularly in high-value purchases.

Footprint With or Without Footfall

As much as they would like to refer to online peer reviews while making a purchase decision, millennials are usually inclined to leave a review for a product or service that they have purchased and used. The reviews are not only about the product/service but usually about their overall experience, including the kind of service they received post purchase. They are willing to share their experiences and change the purchase decisions of others. Sharing is not always in the form of a formal review. Many a time, they are writing blogs or posting their experience or photos on FB or on other social networking sites. They like to voice their opinion and they are also very social minded. They feel almost a sense of redemption to share a poor experience. They also feel elated to share good experiences that they have had. Their social mindedness makes them socially obligatory to share their reviews.

Credit Goes to Credit

Millennials and savings are almost an oxymoron. They often spend more than they earn. Their spending on travel and technology goods or services is very high. They also spend lavishly on clothes and other lifestyle goods. They have little trust on what the future holds for them, and their decision to enjoy the present seems compulsive and often impulsive. A report by the World Youth Student and Educational (WYSE) Travel Confederation, a global not-for-profit membership organization based in Amsterdam showed that 'by 2020, 320 million international trips are expected to be made by youth travellers each year, a staggering 47% increase from 217 million in 2013'. However, their not-so-good incomes and high spending on rent and paying off their loans do not leave them with too much at their disposal. Credit card definitely comes handy and their behaviour with credit cards is quite complex. They spend using credit cards hoping to repay the bill with their next month's income. Many experts argue that millennials' financial behaviour is quite risky and they might be accumulating too much debt. All said and done, credit cards are in demand among millennials. In 2016, JPMorgan Chase released a new travel credit card—the Chase Sapphire Reserve. The demand for these cards became so high that the issuer ran out of cards soon after its release. What is interesting to note is that majority of the applicants were millennials.

All I Can Buy, If Not at Least Try!

Millennials want the right to use more than possession. They would rather own a car and rent a house. Renting has become for many of them a way of accessing a lifestyle that they aspire for and not having to own the same saves them making initial big investments. Millennials are big on renting furniture and other household items. Renting a furniture is not only easy on their pocket, but it also saves them from the hassle of relocation in case they have to move to another location and helps them to set up their home in a new city fast enough. They can also change their furniture and the look of their house at will. Evidence that such trends are catching up in a huge way is the fact that last year, one of India's largest furniture rental company Furlenco raised $30 million in venture capital. The rental market size in India is currently estimated at $10–15 billion and is likely to grow to $25–30 billion by 2020 (Rentomojo in Agarwal, 2015).

Limited Access!

Millennials like to access content or market where they shop at their will, at a time and place of their choice. The market is in the pockets of millennials and the market never sleeps.

Marketplace is more market space for millennials. They can browse through thousands of products and services at the tap of their fingers. Amazon recently added Amazon Global Store in India that allows customers in India to buy products that Amazon sells in other countries as well. Even access of content is more on apps and using Internet, including TV content. Amazon Prime and Netflix have already made their headway into the huge Indian market. Many popular daily shows are launching their second season exclusively on apps like Hotstar.

Browse Boy, Cause I Enjoy!

Millennials are bit of headache for retailers and marketers around the world. While they love to browse through products and services from online markets that are just a finger tap away, they do not buy as much. Popularly called as 'fauxsumerism', it is the latest consumerist fashion trend for millennials, that is, browsing without actually buying anything. A study conducted by the Intelligence Group, a division of Creative Artists Agency, found that millennials research potential purchases online and create their wish lists but will buy only if they feel something is absolutely necessary or something that seems extremely judicious.

We Care for Brands That Share!

Millennials like to associate brands with values. The brands that care are the ones that get most of millennials' share of time and attention. Deloitte Millennial Survey (2016) revealed that the top three values that millennials consider important that every business should demonstrate in letter and spirit are caring for their employees, ethical and honest conduct of business transactions and customer care.

Rules for Engaging Millennial Customers: 1 + 1 = 11

Millennial customers have a multiplier effect. Their experiences can exponentially trend on social media and impact similar customers in some other part of the world. They are social minded and armed with the new media. They love visuals and telling the world about their life, the products they use and how they feel about them using pictures, blogs or videos. One plus one in case of millennial customers is always more than the sum. Hence, very aptly we look at 11 rules of engaging this new-age customer who is hard to get and even more difficult to retain.

Rule # 1: Put Your Money Where There Is Honey

Let us combine two data feeds we have until now—shorter attention span of millennials and their constant desire to stay connected along with the heavy use of mobiles and apps. If their attention is difficult to seek and they are constantly on social networking apps, then what media marketers should be targeting more is a no-brainer. Another data that nails this further is the average CPM when it comes to advertisements over various media.

Media	CPM ($)
Social Media	1–4
YouTube	0.01–6
Radio	1–18
TV	10–30
TV (Prime Time)	35–50

Source: SiteAdWiki (2015).

Social media and YouTube come out to be the cheapest followed by radio, with TV being the costliest. TV is a powerful medium and cannot be completely ignored at this stage. But definitely, the return on investment for a marketer seems to be high on media that millennials use more frequently.

Rule # 2: On or Off, the Line Is Never One

Although online mode of shopping dominates among millennials, it cannot be taken as a thumb rule and the rest be forgotten. The online shopper loves to use mobiles and apps but also likes to browse on websites using a desktop or laptop. Therefore, although mobiles and apps need greater emphasis from marketers, website presence cannot be undermined at the same time. Online e-commerce brands Flipkart and Myntra made the same mistake. Both went app-only for some time before realizing their mistake and came back to relaunch their desktop websites. Buoyed over smartphone boom, both these brands misread the target customers and their behaviour. Another mistake that marketers can make is to think that online is the only mode that millennials will use for shopping. Online dominance does not mean that offline experiences are dead. So while offline retailers are going online with offers and discounts using platforms like Zopper, online retailers are opening limited offline stores for enabling the physical experience of the new-age customer. Babyoye, Zivame, Jabong, all have taken the offline route as well. Pepperfry, one of the leading online furniture and home marketplaces, has opened a concept store called Studio Pepperfry. The store showcases a curated range of furniture from Pepperfry's online portfolio and serves as a design inspiration for customers interested in furnishing their homes. Mobility and apps are definitely the future, but a multi-channel approach is more dynamic and stable.

Rule # 3: Go Social, Go Digital, but Use a Different Vial

Millennials trust indirect messages than traditional advertisements and considering the time they are spending on social media, social media marketing seems to be the best way to reach millennial customers. The number of FB users has increased from a mere 1 million in 2004 to 1.94 billion monthly active FB users for March 2017, an 18 per cent increase year over year (Zephoria, 2017). Twitter and LinkedIn users have also seen a steep spike. Consequently, there has been a huge growth in social media marketing as well. In India, there are over 462 million Internet users and 216.5 million are active social media users. Social media marketing has started getting significant attention and budget of the total marketing budgets of the businesses. India's digital marketing has grown by close to 33 per cent in the last six years (PCQuest, 2017). Digital is the way forward. However, with everyone queuing up for social and digital platforms for marketing their products and services, soon this space could be as cluttered as other platforms. The key is not only in going social or digital, the key is to garner a trust and an experience that millennials will value most. Brands forgetting to focus on friends are committing a huge mistake. Millennials trust people more than brands and brands that connect friends do a good job. Leveraging on social media and digital platforms with age-old advertising techniques of spray and pray will not work. The idea is to connect friends and create engaging stories around brands. A study by the McCarthy Group (2014) strongly suggested that the advertising companies should engage the millennials' friendship circles in order to reach their desired audience. In short, approaching social/ digital marketing like traditional marketing is a huge mistake.

Rule # 4: Tell a Story That Leaves an Impression

Storytelling works big time with millennial customers. We have seen how they do not trust traditional advertising. Building a story around a brand helps create a bond with the brand. The story makes it more authentic, helps to demonstrate behaviours, helps to tell at length and adds emotional value to brands. Gimlet Media even claims that longer stories get more attention of millennials than the shorter pieces. The storytelling gives millennials a sense of control over the brands, making them even more comfortable. The stories can be spun along the horizon of their lives. Their aspirations, insecurities, desires, all can be captured in such stories, helping brands to relate to them better and thereby create deeper engagement. Millennials are tremendously media savvy, and storytelling is a great way for marketers to credibly build their brand through authentic partnerships with cause-focused organizations. Brands such as Apple, Mahindra, Lufthansa, McDonald's and Nestle have succeeded in telling engaging stories that connected them to their customers.

Rule # 5: Create Brands with a Heart

The 'buy one, give one' business model of 'Toms Shoes' has inspired many other for-profit companies to create brands with a heart. The California-based shoe company started this unique model whereby whenever a person buys a pair of shoes, another pair is given away to someone needy. Reportedly, Toms

Shoes has given away more than 10 million pairs of shoes until date, helping many needy people to have a footwear. 'Mealshare' is another such model inspired by Toms Shoes. Whenever one orders food through Mealshare from any of the partners' restaurant Mealshare menu, a person in need receives a meal as well. Mealshare has reportedly served 1.337017 million meals to date. Similarly, whenever one order's a blanket for a child from 'Everything Happy', a needy child receives a blanket as well. There are other models too, whereby companies pledge to support social sustainability causes and donate a portion of their sales or profits to charities. The idea is to create a genuine image of a brand that it cares about human values and supports the causes important to this planet and humanity. This is a great way to attract millennial customers. Research also shows that millennials are extremely inclined on social impact investing or, in other words, investing in companies that care about environmental sustainability and social issues.

Rule # 6: Do Not Sell a Product

Before you jump to conclusions, marketers trying to sell a product or service to a millennials customer are missing the big picture. Millennials value experience over anything and more than any other cohort of customers. Why multiplexes continue to attract crowd mostly of young people despite the movies reaching smartphones of customers via legal routes like Netflix and Amazon Prime and illegal routes of piracy is again because of experience. The experience starts with their prospecting for the product or service, to their experience in purchasing/renting the same and post-purchase customer service. The promises made by the marketer, their level of commitment and honesty in fulfilling those promises and their quality of service that includes, promptness, timeliness, empathy and courteousness, all make up the value proposition that appeal to millennial customers.

Kishan Chakraborty was travelling along with his pregnant wife Ria from New York (NY) to Kolkata to participate in Durga Puja, a Bengali festival. The Qatar Airways tickets had been purchased by Kishan's company. The flight had a changeover at Doha. Kishan was a bit anxious about the low transit time between the two flights. The transit time between the NY-Doha flight and Doha-Kolkata flight was only one hour. Considering that his wife was six-months pregnant and she would not be able to move very fast, Kishan alerted the Qatar Airways' customer care about the condition of his wife before he started from NY and also requested assistance on ground for a smooth transit between the flights. Kishan's repeated calls to the airline's customer care were met with very polite response and assurance of all help. They assured him that an hour for transit would be enough and they will provide all assistance to him and his wife so that they do not have any hiccups. Kishan was assured and they embarked on the first leg of their flight. From NY, the flight took off about 40 minutes late. This did little for Kishan's comfort. He told the flight attendants about his problem and was assured that flight would reach on time and he will be extended all assistance at Doha. The flight landed 10 minutes late and for reaching the terminal, there was no air bridge. They were taxied to the terminal and the driver drove so atrociously slow that it took close to 45 minutes to reach the terminal. Kishan repeatedly kept calling the customer care and every time, he was assured of help. Upon reaching the terminal, another problem awaited Kishan and his expecting wife. Doha Airport was undergoing renovation and the place was in total mess. The directions for reaching other terminal and airline counters were all over the place. Somehow with a lot of difficulty, Kishan and his wife reached the Qatar Airways counter. Kishan was sure that they had missed their connecting flight. He explained how because of the delays caused for no fault of theirs they had been delayed. He also told the lady at the counter of his wife's state and how he had been contacting the airline's customer care all this while requesting for help. However, to his utter shock, he was told on his face by the airline official that the delay was completely his fault and so he was missing the connecting flight. Least he was expecting at this stage was a bit of empathy. That was too much to expect, perhaps! He was told that he will have to buy tickets for the next flight that was only available the next day. And since missing the flight was his fault, the airline would not even arrange for a hotel. Waiting with a lady in that condition, where she needed rest, sleep and comfort, in the airport lounge was unimaginable. Kishan felt helpless and in the 'middle of a sea'. He was appalled by the manner in which they were transferring their mistake on the passenger, the rudeness of the airline official and their complete lack of empathy. They did not have any consideration for his wife who needed to lie down every hour and take some rest. When he lost his cool and argued his case with the manager, only then he was assured of some help. He waited for another hour, after which the manager told him that since it was festival time and all flights were over booked, they could only arrange a flight to Mumbai from where there will be a domestic connecting flight to Kolkata. This was making the route longer and increasing their travel time. Added to this, they weren't given adjacent seats on the flight. But some solution was better than remaining stranded at Doha Airport. Kishan took the offer and by requesting his co-passengers, he was able to arrange a seat next to his wife on the flight. In Mumbai also, the transit was not completed properly by Qatar, which meant that he had to collect his entire luggage in Mumbai and book them again on the domestic connector. This was small worry compared to the fact that out of his five pieces of luggage, only two had reached Mumbai. The other three were missing. He had no one from Qatar Airways to help him in Mumbai and he had a tough time with custom officials. He registered the lost luggage complaint with Qatar's Mumbai office. His ordeal did not end even after reaching Kolkata as he had to keep following up with airline officials about his missing luggage. He received them in instalments over the next five days, which disrupted all his plans. The gifts that he had bought for his near and dear ones could not be given to them. He recalls that he was not the only one who had missed his flight due to the callousness of the airline; there were other stranded passengers as well. Among them was an *old lady who could not speak fluent English. Kishan says, 'I don't know what happened to her. At that time I was so consumed with my own problem that I could not offer her any help'. Kishan registered a complaint with the airlines about his whole experience and the problems that he faced. As expected, there was no response from the airline. Kishan signs off by saying,*

> *I was very excited to fly Qatar because they use Airbus A350 planes. For these planes, I have done the programming for their fuel systems. It is exciting to fly a plane that runs on fuel system for which you have written codes. But while the plane was fabulous, the experience was so bad that in my life I will never board a Qatar Airways flight.*

Kishan's vow is not wasted on us. Not that I am taking one now, but surely I will think twice before I take a United or a Qatar.

Experiences more than possession of physical goods attract millennials. A research by the Harris/Eventbrite researchers found that 78 per cent of .millennials were more willing to spend money on a desirable experience than buy popular goods, and 72 per cent of millennials actually wanted to increase their spending on experiences in the coming year, in lieu of physical possessions.

Going back to our airline experience, a research in the USA found that millennials were willing to settle for lesser legroom and lesser frills if that makes travel more affordable but count on experiences to make up for the same. A pilot of Southwest Airlines reportedly became famous for clicking selfies with passengers before the flight took off. That helped strengthen the fun nature of the brand. Millennials are said to be the top influencers in the toppling of Delta by American Airlines and relegation of United Airlines to the fifth spot among the best full-service airlines in America in the 2017 Harris Poll EquiTrend® Rankings (see Table 9.1). Trust on the

Table 9.1. Best Full-Service Airlines: America

Rank	2013	2014	2015	2016	2017
1	Alaska/ Horizon Airlines	Alaska/ Horizon Airlines	Delta Airlines	Delta Airlines	American Airlines
2	Hawaiian Airlines	Hawaiian Airlines	Alaska/ Horizon Airlines	Alaska/ Horizon Airlines	Alaska/ Horizon Airlines
3	Delta Airlines	Delta Airlines	Hawaiian Airlines	American Airlines	Hawaiian Airlines
4	United Airlines	American Airlines		Hawaiian Airlines	Delta Airlines
5				United Airlines	United Airlines

Source: Harris Poll EquiTrend (2017).

airline brand and the kind of experiences that it offers seems to be setting up the agenda.

Strengthening the experience argument in favour of millennials is another study by flight update app company FlightView (2017) that finds that more millennials (as much as three-fourths of millennials flyers) compared to other flyers are willing to pay extra for certain conveniences such as special radio-frequency identification (RFID) baggage tags (to reduce the likelihood of lost suitcases), check luggage at airport gates (so as not to carry them to airport restaurants and restrooms), purchase high-performance Wi-Fi (to stream video) or pay for in-seat electrical outlets (charging devices). By 2020, half of the world's flyers will be millennials. This calls for an urgent need to refocus and realign customer-winning strategies so as to boost the experience aspect. However, this is not limited to airline industry. Experience-seeking millennials crave for the same in most of their purchases. A look at Business Insider's (2016) top 100 brands that millennials prefer gives a good glimpse into the behaviour of millennial customers. Experience and value reign supreme among other factors for their preference and brand loyalty.

Rule # 7: Innovative Ways 'Own' the Race

It is very important for marketers to find out innovative ways in which they can encourage ownership among millennials. Remember, millennials are a bit cash-strapped. At the same time, they are likely to delay ownership of some high-involvement assets, if not all. Easy financing may not be the only way out to penetrate millennial customers. The overall deal has to be made attractive and lucrative for millennials to take the plunge. The offer has to appear very reasonable and irresistible in terms of benefits that it holds, that again must be manifold.

Zoomcar, one of India's prominent car rental services companies, has recently launched Zoomcar Associate Program (ZAP). Under ZAP, Zoomcar allows individuals to purchase one or more vehicles, lease the vehicles to Zoomcar and then share in the revenue. In other words, it allows a person to own a car and rent it out on idle days, raking in moolah that helps to repay the car loan EMI. The company also helps interested individuals to secure a bank loan for purchasing the car. The ZAP is a win-win strategy by Zoomcar. On the one hand, it reduces their investment as their need for ownership will go down with this programme. On the other hand, individuals' renting out their car helps them to own the car while being light on their pockets, use it when they need and rent it when they don't.

Very recently, Amazon India declared sale on its site. However, that was not the only attraction. Along with the sale, Amazon announced that every hour of the sale, it would pick some buyers randomly and ask them some questions. The winners would receive ₹0.1 million in their Amazon wallet. Ninety-six winners were declared using this scheme, with ₹1,000 added to their Amazon wallets. More importantly, thousands flocked the sale.

Rule # 8: All Is Not Fair in Love and War!

To engage a particular customer segment, one has to first understand them and decipher what issues are close to their heart. Millennials' distrust of the corporate world has not been without reason. If trust is what they expect, then value for money is what they expect out of every transaction. To be treated fairly is a basic expectation; however, millennials are very informed customers, have plenty of choices and are vocal about their experiences on social media. Hence, an unfair treatment is more likely to get reported on social media, get inked in reviews across various seller sites and may even get blogged about. In the case of service offerings, many a time it is the last-mile offering that needs to be taken care of. The company may be using associates or partners to deliver the service finally to the customer and even if the company is honest, but the partner is not fair in dealings, the experience of the customer is bound to be spoilt. Remember, it is the brand that takes the hit and not the partner. Take Pinki's case for instance.

Pinki Laskar narrates her poor experience riding with Ola Cabs. The driver took a longer route than usual and the bill amount was naturally more. Pinki knew as she has been travelling on that route quite often and despite her insistence to take the usual route, the driver took the longer route on the pretext that the usual route was experiencing a traffic jam. Upon reaching the destination, the driver insisted on cash payment. Pinki was having enough money in her Ola Money wallet to pay for the ride; however, she was not carrying enough cash. Her requests for making the payment using her Ola Money wallet fell on deaf ears and the driver rudely insisted on cash payment. She stood in the middle of the road, trying to call the Ola customer care, but she could not put her word across. The rude and intimidating behaviour of the driver scared Pinki as well. Finally, she had to rush to the nearest ATM, withdraw cash and make the payment. After the cab left, she further discovered that some amount had been deducted from her Ola Money wallet as well. Since she had paid the entire bill amount vide cash, the deduction from the Ola Money wallet was wrongful deduction. She says that she had registered her compliant with Ola customer care and had followed up couple of times for getting back her money. However, until date she has been unable to get the money back. Pinki signs off by saying, 'from that day I stopped taking an Ola'.

Keerthi still laments buying an external hard disk from Snapdeal. She bought a 1 terabyte hard disk from the e-commerce site. As compared to other sites, Snapdeal was showing the same product ₹500 cheaper. Keerthi opened the product one month after receiving the same and that turned out to be her biggest mistake. Her assumed trust on the e-tailer and her other pre-occupation made her keep the product she received with assurance that it will be of good quality. The product on opening not only turned out to be defective, but her attempts to seek a replacement from Snapdeal were also turned down on the pretext that the order was more than three weeks old. She was directed to the manufacturer Transcend for resolution. The manufacturer on the other hand asked her to deal with Snapdeal. She was caught in a volley between Snapdeal and Transcend and finally decided to give up and swallow the loss instead of incurring more cost on trying to find a resolution of her problem.

Varsha Jain, on the contrary, has a good experience to relate. In one instance her brother in Mumbai and in another she herself in Bengaluru forgot their phones in an Uber cab, and in both the instances, the respective drivers came back to return their phones. Although the absence of a helpline number of Uber customer care gave her some nightmares, but eventually both she and her brother got back their phones.

Rule # 9: Do Not Rub Them the Wrong Way

Connecting with issues close to their heart and treating them well goes a long way in engaging millennials customers. Millennial customers love experience as we have discussed earlier, and want to be treated with respect. They love personalized services and value genuine attention and care.

Shan likes the fact that KTM bikes dealers have sales personnel who are of his age. Shan says,

It is very easy talking to them. Plus they have very good knowledge about super bikes and explain their product really well. I have been to Honda and Yamaha showrooms. They have older sales people who are good but they do not know that much about

superbikes and their features. The dealer also make you feel a part of their family.

KTM also organizes 'Orange Day Racing' exclusively for KTM bike owners. Shan was offered sponsorship for racing for one such race by his dealer. While Shan relishes every bit of his KTM bike experience, he is not so upbeat about his recent experience at a Raymond outlet. He had visited the store to get a stitched suit for himself. The sales people assumed that he would have a shoestring budget since he was a student. They treated him with slight disdain and showed him cheaper materials. Despite his insistence, they kept on asking him embarrassing questions such as what his budget was and whether he could afford costlier suits. He did not like the stereotyping that store sales people seemed to make and the way they treated him. He felt even more humiliated as he was accompanied by his girlfriend to the Raymond outlet. The 'Complete Man' seems to be a rich one too!

Rule # 10: Encourage Online Reviews

Millennials like to share their experiences as customers as well as read and believe the reviews by other customers while making a purchase. A smart marketer would always encourage his millennial customer to write reviews on various online sites that are frequented by other millennial customers. Such opportunities for sharing reviews make millennial customers feel more empowered, make them feel a part of the influencer group and at the same time help the brand as well. Real reviews help more than just plain good reviews. Millennials tend to believe real reviews that is not out-and-out sugar coated but talks mostly positive about the brand. A blog post that I wrote on our good experience at a McDonald's outlet (Some Balloons Fly) on my blog has still got the largest number of hits.

Rule # 11: Let Us Co-create!

Millennials love collaboration opportunities to co-create brands or products. Letting millennial customers do the same is one of the secrets of success. Lego Blocks encourages its fans to submit new creation ideas as well as lets them vote for creations submitted by other fans. If a creation gets the requisite number of votes, it gets the official Lego ideas award and goes into commercial production. Millennials' love for co-creation has helped companies use crowdsourcing to infuse new ideas into the company. Considering that millennials live a paradox dotted life, their trials and tribulations are best understood by them. Hence, letting them participate in designing product, services or marketing campaigns helps bring in ideas that can really help millennial customers and has high appeal and recall. Every year, DHL, a global logistics company, brings its customers and service partners under one roof at specially designed innovation centres to conduct workshops that not only help share best practices but also create valuable insights into better ways of managing logistics.

Value Interactions

Technology and social media have transformed the market and revolutionized the concept of marketing. Millennial customers are different. They are tech-savvy, armed with plenty of information, spoilt for choices, browse at will with no compulsion to buy, trust reviews more than advertisements and continuously look for value, not hesitating to hold brands accountable for the same. Brands would do themselves good by forming meaningful, ongoing relationships that involves frequent online interactions mostly through social networking channels.

In the end, it all boils down to how much companies understand millennial customers and the effort they make to reach out to this new customer cohort. Engaging millennial customers may many a time mean treading more paths than one, doing more things and reinventing in terms of new offerings and newer ways to offer.

10
ENGAGING MILLENNIALS
IN THE SOCIETY

In our effort to define workplace and marketplace contexts and learn new ways of engaging the millennials, we must not forget that millennials are social beings first and therefore besides these two contexts, the societal context is also important. In fact, understanding the millennial dynamics in the societal context may have important ramifications in how we engage them as employees and customers as well.

Engaging them in the societal context has different shades. There are various sub-contexts within the societal context where engagement of millennials is both sought and desired. We discuss in this chapter three such sub-contexts.

Millennials and Volunteerism

Research indicates that millennials have high concern for sustainability issues addressing societal challenges in the areas of deepest concerns: resource scarcity, climate change and income inequality (Williams, 2014). Millennials are a generation that has grown up in a society of eco-consciousness, and many believe that they have a holistic outlook of the world and social enterprises will help enable this. They want to simultaneously reach levels of financial well-being as well as achieving social good (Seager, 2014). Most of them feel that business can do much more to address the societal concerns and challenges. They believe that success of a business should be measured not only in terms of its financial performance but also in terms of its focus on improving society. Millennials are also charitable and keen to participate in public life. A 2014 Deloitte study found that a large percentage of millennials either gave to charities or actively volunteered or were members of community organizations, and a significant number of them had also signed e-petitions for issues they believed in (Deloitte, 2014).

Contextual Motivations

Volunteerism is thought to be a powerful tool for engaging people in tackling development challenges. It has the potential to transform the pace and nature of development of a region or a country. It benefits both the society at large and the individual volunteer by strengthening trust, solidarity and reciprocity among citizens, and by purposefully creating opportunities for participation. Millennials world over are keen on volunteerism and like to volunteer for social causes. Interestingly, though the motivation to undertake volunteerism is context specific. In Israel, where the Jewish religion is dominant, the Bible has a lot to do with volunteering. One of the tenets of the Bible, 'Love thy neighbour as yourself' reflects the importance of helping people in need.

In the USA, social responsibility is a way to make yourself look good on paper. Using community service to get credits in colleges/universities and also pad one's resume are key motivations for millennials to take up volunteerism (McGlone, Spain, & McGlone, 2011). However, the indirect benefits of volunteering for millennials are not limited to career aspects alone. Students who have volunteered during high school have been found to have a lower probability of being arrested when they reach adulthood (Uggen & Janikula, 1999). Another pattern noticed in the USA is the tendency of continuing volunteerism if they begin during their teens (Oesterle, Johnson, & Mortimer, 2004).

Research on related grounds from an Italian perspective reveals that distinctive and composite self and other motivational factors exist. Volunteerism is used as a way to reduce guilt by giving back to the society, a career booster, and self-efficacy and self-esteem enhancer (Marta, Gulielmetti, & Pozzi, 2006).

Specific to Canada, 'Members of Millennials are generally more civic minded and appear to be predisposed to being more actively involved in volunteering than individuals in previous generations' (Pooley, 2005).

The size of one's social network has a lot to do with millennials to volunteer. The larger the social network, the greater the odds that an individual may volunteer (Puntam, 2000).

Millennials go the extra mile when it comes to making a social presence for a good cause. They not only volunteer but also choose to be customers and work for organizations that have meaningful CSR initiatives (Litauen & Miller, 2012). In fact, 69 per cent of millennials refuse to work for companies that are not socially responsible (Cone, 2008).

In a similar research study done in India, I found that passion to serve and personal satisfaction were the most dominant motivational factors behind millennials taking up volunteerism. It is also interesting to note that most of them have volunteered for social causes close to their heart.

Sneha (21), for instance, participated as a volunteer for organizing free eye camps in villages and primary schools. She did this while pursuing her engineering studies and as a part of her college NSS camp. Although she received a certificate from her college for her participation as a volunteer, she vouches for the fact that she would have still gone ahead and done the volunteering job even if she had not been recognized for the same. She continues to participate in social cause drives and anonymously donates monetarily as well.

Ramya (23), also a BTech, worked in a premier IT company in India. She on her own initiative collected donations for cancer patients. When she later came to know that her organization also had similar initiatives, she happily participated in them as well. She by her own confession is driven by an urge to do something for those in distress and finds emotional comfort in comforting them.

Padma (22) from Chennai has volunteered for a well-known NGO in India that works for child rights. She has an interesting story as to how an incident changed her life and made her to think about taking up volunteering. She was once 'hanging out' with her friends at the famous 'Marina Beach' in Chennai. They were having some snacks and were casually throwing away some leftover food. Padma noticed after some time that some underprivileged children begging on the beach were picking up the food thrown away by them and eating to quell their hunger. This incident moved her from within and that very moment she decided to do something for the underprivileged kids in India. This NGO that apparently works for child issues attracted Padma and she associated with this organization. She participated in their fund-raising events and had also volunteered to teach small kids in slums. In her own words, 'Because of me if some children are happy, even for some time, then I feel blessed'. Padma does not feel too good telling others about her contributions to such causes and has never tried to secure any personal gains through such involvements.

Mohammad Abdul Samad (22), a pharmacy graduate, has worked as a scribe for blind children in a blind school in Secunderabad. After getting a random call from an agency, he decided to volunteer as a scribe for blind children. He also spread the word in his pharmacy college and made a team of like-minded students who also volunteered as scribes. He did it for his personal satisfaction and every time he volunteered for these children, he felt happy. In fact, he opines that he found blind children very talented and sometime more knowledgeable than normal kids. He often found brilliant mental imagery among these students while they were dictating answers to him to scribe them. Hence, he never felt he was doing any favour to these students by acting as their scribe. Instead, he felt a sense of satisfaction at getting an opportunity to serve.

Arjun Ajit (25) lost his mother when he was 19 years old and according to him, that loss eroded his faith in God. But his life turned around when he associated with a social service organization. As a part of their team, he started cooking and distributing free food to the patients below poverty level in the city government hospital on Sundays. He drew immense comfort and inner satisfaction from his act. He believed in the motto of the organization with which he associated that read: 'Service to mankind is Service to God'. He spent his many Sundays working for the needy and sick, rather than engaging in leisure and entertainment. Today, he is a much fulfilled man and believes that his volunteering act has healed his inner wounds.

For Krishna Teja Koya (23) from Bengaluru, the casual opportunity to visit a social missionary organization to which his father is a donator to oversee the work done by them turned into a life-changing experience. Moved by the work done by the NGO for the local tribal and their families having minimum access to basic amenities of life, he decided to make his bit of contribution. Since then he has been a regular at the NGO and has involved himself in various activities like teaching computers to the tribal kids. He has derived tremendous happiness and satisfaction through such endeavours.

Udita Sengupta (22) from Kolkata along with her 'gang' of friends does event management activities. However, in their leisure hours, they get together and try to do something for the society. They have in the past distributed winter clothes to the slum dwellers in Kolkata; they also frequent orphanages for *distributing gifts to the children. Udita likes to see the happiness on the faces of the orphans or the slum dwellers and feels a sense of satisfaction by being a source of joy to them. She and her friends derive a sense of meaning for life and it is their way of 'giving back'. By her own confession, Udita would do more of such volunteering activities, but for the paucity of time.*

Abhishek Bhattacharya (20), also from Kolkata, has involved himself in different kinds of volunteering activities and his reasons for doing so interestingly have not been much different from others. He has been a volunteer in his school sports activities, in his college fests and in organizing various cultural and sporting activities in his social community centre. Abhishek likes to help, and he feels good when he works as a volunteer. No gain beyond such personal fulfilment has ever crossed Abhishek's mind in becoming a volunteer, although such activities have made him very popular.

Implications for Employers

As discussed in the previous section, research has clearly indicated that millennials not only like to volunteer for social causes but also choose to be customers and work for organizations that are having meaningful CSR initiatives (Litauen & Miller, 2012), and that majority of millennials refuse to work for companies that are not socially responsible (Cone, 2008).

MSLGROUP, the flagship strategic communications and engagement consultancy of Publicis Groupe, and the largest brand and reputation advisory network in Asia and Europe, sometime ago released 'The Future of Business Citizenship' report, a 17-market study of millennials' views on citizenship and the role businesses play in tackling critical macro and micro issues. The study revealed that 73 per cent of the 8,000 millennials surveyed worldwide felt that governments can't solve societal issues by themselves, and 83 per cent want to see corporations actively involved. Interestingly, more than 86 per cent of millennials surveyed were from Asia that included Mainland China, Hong Kong, India, Japan and Singapore, and they expect businesses to be actively involved in solving important issues in areas such as economy, environment and health care. In India, an overwhelming 93 per cent of millennials want to do something to get involved in making the world a better place and believe they can do so (MSL, 2014).

India is the first country in the world to mandate CSR. On 1 April 2014, the Government of India implemented new CSR guidelines, requiring companies to spend 2 per cent of their net profit on social development. The Ministry of Corporate Affairs (MCA) has notified Section 135 and Schedule VII of the Companies Act, 2013, which relate to CSR and mandate companies to spend 2 per cent of their three-year average annual net profit on CSR activities in each financial year, starting from financial year 2015. The new provision also clearly states that CSR activities should be undertaken only in 'project/programme' mode (ENS Economic Bureau, 2014; Jones Day, 2014; Prasad, 2014; PTI, 2014).

Considering the findings of this research, it will be prudent for companies to provide their millennial employees with an opportunity to volunteer for social causes. If the company has institutionalized a CSR programme, then it is a great opportunity to provide millennial employees a chance to volunteer. This may help in not only attracting millennial talent but also meaningfully engaging them at the workplace where they derive more meaning to their lives, not just through their work. Additionally, it helps companies create a responsible consumer brand as well that appeals to millennial customers.

Part of the wHole

PotHoleRajaTM is a unique pothole-free-India mission from GroundReality Enterprises Pvt. Ltd and GroundReality Trust, a private organization and NGO, which is aiming for safer roads and filling the potholes across India through a public–private partnership (PPP) model. Prathaap Bhimsen Rao, the founder and CEO and the brain behind this initiative, says,

> Our vision is to make Indian roads pothole free for safer commutation. Until now, we have identified and fixed over 350 potholes in Bengaluru in a very short span of time. We have ensured that technology integration ensures live view of potholes online. On a daily basis, 8+ potholes are reported by public and employees of different companies to +91 814 POTHOLE number. With media support across newspaper, radio, TV and online, the reach to public at large about this initiative has started spreading like wild fire.

PotHoleRajaTM has broken several social perceptions about road safety and one of them has been that only government is responsible for maintenance of roads. In a country where using and damaging roads for private usage is a norm, voluntary citizen participation is significant to address the problem.

Another social perception that PotHoleRajaTM seems to be challenging is that private companies can do nothing about public roads and worse still that employees have nothing to do with the CSR fund that a company spends.

Prathaap very aptly adds,

> Most of the times the companies give away their CSR fund to NGOs or public institutions with zero accountability of

impact that it makes on the society. There was an instance I know with a company that had spent several crores from its CSR funds and then during their financial audit, they discovered that they had actually spent Rs.7.5 million less than what they should have. It was clear that there was no track of CSR fund spending. It was limited to cheques and just ensuring that legal compliance was made in terms of the company law. Through our PotHoleRajaTM initiative, we have tried to break this mental model, sensitizing and encouraging companies who participate in the PotHoleRajaTM to involve their employees in this initiative. The results are very encouraging.

Bengaluru-based QwikCilver Solutions Pvt. Ltd is one such company that has not only supported the PotHoleRajaTM mission under its CSR initiative but has also encouraged voluntary participation from its employees. The CTO of the company Mr Sanjay who lost his daughter in a road accident has been at the forefront of this initiative on part of QwikCilver. Before the pothole things happened to QwikCilver, less than 5 per cent of employees used to participate in the CSR activities of the company. These were generally the managers in the 35–40-year-old age bracket. The company's larger workforce of millennials were hardly involved in such activities. However, the way pothole fixing mission was conceptualized, it made it very simple for all employees to participate and make themselves a part of this activity. Three levels of participation were seen as a part of employee initiative.

The task was to ensure that public roads in and around QwikCilver offices in Koramangala region of Bengaluru were made pothole free. Hence, the first task was to identify the potholes and mark them. The employees did the first set of identification of potholes in groups of four. When they stepped out for lunch, during their walk to the restaurant and back to the office, wherever they saw potholes, they just took a picture of the same and marked the location. In just a matter of two days, close to 20 potholes were identified in the 1 km periphery of the QwikCilver offices.

The employees with support from the HR team at the company also raised funds for fixing potholes. They conducted a social event in which the food that was served was cooked by the employees themselves. They raised funds through this event. This same fund was used for fixing the potholes.

The employees also volunteered in fixing the potholes themselves with support from PotHoleRajaTM that uses a very easy, eco-friendly and innovative way of fixing potholes. The same group of employees fixed the potholes that had identified them. The work was done during early mornings or late nights or over weekends when the vehicular traffic on the roads was less.

Prathaap proudly announces,

Never before had any CSR initiative at QwikCilver received such a tremendous response and participation from the employees and neither had anyone so actively sought their voluntary participation. The feedback after the programme was that no other CSR initiative had given such a huge sense of fulfilment and engagement among the employees as had the pothole management activity. This can be a model for every company who can create engagement among their millennial employees by encouraging volunteerism among them for the CSR activities supported by the firm.

PotHoleRajaTM is planning a similar initiative for another company—Bosch—that has a huge percentage of millennial population among their workforce. Prathaap has developed three levels of this initiative where Bosch can not only productively use their CSR funds but also involve and engage a large millennial workforce to volunteer for pothole management.

The first idea is to ensure that 1–2 km stretch of public roads that lead up to the Bosch properties are made pothole free. The volunteering employees would identify and fix the potholes.

The second idea is to encourage the employees living in different part of the city to identify and fix potholes on the public roads close to their locality. This also helps employees to sensitize and involve other citizens living in the area in this initiative, thereby creating a lot of goodwill for themselves.

The third idea is to create model roads that lead up to Bosch properties, at least a kilometre or two stretch of it. This would go beyond pothole management and would also include making wider roads, fixing the road lights, creating marking on roads and installing safety devices to ensure safety of drivers and pedestrians.

Millennial employees at Bosch have different informal interest groups such as the runners group, cyclists group and bikers group. The idea is to involve these groups who identify and fix potholes on the roads they frequent.

The technical assistance for fixing potholes will be provided by PotHoleRajaTM, while Bosch would fund all such drives.

Prathaap adds,

> Millennials do not have any hang-ups. For instance, they do not feel shy to fix potholes on the roads. It is very easy to work with them. They feel good and have a sense of giving back to the society, when they are encouraged to volunteer.

Go Social

Millennials are much more social-minded and willing to donate for social causes then we think. Despite the mythical tag of being self-centred and the fact that they are actually cash-strapped, millennials are a well-informed generation, willing and wanting to do good and joining with causes and issues they care about. A research report of Blackbaud indicates the fact that more millennials donate compared to members of the previous generation, with many of them actually making donations using mobile applications. According to the Millennial Impact Report by the research group Achieve, a substantial 84 per cent of millennials made a charitable donation in 2014, and 70 per cent spent at least an hour volunteering (CNBC, 2015). Study after study have only confirmed the high levels of social consciousness of millennials and their willingness and preference to associate with brands that are socially responsible. A study from the Stanford Graduate School of Business revealed that 90 per cent of business graduates from business schools in Europe and North America prefer working for organizations committed to social responsibility. Millennials' preference for ethics and integrity over financial reward is well known (Stanford Business, 2004).

The 2015 Cone Communications Millennial CSR Study confirms that millennials' engagement with CSR efforts was universal. The study revealed that more than 90 per cent of the millennials would switch brands to be associated with brands genuinely supporting a cause. More than 75 per cent use social media to engage in CSR activities (Sustainable Brands, 2015). I have always argued that CSR spends of a company can bring symbiotic benefits to the company as well. With a huge millennial working population and more entering the workforce in large numbers in coming years, also remembering that they are highly social minded and prefer to work for socially responsible organization, many of them involving themselves in volunteering work through NGOs, companies have huge opportunity to turn their CSR fund into millennial engagement fund by encouraging such employees to participate voluntarily in social events and activities funded by the company. This way the company not only gets to know the direct benefits of its CSR funds but also fulfils a psychological and social need of its millennial employees in the form of providing a platform and opportunity to volunteer for social causes. Not to forget that when these millennials double up as customers, then a similar factor may create a favour among millennial customers. Millennials are not only willing to pay more for sustainable brands but are also likely to pay extra money for offerings that are sustainable in nature, as per the Nielsen Global Corporate Sustainability Report (2015). Enough pointers are there to say very safely that the social purpose of a brand has a major influence on the purchase decisions of the millennial customers.

Hence, engaging millennials in the societal context influences engagement in both workplace and marketplace business contexts. Their affinity for social causes may be the product of their own lives characterized by deficit in their state of wellness. But societal engagement is a good way to not only better recognize how different they are but also use that knowledge to engage them better.

Millepreneurs: A New Generation of Entrepreneurs

Millennials have grown up in a chaotic world, a world full of uncertainties and volatility. Their inherent suspicion and distrust for corporations, the high instability in their jobs, the shrinking job market and loss of jobs, combined with their desire for freedom and career ambition—due to all these factors, most of the members of this generation prefer to be entrepreneurs. Entrepreneurship also gives them the flexibility that they yearn for but hardly get while working for most corporations. A top executive of a German multinational bank speaking on anonymity says that most organizations are scared of giving flexibility to millennial workers. They are still used to tracking, monitoring and closely supervising millennial workers. According to him, there are trust issues and older managers are not used to place their trust on them (see Figure 10.1). However, he feels that millennial workers do much better when trust is placed on them by their organizations and managers.

The percentage of millennials who wish to become entrepreneurs is so overwhelming that it will not be wrong to call this new generation of entrepreneurs as 'millepreneurs'. These preferences have been found to be similar in various studies taken in various parts of the world. A study by Bentley University (2014) on preference of American millennials towards entrepreneurship found that close to 67 per cent of them wanted to start their own venture.

According to a 2015 study Amway Global Entrepreneurship Report (AGER), 93 per cent of the Indians wish to take up entrepreneurship (Chandna, 2016). A global study that found millennials around the globe showing high preference for entrepreneurship ranked India highest among 44 countries worldwide in entrepreneurial spirit. Indian millennials also effuse high degree of optimism for

Figure 10.1   Why Team Members Do Not Respect Their Boss?

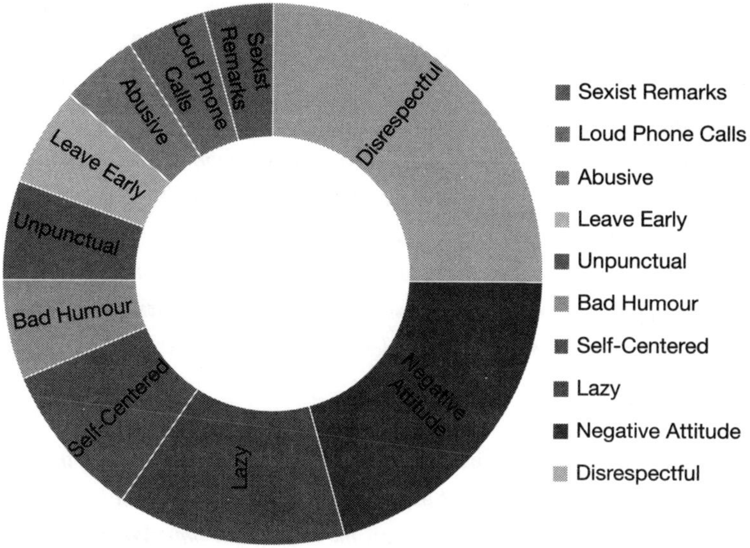

- ■ Sexist Remarks
- ■ Loud Phone Calls
- ■ Abusive
- ▨ Leave Early
- ■ Unpunctual
- ■ Bad Humour
- ■ Self-Centered
- ■ Lazy
- ■ Negative Attitude
- ▨ Disrespectful

Source: Statista and Glassdoor (2017).

entrepreneurial prospects in their country and believe that they have an opportunity to undertake entrepreneurship. As much as 87 per cent of the Indian millennials believe that the time is opportune for them to start an entrepreneurial venture, as per the findings of telecommunications major Telefónica (2013) study done in association with *Financial Times*.

Vivek who works as a software engineer at one of the top Indian IT majors is one of these millennipreneurs who wants to give up his IT job and start a venture on organic farming in partnership with a friend who is also planning to give up his booming salesman job. Vivek is actually doing quite well in his company, having spent close to eight years, having had opportunities to work on on-site at the USA and drawing a good healthy pay package. But Vivek by his own confession feels a sense of monotony with IT work, having very little to try something new.

Kumail Kirmani, nephew of legendary Indian cricketer Syed Kirmani, is the first-generation entrepreneur in his family. Inspired by the passion and an attitude to follow one's own heart and pursue one's dreams of his illustrious uncle Syed Kirmani, Kumail decided to embark upon his entrepreneurial journey after working in sales and marketing domain for few organizations, quite early in his career. Kumail owns a business consulting firm Sreshtha Global. He has two more partners in the business who are also millennials. His Bengaluru-based firm offers an array of business consulting services to various corporations, which include financial services, HR services and marketing support. Kumail says,

> I have seen people's lives and careers stagnating by the time they reach their mid-30s. I did not want that to happen to me. I had a good stint as an employee. But entrepreneurship gives me a boundless opportunity to try things that I want to! I have a lot of freedom and flexibility as an entrepreneur.

Kumail acknowledges that his entrepreneurial journey until now has not been without its share of troubles and challenges. He adds,

> As a start-up and as young people running a consulting firm, public perception has been our biggest challenge. Generally, companies associate business consulting with grey-haired people and feel comfortable with established consulting brands. It takes us lot of time and effort to break these stereotypes and persuade companies that we can offer them equally good services.

Actually, reports suggest that millennials are doing much better as entrepreneurs compared to the previous generations. The findings of 2016 BNP Paribas Global Entrepreneur Report shows that millennials are not only starting more businesses but also targeting higher profits (Petrilla, 2016).

Table 10.1. Top 20 Cities with Fastest-growing Start-up Ecosystem

Rank	2015 Ranking	2017 Ranking	Change
1	Silicon Valley	Silicon Valley	No change
2	New York	New York	No change
3	Los Angeles	London	+3
4	Boston	Beijing	New entrant
5	Tel Aviv	Boston	−1
6	London	Tel Aviv	−1
7	Chicago	Berlin	+2
8	Seattle	Shanghai	New entrant
9	Berlin	Los Angeles	−6
10	Singapore	Seattle	−2
11	Paris	Paris	No change
12	Sau Paulo	Singapore	−2
13	Moscow	Austin	+1
14	Austin	Stockholm	New entrant
15	Bengaluru	Vancouver	+3
16	Sydney	Toronto	+1
17	Toronto	Sydney	−1
18	Vancouver	Chicago	−11
19	Amsterdam	Amsterdam	No change
20	Montreal	Bengaluru	−5

Source: Startup Genome (2017).

Kumail's vision for his firm is to be able to change a perception among Indian companies that all good things can come from West, or can be delivered only by established consulting brands.

The last decade has largely been a persistent jobless growth characterized by growth of consumerism, but not matched with growth of the job market. 'The term "persistent jobless growth" refers to the phenomenon in which economies exiting recessions demonstrate economic growth while merely maintaining—or, in some cases, decreasing—their level of employment' (World Economic Forum, 2015). Entrepreneurship among millennials seems the only viable way to deal with this jobless growth that will on the one hand provide self-employment to many millennials and on the other hand create new job opportunities for others. Entrepreneurship among millennials is a way ahead for a bright future of the world. Both governments and societies have a huge role to play in ensuring that this millennial aspiration for entrepreneurship is backed by strong policy support and breaking of social stereotypes, giving young entrepreneurs an opportunity to prove their worth. Companies like 3M have kept the entrepreneurial spirit alive in the company by encouraging intrapreneurship. An intrapreneur is an employee within a company who takes risks in an effort to solve a given problem. Companies like 3M have not only encouraged such employees but also provided opportunities to head their own entrepreneurial ventures at some stage with the parent company doing the seed funding. This way, it keeps innovation alive in their companies, retains intrapreneurial talent and also helps them to diversify their portfolio of offerings. For employees, it is a more challenging work, a way to satisfy their entrepreneurial urge and a platform to show their entrepreneurial skills. Encouraging and fostering entrepreneurship among millennials is a great way to engage them in the society.

Engaging Millennials as Learners

The context of learning with respect to millennials has two connotations—it refers to millennials who are still in college and are active student learners; it also refers to corporate learners who during the course of their employment are exposed to various formal learning forums such as coaching, training and management development.

The focus here is on the first group of learners, that is, the millennials who are still in their college completing their formal education. Therefore, we are looking at millennial college graduates and professional studies. This is not without a reason. The past few years have seen a steep fall in the employability among college graduates. In very simple words, it means that majority of the millennials who are graduating every year from various colleges do not have skill sets that are needed by the industry. Take India for instance. Despite the rapid proliferation of professional education landscape, the quality of graduates has been very inconsistent. Barring the top colleges, most other colleges have churned out graduates who are not ready for the job market. This is true for both public and private universities. If statistics can speak more of this sad reality, then there is a mountain load of them available. Out of the 3 million graduates who join the Indian job market every year, only about 0.5 million are considered employable, which is just about 16–17 per cent. Discipline-wise, the percentage is even lower (PTI, 2017). Only about 7 per cent of the engineers who pass out every year were found to be employable. An employability-focused study by New Delhi-based consulting firm Aspiring Minds who surveyed 150,000 engineering students revealed this shocking reality.

Employability of management graduates in functional domains remains below 10 per cent. Whereas employability for management students ranges between 10–20 per cent for roles involving client interaction, it remains below 10 per cent for any functional role in the field of HR, marketing or finance. Whereas 32 per cent management graduates lose out because of lack of English and cognitive skills, at least 50 per cent students are not employable in functional domains  for lack of knowledge and conceptual understanding of the domain (National Employability Report, 2012).

Skill gap or employability gap is not only an India-specific problem, but it is also prevalent even among the developed economies. 'The global skill gap is here to stay for as long as technological advances, globalisation and demography continue to redefine work' (*Gratton*, 2011). The biggest demographical factor has been the millennials who populate both colleges and corporate, and in this campus to corporate journey for majority of them the skills do not seem to be coming their way. I quote *The Globe and Mail* here which attributes skill gaps to 'government policy, the efficiency of educational institutions in turning out graduates with the right skills, and how effectively employers train their workers'.

Clearly, the onus has been put on the institutions of higher learning to ensure that millennial graduates are empowered with skills and not just theoretical knowledge to make them more employable. Most of the institution-based courses and programmes as well as workplace learning are planned, organized and led by instructors, leading to formal learning. While the curriculum has been easy to develop and easy to copy, teaching styles have not evolved with the change of audience in the classroom. The teaching is still heavily dependent on text and lecturing style. The large number of millennials in college and the overwhelming skill or employability gap indicate that traditional pedagogical tool used in business school may be outdated (Noble, 2013). There is a need to have a relook at the choice of tools as this could have significant impact on assurance of learning among business graduates (Uthra, 2014). Since learning styles have huge impact on learning effectiveness, understanding and mapping learning styles with pedagogical tools should be a logical approach to choose the former to address deep understanding, industry-specific skills and vocational training in business schools. The process of learning has to become engaging enough for it to become productive.

Relationship Between Learning Styles and Instructional Methods

A learning style replicates to the ideal and consistent way in requisites of behaviour and approaches, how one responds to and uses stimuli in an educational site (Clark, 2000; Litzinger & Osif, 1993). It reflects the 'characteristic cognitive, affective, and physiological behaviours that provide as moderately steady indicators of how learners perceive, interact with, and respond to the learning environment'.

Learning styles can be broadly categorized in three different styles which are dominant in most learners' perspective. The most utilized approach to learning style analysis is the VAK model (visual, auditory and kinaesthetic). The VAK model is based on three sensory receivers: visual, auditory, and kinaesthetic, where one or more of the receiving styles dominate one's preferred approach to learning. These biologically imposed learning modalities of this model—visual, auditory and kinaesthetic perceptions—have evolved within an individual over time.

Individuals with visual learning style learn best using pictorial aids and text materials, such as optical aid, figures and video clips. Auditory learners learn best by listening. While kinaesthetic learners are tactile learners who learn best by doing an activity.

Several research studies have indicated that learning styles are effective means by which teachers can identify the different needs of the students by applying the same in the classroom teaching. An understanding of the way students learn improves the selection of teaching strategies best suited to student learning and enables teachers to knowledgably develop a variety of instructional methods. The greater consistency between course design and student learning styles leads to less stress in the learning environment, higher motivation to learn and better performance. In short, the research supports that individuals learn better when they are presented instruction in the modality that capitalizes on their learning style preference.

To further ascertain the learning style of millennial students, a sample size of 300 millennial students doing their professional studies in business management were chosen using purposive sampling method. The learning styles of these students were analysed using three separate reliable open source tools and the results were matched. The millennial students were from 25 different cities in India, out of which 180 were males and 120 were females. The sample was restricted to students of business schools in India.

All of them undertook the learning style tests under researcher's supervision. The results were compared and studied. Majority of them had multimodal style of learning; however, almost all of them had kinaesthetic learning style. 'Kinaesthetic learning style' was followed by visual as the next dominant learning style.

Interestingly, these findings match with similar learning style studies conducted among millennial students of disciplines other than business administration in other colleges in India.

Study 1

Target: First semester medical students enrolled in India

Sample Size: 100

Tool Used: The visual, auditory, read/write and kinaesthetic (VARK) questionnaire, version 7.1

Results:

- The majority (61%) of the students had multimodal VARK preferences.
- Among them, 41 per cent, 14 per cent and 6 per cent preferred the bimodal, trimodal and quadrimodal ways of information presentation respectively.
- Out of all the respondents, 39 per cent had one strong (unimodal) learning preference.

- The most common unimodal preference was 'kinaesthetic', followed by visual, auditory and read/write (Kharb, Samanta, Jindal, & Singh, 2013).

Study 2

Target: Undergraduate medical students

Sample Size: 2,000 (approximately)

Tool Used: The 16-point multiple choice VARK questionnaire, version 7.1

Results:

- Seventy-nine students (86.8%) were multimodal in their learning preference, and 12 students (13.8%) were unimodal.
- The highest unimodal preference was K-7.7 per cent.
- Bimodal preference: AK (33%), AR (16.5%) category.
- Trimodal preference: ARK (8.9%).
- Auditory and 'kinaesthetic' being the highest preference (Prithishkumar & Michael, 2014).

Study 3

Target: Physiotherapy undergraduate students

Sample Size: 12 (outstanding students)

Results:

- Multimodal learning style: 58.34 per cent with higher preference for 'kinaesthetic'.
- Unimodal kinaesthetic: 33.33 per cent.
- Unimodal learning style: 41.66 per cent (Rai & Khatri, 2014).

These results are no different from the preferred learning style findings in other parts of the world. McCrindle Research reported a research conducted on Australian students and found that 52 per cent prefer to be taught kinaesthetically and 42 per cent visually, although 6 per cent are primarily auditory learners (McCrindle Research, 2006).

Impact of Millennial Students' Learning Styles on Choice of Pedagogical Tools

Previous researches as well as the current research have conclusively proven that millennials are dominantly kinaesthetic learners, that is, tactile learners. Kinaesthetic learners prefer to learn through concrete examples and applications. Kinaesthetic learners like field trips, trial and error, doing things to understand them, laboratories, recipes and solutions to problems, hands-on approaches, using their senses and collections of samples.

'Effective teachers must evolve to achieve success within a constantly changing environment (Hawk & Shah, 2007)'. The millennial students who populate various professional schools today and will do so for good number of years to come are primarily kinaesthetic learners. It is important to match their learning styles with the pedagogical tools being employed in the teaching–learning process. The emphasis clearly has to be on tools that encourage 'learning by doing'.

Matching pedagogical tools with learning styles will not only enhance learning and retention but since choice of tools will start skewing towards more learning by doing, they may also improve the skill set of students and enhance their employability. Fleming and Mills (1992) also observed that there exists a relationship between learning styles and performance of

Pedagogy	Instruction Element	Description	Learning Styles			
			Visual	Aural	Read/Write	Kinaesthetic
Demonstration-based training (DBT)	Observational learning	Activities that help learners to learn from a demonstration				X
	Attentional cueing	Includes verbal or written indicators of key information			X	
	Instructional narratives	Explain the reasoning behind behaviours demonstrated				X
	Note taking	Facilitates guided note taking to improve retention of concepts			X	
	Group discussion	GD to follow the demonstrations to emphasize learning objectives		X		
	Imagery exercises	Learners must be able to have an appropriate mental model of demonstrated behaviours	X			
	Imitations	Indulge the learners to imitate the appropriate demonstrated behaviours				X

Pedagogy	Instruction Element	Description	Learning Styles			
			Visual	Aural	Read/Write	Kinaesthetic
	Practice	Motivates learners to generate their own practice scenarios				X
	Goal setting	Prompt learners to develop goals on how they implement			X	
Active learning	Homework problems/books/handouts	Mirror the examples provided with courseware			X	
	Diagrams/graphs/charts/designs		X			
	Video	Access through video-based learning through Internet/intranet	X			
	Case studies, vignettes and scenarios	Real-time cases usually adapted from real-time business used in classrooms to teach a concept		X		

(Continued)

(Continued)

Pedagogy	Instruction Element	Description	Learning Styles			
			Visual	Aural	Read/Write	Kinaesthetic
	Seminar presentations	Students make presentations to teachers based on assigned case study		X		
	Group assignments	Assignments given to students which typically include exploration of concepts studied in class				X
	Simulations/ constructing ideas/ working models	A unique way of gamifying the learning to practise the concepts learnt simultaneously for better retention				X
	Class discussions/ debates	Making students to argue to arrive at decisions on a case within classrooms		X		
	Quiz	Formative assessment of concepts learnt			X	
	Field trips	Experience/exposure to real-time world scenario based on concept learnt				X

Pedagogy	Instruction Element	Description	Learning Styles			
			Visual	Aural	Read/Write	Kinaesthetic
	Reflective learning	Use of reflection logs, diaries, blogs, discussion forums				X
	Guest lectures	Expert talk by an industry expert				X
	Projects	Solving a real-time case/mini case by a group of students				X
	Polling devices	Devices to instantly gauge the responses of participants				X
	Peer review/feedback				X	
	Role play	Enacting a scenario and arriving at best demonstrated behaviours at work				X
Student-centred approach	Client-based learning	Working on real-time business problems; usually organized as cohorts in corporate universities				X

students (Leung, McGegor, Sabiston, & Vriliotisi, 2014). Evidence also suggests that the learning styles impact the teaching effectiveness.

Understanding millennials' learning styles may go a long way in engaging them as learners and creating greater employability among them. Poor employability not only impacts businesses by shrinking their talent pool but also shoots up their training budgets. At times when businesses have to settle for substandard skills, it impacts customers as well, since they are left with poor products and services.

In this chapter, we have discussed three sub-contexts within the societal context of engaging millennials—engaging them as volunteers, learners and entrepreneurs. All of them have huge implications not only on the society but also on the business. There can be some other sub-contexts too within the societal context but the key is to remember the deep empathy that we continuously talk about in this book. As long as we remember that and make concerted efforts to understand the mindsets, behaviour and lives of millennials, we should be able to understand how to engage them in various other social contexts.

11
CORPORATE LEADERSHIP AND THE FUTURE OF MILLENNIAL ENGAGEMENT

It has always bewildered me that the health of a company is always and only measured in financial terms. Return on assets (ROA), return on investment (ROI), earning per share (EPS), return on net assets (RONA), return on invested capital (ROIC), return on capital employed (ROCE), internal rate of return (IRR), adjusted present value (APV) and so on are variety of measures available to know how a company is doing. It all boils down to the balance sheet, despite knowing well that financial outcomes are dependent largely on human resources. Their attitudes and behaviour, their performance, their decisions, all cumulatively decide how the company performs amidst competition. The creation of value within a firm depends on how the value chain elements interact among themselves. Among the value chain elements, human resource is the only animate asset that helps in enhancing all other aspects of the firm such as technology, infrastructure, internal processes, sales and marketing and services. Yet most companies and most leaders spend more time and effort in managing financial capital, rather than the human capital. As per the Bain's Macro Trends Group, the global supply of capital stands at nearly 10 times the global GDP. Despite the ample abundancy of financial capital, the focus is so skewed in its favour that many a time companies and societies forget to focus on the human capital. The fact that millennials are rapidly proliferating the workspace and the marketplace with most companies still not completely prepared for them and recording abysmal levels of engagement, such ignorance of the human capital could prove very, very costly and disastrous. The future of millennial engagement depends a lot on the realization and readiness of the leadership that they need to change their understanding and mindsets about millennials and redesign their organizations to engage this cohort. There are few companies though which some by conscious design and others by the strength of their culture have been able to create an ecosystem that engages millennials. I would now like to introduce you to three narratives—foreign bank that is reinventing its business model to appeal to millennial customers, a medium-scale enterprise and a leading Ayurvedic hospital and wellness centre—all of which have created a unique culture that attracts and engages millennials.

Millennials Can Bank on This Bank

Mashreq Bank, one of the largest banks in UAE, would soon be launching Mashreq Neo—a bank designed for the millennials. A digital spin-off of the 50-year-old bank, the bank is getting modern as it targets new-age millennial customers.

The new bank dubbed as 'bank without boundaries' will be a completely branchless bank that will be using digital technologies to make all its services accessible to the customers via mobiles and apps. The announcement to this effect was made on the 50th anniversary of the bank as it looks to become the progressive bank in the region and remains shoulder-high than the rest of the competition that is undergoing consolidation. Recently, Abu Dhabi's biggest lenders National Bank of Abu Dhabi (NBAD) and First Gulf Bank (FGB) recently completed their formal merger earlier this year to create the renamed First Abu Dhabi Bank (FAB). The Qatari banks Masraf Al Rayan, Barwa Bank and International Bank of Qatar are also reportedly contemplating a merger at the moment. If that materializes, it will create Qatar's largest Islamic bank and second largest lender. Among this formidable competition, Mashreq's strategy seems to on the differentiator path as they plan to adopt a more open and accessible IT system and reach out to their millennial customers that will become the biggest customer base in the future.

UAE has a large percentage of the population that is made up of millennials. Roughly 40 per cent of UAE's population comprises millennials. A recent survey by WEF also revealed that more and more millennials living outside of UAE see it as a destination of choice with respect to their careers. Economic growth, favourable tax conditions, year-round sunshine and an exciting social calendar, all add up to an attractive package and make UAE an attractive destination for millennials. Given the bustling local population of millennials, doubled up by expat millennials rushing there to give their career a boost, the multi-cultural context of UAE makes millennial engagement an even greater imperative for companies operating in this region.

Mashreq Bank understands the pulse of the millennial customers who demand a 24×7 customer service, want their
banks to be convenient and accessible at the fingertips, and
also demand an easy-to-use interface, banking that they can do
using mobiles and apps. Mashreq Neo will be a customized
bank for the millennials that will be a bank without branches
and will leverage on digital technology, artificial intelligence
and automation.

Internal Programming

What makes Mashreq's case very interesting is the fact that
along with developing a strategy to attract and engage their
millennial customers, they are making serious efforts to better
engage their millennial employees. Backed by the bank's retail
division, it has launched a focused effort to coach and train all
its managers on how they engage millennial employees better.
They want their managers to realize that millennial employees
are different and they must be managed and engaged differently as well.

Says Yuvakumar, organizational mentor, executive coach
based in UAE and head of Mashreq Learning Systems,

> Mashreq has been well recognized as a true learning organiza-
> tion in the region, with many firsts to its credit in both its
> business and people practices. Its pragmatic training beliefs
> and proactive training measures are aimed at continually
> developing and retaining talent. Considering the changing
> landscape of the workforce, winning organizations have
> started bringing in fresh organizational design and learning
> strategies to tap and nurture the millennial mindset. Effective
> millennial management will indeed be a cornerstone for

sustained organizational effectiveness. Therefore, increasingly learning functions are preparing their corporate managers to learn faster than their competition. There is a new emphasis that managers regard the nuances of this new workplace design and leadership style that addresses the millennials' expectations and sparks their engagement psyche.

The internal programming to ensure that external programmes run smoothly and succeed shows how the bank has moved with the times and has come of age since its humble beginnings way back in 1967 as the Bank of Oman with just 10 employees. Today, it is one of the biggest banks of UAE with around 5,000 employees and counting. The bank wishes to charter the next 50 years buoyed on technology to become the most liked bank of the millennials. Here is definitely one bank that millennials can bank on!

More Power to Others

Mathew Mampra, founder and CEO of BPC Power Rentals, started his company way back in 1988. Today, his company is the largest industrial power rental company in Karnataka, one of the prominent southern states in India, home to the Silicon Valley of India—Bengaluru. BPC Power Rentals was like any other start-up; however, it came into existence at a time when start-up revolution had not set into force. The company started with just two people, Mathew himself and his first employee who after more than 27 years still continues to work for him. Today, as Mathew recalls his journey through these three decades of his entrepreneurial journey, there have been many ups and downs but his determination, integrity and strong focus on people has kept him and his company in the leader position in the power rental sector. BPC started as a sub-contractor handling the installation and maintenance on annual contract basis between the power generator supplier and the business houses (client) who are renting generators. Today, BPC owns its own generation units and rents them directly to leading corporate houses, boasting of clientele such as Infosys, SAP Labs, GE Healthcare, Alstom, Life Insurance Corporation of India (LIC).

Mathew, a scholar himself, is very cognizant of the millennials population and the force that it reckons in today's times. He says,

> My entrepreneurial journey has not let me go away from my passion for learning. I am on the verge of finishing my doctoral degree in human resource management. I have always felt that people are the core of any business. In my company, we do power generator installation and maintenance for big corporate houses and my people are my strength. If they let me down, then the company cannot deliver the kind of service that it promises. Over the last few years, most of my new recruits are millennials. The same is true for our clients. These days most managers at the client end who we deal with are millennials. We have very consciously created a culture that is flexible enough to make room for changes that we have to make in order to appeal to sensibilities of this new generation.

Serving Millennial Customers

The managers from the client side with whom BPC deals are mostly young people. Considering that they expect quick and complete solutions, BPC offers unmatched customer service in the industry, delivering most of the times above expectations of the clients. One such service is securing the statutory permission from the government that is necessary for installation of any generator. In normal course, it is the responsibility of the customer to secure the same. However, BPC ensures that its clients are saved from this hassle and facilitates the approval process for the client. Mathew adds,

> This saves a lot of time and effort on part of the client managers. They love it. Even the generator manufacturing companies are happy because this helps them in getting more clients. And it does not cost us much as being in business for so long we have built good professional relations with various agencies. While our other competitors who are in similar businesses do not offer such facilitation, we take upon ourselves every project as a turnkey one and deliver beyond what our client expects from us.

BPC operators at the client side are not very highly educated but are well-versed in the culture of the company. It is their honesty and behaviour that many a time gets fresh business for the company. Mathews adds, 'I tell each of them that they are BPC for the client. If they make a mistake or behave poorly, the BPC image takes a hit. They are our brand ambassadors'.

Accessibility and promptness in response is another thing that BPC offers to its clients. None less than the CEO remains just a call away from the client. Periodically, Mathew himself visits the client offices and meets their managers to check on their satisfaction with the services offered by his company. 'My client's young managers are very happy with this kind of instant response that they get from our company. My closeness with my clients also keeps my other employees alert and proactive', says Mathew.

A Day with the CEO

Any new recruit has his first day with the CEO. Mathews says,

> It is very important to ingrain the millennial recruits in the culture of the company. And despite the fact that we have grown in size and numbers, I still take time out for each new employee to explain him about the culture of the company and the way we do our work. For us at BPC, our customer is supreme and we do not compromise on ethics. At times new employees in their bid to please their managers try to do some tricks with customer to rake in some extra profit. It is a strict no in our company. We make it very clear to our new employees—they should never do anything unethical, neither should they get cheated by anyone. In either case, they will not be appreciated.

Tolerance for Mistakes, Not For Unethical Conduct

Mathew narrates an instance when one of his new employees committed an unethical act.

> While returning from the client location, post installation of the generator, he carried a huge bundle of cable from the client location, which was worth thousands of rupees. He actually came and announced very proudly of his misadventure. I took upon myself to teach this employee a lesson and ensure that this is a lesson for others. That same employee was made to return the cable to the client with an apology. The very next day I myself visited the client and apologized for the act. I told them that the employee was new to the company and in his

ignorance he had committed such an act. Frankly, the client was at first very annoyed, but later they appreciated our honesty as a company and continued the relationship. We also forgave the employee as he was new. It was also a message to everyone else that no such actions where ethics are compromised would be tolerated. On the contrary if I had encouraged such things, tomorrow the same people would cheat my company.

You Might Fail, But Thou Shall Not Fall!

The employees are completely empowered to take decisions. Mathew says,

I do not interfere with what they do, nor do I allow their super-visors to do it as well. They sometimes make mistakes but that is fine. We can always give them the right feedback. The employee feels he is the boss and so many times they have helped customer save more and bring more credit to our company.

Managers and supervisors at BPC are encouraged to give the employees both corrective and appreciative feedback on prior-ity. Mathew himself runs a mentoring programme for his employees. 'We give them the confidence to fly by giving them wings, but if they falter we are there to support them', adds Mathew.

Open Inclusive Culture

From the very beginning, a very open and inclusive culture has been created in the company by design. Such a culture has come to be very handy with growing number of millennials who prefer such culture and like being included in the important affairs of the company. Starting from the CEO's cabin that has glass walls and an open door, every bit of important information and decisions is shared with all key members of the team. There are no secrets. Everyone is informed and empowered. Mathew adds,

> I have always emphasized to our small leadership team to be transparent in their functioning and refrain from making any unnecessary promises neither to employees nor to customers. If a promise is made, then we all must collectively ensure that we fulfil the same. Unfulfilled promises always strain relationships.

Culture of Unity

'One for all, all for one' is not just a rhetoric at BPC. The relationship of employees with the company is not limited to mere work and goes beyond plain conduct of business. Recently, when an employee fell sick and had to be hospitalized, his colleagues took turns to be with him and take care of him as his family was away at that time. The company does not mind the employees spending their work hours in caring for their peer. Mathew says,

> All this is not just because they are a part of business. It is a genuine culture of unity we have created. We know our employees, especially millennial workers, lack social support system. We do our bit to make life a bit easy for them.

No Attendance, No Fixed Hours

The company has no formal attendance system nor any formal work hours. The timings are flexible. If the workload is heavy, then employees take upon themselves to reach office early. And if the work is a bit lean, then coming late to the office on such days is acceptable. The attendance registered is maintained and checked by the employees themselves and so is the overtime register. There is no cross-checking by the management. Although termed naïve by well-wishers, Mathew created this system. The trust that he has placed on his employees has not gone in vain. The attendance and overtime records are very honest and there is hardly any misreporting. Since leaves, work timings, all are decided by the employees themselves, hence absenteeism or punctuality issues are unheard of at BPC.

Dignity of Labour

The company insists on treating everyone with respect and maintaining their dignity even when they make mistakes. It starts with the lowest level of worker. No one is looked down for being lesser qualified or lesser paid. Everyone is doing their job and is ought to be respected for that. There is dignity of labour. Any discrimination based on caste, ethnicity and gender is not tolerated.

Team That Celebrates Together Stays Together

Every small achievement is celebrated in the company and the achievers are recognized. The achievers are rewarded and applauded that gives them a sense of self-worth and they feel good since their efforts are recognized. The company has no dedicated sales team. The service personnel through the good-will they create help get additional orders from existing clients or new clients at times. Each such personnel who helps get more business for the company is recognized and rewarded.

All Is Well in the Family

BPC has been very cognizant that engagement does not stop with employees but extends to families as well. The company bears the cost of the entire annual school/college tuition fees of the employees' kids. Mathew himself keeps a track of the academic performance of his employees' kids and interacts with them on a regular basis. This benefit extends to all the employees and their kids, up to two children per employee.

The company also offers interest-free loan to employees to meet initial expenses on their kids' uniform, books, transport, and so on. at the beginning of each academic year. Mathew says,

> I have seen people struggling during such times even when I was an employee in a firm. They would borrow from private chit funds and will pay high interest rates. When I started my company, I decided not to let my employees go through such troubles.

The company also organizes occasional families' day out where the spouses and kids of the employees are invited to be a part of the celebrations during festivals and religious occasions. On such days, they all have lunch together and gifts are given to spouses and kids of the employees.

The company also offers free housing to most of the employees and their families.

Mathew very aptly remarks,

> What we do for our employees is definitely with a genuine intention to take good care of them and their families, but I am not sure if I should call that philanthropic. I take care of them, in turn they take care of my company. The nature of my business is such that employees might have to deal with emergencies at client's end at odd hours. When families are engaged, they understand they are much more supportive towards the employee and the company. Our employees staying on various properties that we have built in turn secure them. So it a win-win proposition.

Security Is Through Care

Mathew narrates an incident when upon untimely death of one of his employees and considering that his spouse was suffering from mental disorder, the company adopted two of his small kids. The fact that the employee was not very useful to the company did not prevent Mathew from doing this humane act. The company sponsored entire education and expenses of these two kids, out of whom the boy is now employed and the girl is on her way to study medicine. Mathew is still bearing the expense. 'I know my other employees are watching this and they know somewhere subconsciously that even if God forbid something happens to them, the company will stand by their family and we will!' signs off Mathew.

Culture Rocks the Cradle

Vaidyagrama literally means a healing village. Vaidyagrama is an Ayurvedic hospital and wellness institution. Led by Dr Ramkumar, an Ayurveda *vaidya* (doctor) hailing from a traditional Ayurveda family Punarnava Ayurveda in Coimbatore, South India, Vaidyagrama has a vision of 'Authentic Ayurveda for Universal Well-being'. While there are Ayurveda centres galore, Vaidyagrama is no run-of-the-mill types. While most other Ayurvedic centres have diluted treatment methods and sugar-coated bitter medicines under commercial pressures, Vaidyagrama has on the other hand embraced authentic Ayurveda in the truest sense. It offers an Ayurveda healing place that is authentic plus natural. Vaidyagrama attempts to cater to the demand of authentic Ayurveda, the traditional way, as well as go natural, the contemporary way. It has authentic Ayurveda made contemporary. This is what differentiates Vaidyagrama from the rest and makes it a compelling case. Having been host to World Ayurveda Conference and clientele from more than 50 countries of the world, Vaidyagrama is a successful model that thrives on its unique culture. However, the same is becoming an oxymoron as the fear of losing the same is coming in the way of expansion through franchising model.

Appealing to Millennial Customers

It is offering fruits of authentic Ayurveda to a large national and international community, having clientele from more than 31 countries of the world. It is faced with a growing demand, increased availability of funding and the boost of medical tourism in India. The growing number of millennial customers who suffer from largely a wellness deficit is both an opportunity and challenge for Vaidyagrama.

The demand for yoga and Ayurveda is on the rise and society as a whole is moving towards a concept of wellness and not just of treating illness. People in general are also disillusioned with clinical medicines and treatment methods owing to high cost and side effects of treatment that cures the illness but does little to promote wellness. Vaidyagrama has a huge opportunity to ride on the crest of such change of social perceptions.

Millennials are also extremely sensitive on sustainability issue and issues close to saving the environment and the planet. Vaidyagrama scores very high on such perceptions as well. It is a wellness community that focuses on healing of mind, body and spirit. It prides itself in its traditional and authentic approach to Ayurveda and wellness. It was started with a vision of practising holistic (and not reductionist) and authentic Ayurveda. As advocated by the ancient texts and scriptures along with the right medicinal and treatment methodologies, the concept of holistic is also extended to environment and surrounding communities. The idea was to create a self-sustainable, eco-friendly healing community based on Ayurveda and natural farming. Today, Vaidyagrama is not only a hospital but also a wellness community. It has not only co-existed with nature but also contributed in promoting environmental sustainability. The villages that live around Vaidyagrama are being slowly integrated with the organization in a manner that they have become a self-sustainable community and people can live off the land itself, rather than migrating to the city and becoming daily wage labourers or construction workers, thereby inviting all negative social practices. Vaidyagrama aims to create and maintain healing energy.

Dr Kalpana Sampath, director of Punarnava, informs that Vaidyagrama gets a lot of millennial patients across the world suffering from variety of physical ailments, mostly related to lifestyle disorders. It also gets millennial patients suffering from anxiety and depression.

Earlier, relationships used to start at the age of 21. In case of millennials, it starts from 13 itself. Hence, by the time they reach adulthood they have broken relationships and bruised emotions. Culmination of these things is a lot of toxicity in the body that gets accumulated over a period of time and the soul is lost. They come in search of their soul. The environment of Vaidyagrama is peaceful, integrated, healing and aligned with what they want to do. Therefore, it attracts them. Vaidyagrama is not only a place to cure, it is a way of life! Many of the millennials who come to us as patients are attention-deficient. When they come here and find so much love and attention, they feel healed. That cures half of their diseases. Once they experience the culture of Vaidyagrama, many of them want to stay back. We had instances when millennials came as customers and then wanted to stay back and therefore joined us as employees. Others who cannot join us full time support us and keep coming back as volunteers and lend their expertise in improving facilities, infrastructure or services of Vaidyagrama. This is an amazing experience.

Vaidyagrama gets a lot of school dropouts, from underprivileged and lower middle class families, who come to work as therapists. Usually, they come through referrals. Vaidyagrama not only gives them an employment but also encourages them to complete their education. It has tied up with government to enable these set of employees to take up a certification in therapy, all cost borne by Vaidyagrama. Although some of these employees later leave, especially girls after they get married, still Vaidyagrama takes pride in the fact that they helped them to become employable and earn their livelihood.

In fact, many teens come as caretakers of older patients and get a chance to experience the life at Vaidyagrama. They also come back later with a willingness to work for the organization.

Dr Kalpana adds,

> These youngsters are an easy bunch of people to work with. Although I find them not very focused in terms of their future and hardly save any of their earnings, but they come with no preconceived notions and are open to learning and experiences. We have understood that they like freedom, be involved in the decision-making and like peer group appreciation. Hence, all the events or celebrations that happen at Vaidyagrama throughout the year are completely planned and executed by them.

She narrates an incident when one of her house help's sons, who did not do well in college, took up a storekeeper's job at Vaidyagrama. Today, he is such a happy person. He feels important there as everyone comes and asks him about supplies.

> The variety that Vaidyagrama offers is also a big draw for the millennials. The patients come in from all parts of the world. They stay for short duration and then new set of people come. This opportunity of meeting new people, learning English from them, learning about new cultures and the

excitement of making new friends attracts them to this place. This would not have been same with older generations, who might feel a sense of fatigue meeting so many new people every few days. Not the case with millennials; they on the other hand relish the experience.

These young workers at Vaidyagrama also help a lot in brand building. They are active on social media, make friends with visiting patients, and share pictures and videos of events and celebrations at Vaidyagrama. That spreads the positive message across a large network, and community that is engaged to us keeps expanding.

Although the organization does not have a written policy manual on millennials, the culture at Vaidyagrama has helped evolution of an attitude towards amalgamation of millennials into the system. Dr Kalpana says,

> Not that we never had any problems. We had occasional resistance from some quarters regarding the freedom and latitude given to the millennials. But I think our culture that we consciously created for first five years has helped a lot in ironing out such differences. We still are a long shot from what we aspire to be as per our own standards, and we need to work with more purpose to make that happen in the future.

The leaders at Vaidyagrama use a lot of informal random conversations with the members of Vaidyagrama to help their acculturalization. The idea is to put a thought in the consciousness of the people who run the place and create a sense of community.

Unique Culture

The culture of Vaidyagrama is in line with its vision to become a healing community dedicated to universal wellness. The culture very unlike the typical corporate culture thrives on building strong relationships. Vaidyagrama does not offer to its recruits the typical perks associated with city life. The place is away from the city, having limited options with hardly any conventional source of entertainment. The food is very plain and not the usual gourmet servings. In short, all these factors could prove a challenge in attracting and retaining people. The retention policy is not based on hefty compensation packages or perks; instead, the idea is to keep sharing the core values and vision of Vaidyagrama and hope that those who buy in to the same will stay much longer. The same has happened. Vaidyagrama not only has high retention rates, but it has also been able to attract back those who left it for seemingly greener pastures. Some of them who left Vaidyagrama to join certain hotels and resorts were soon disillusioned by the different culture and returned to the former's fold happily. Although the compensation was more in hotels and resorts, there were longer working hours and concerns of safety especially for the women therapists. Then most of these jobs were contract based and lasted only the peak tourist season months. Rest of the months there was hardly any income. Contrastingly, Vaidyagrama offers a permanent 12-month employment, a safe and sound working environment and care of a family. All employees of Vaidyagrama get food free of cost and are provided with accommodation facilities. They are also given the best of space to work. Most hires come from nearby villages and such a caring environment, plus their native innocence, has ensured strong bonding between the patients and the staff. Vaidyagrama is more home than hospital, more personal than businesslike. The client satisfaction is extremely high owing to the spirit with which the service is delivered.

Dignity of labour is a part of the Vaidyagrama culture. The doctors or vaidyas not only involve themselves as clinicians, but they also participate in preparing medicines, serve food, answer the queries of the patients, initiate group discussions for clearing doubts in the minds of patients regarding Ayurveda and treatment methods, and even participate in repair and maintenance activities. In other words, they involve themselves like anyone will work in their own home. This behaviour per-colates to everyone else at Vaidyagrama and no one really feels ashamed of doing anything. A sense of ownership prevails throughout the organization. Vaidyagrama encourages its employees to have the sense of ownership in the literal sense as well. Any employee who completes five years of service in the organization is offered a shareholding in the parent com-pany Punarnava.

Even structurally, Vaidyagrama is organized as three small hospitals. Each of these sections have 3 blocks of 4 rooms each, making a total of 36 rooms. Each of these sections have their own medical director who along with his/her family resides in the same complex. Each section has its set of staff attached with the same. This is a unique arrangement wherein the doctor lives with the patients like the ancient system. The doctor is involved in holistic wellness of the patient, unlike the minute-based consultation.

Critical Incidents That Defined Culture of Vaidyagrama

Annadaan Programme
Vaidygrama decided to start an *annadaan* programme to donate food to surrounding villages. Initially, the staff's reaction was

negative and they resisted the same. The idea was to share with everyone whatever organization could provide. As the programme started, it received very positive reaction and the surrounding community not only became very supportive of the organization but also grew increasingly empathetic of its cause. Over a period of time, it received strong backing of the staff and they willingly involved themselves in the programme.

Dealing with Theft

Vaidygrama has a practice of daily meetings that are organized in the morning. In these meetings, everything under the sun is discussed, anyone who commits a mistake renders apology and cites out learning from the mistake that they committed and action points are articulated for the day. In one such meetings, it was brought to the notice that two people had committed theft. The culprits confessed to committing the crime. All the employees decided in one of the daily meetings to pardon them, not handover them to police but ask them to leave their jobs. After discussions, everyone in Vaidyagrama agreed to the decision of pardoning them since it was their first mistake and also decided to let them continue their services. These two people have gone on to become good custodians of the property and interests of Vaidyagrama.

'Tip of the Iceberg'

An arrangement was made whereby tips received by various staff at Vaidyagrama were to be collected in a single box, instead of being retained by the individual staff member. At the end of the month, it was to be distributed equally among all staff, barring 20 per cent of the amount that would be retained for any exigency for any of the staff. This was initially not liked by the staff. However, after sometime, when one of the staff members became critically ill and all his medical expenses were met by the 20 per cent exigency fund, then everyone realized the advantage of such an arrangement. Thereafter, everyone wholeheartedly supported the initiative.

What makes Vaidyagrama unique is its community and family culture. The community and family culture has enabled a customer-centric environment that makes its clients feel at home when they arrive for treatments and rejuvenation. The activities and group discussions are also value added as this helps in changing mental models of their clients. The group discussions allow for dialogue and as such reflect on their current habits and reconsider the actions that are best for their health. This leads to a more holistic approach to treatment that increases the chances of patients sticking to the regiments.

Just a Beginning

Managing engagement touch points becomes primal to engaging the stakeholders. Every time a brand comes in touch with a customer, employee or a channel partner, it is defined as a touch point. Aggregate of such interaction goes on to define a brand.

Discovering Engagement Touch Points

Tube Hotels, a hotel chain in Southeast Asia, found out that customers, out of all the facilities and services in the hotel, valued their bed, the TV in their rooms and the shower in their bathrooms the most. Consequently, they made sure that these three aspects in every room were very well taken care of and rest of the facilities were meeting the minimum standards. As a result, the customer satisfaction saw a considerable increase.

Apollo Hospitals gets patients from 100+ countries. Along with ensuring that the patient gets best medical attention, Apollo also ensures that the patient's attendant gets adequate care and is looked after well, often ensuring that they get their native cuisines in their food.

ITC's food division was taken by surprise when a customer from Gujarat asked them which of their food products did not contain onion or garlic. After some effort, the customer's query was answered but it exposed a hitherto unexplored touch point. Gujarat, a predominantly vegetarian state, would have many such consumers who will be sensitive to presence of even onion and garlic in the food products. Some other northern states of India had similar consumer population. In fact, world over more and more millennials are showing preference for vegetarian food. A study by Chicago-based food research firm Technomic concluded that vegetarian and vegan meals were a great way for restaurants to attract millennial customers. The report showed that 45 per cent of younger consumers either regularly eat vegetarian and vegan food or follow a vegetarian diet, compared to just about 30 per cent of the older generation having similar preferences.

Flipkart introduced COD (cash on delivery) and '30-days return' policies understanding customer sensibilities. Many young customers want to pay only after they have received the product. The customers also wish to have the flexibility to return the product if they are not happy with the same, once they start using it.

Different Individuals, Different Touch Points

As much as discovering engagement touch points is important, generalizing such touch points when the consumer base is heterogeneous is not a good idea. Hence, discovering touch points of millennial customers assumes significance.

Club Mahindra, a family holiday destination resort, generally gets a lot of young couples and families with small kids in their resorts. A typical family comprising of 'father', 'mother' and kids has different needs and hence different touch points. While the 'father' wants a lazy holiday, preferring no connectivity of any kind with the outside world, if possible, the 'mother' wants a more active holiday with yoga, exercise, etc. Young kids are hyperactive during holidays and want to run around and have as much fun as possible. Contrary to this, the teenage kids want Wi-Fi connectivity and just need a cosy corner for themselves with their gadgets. Understanding these different touch points and addressing them becomes significant in engaging the entire family.

A 100-year-old jewellery chain, C. Krishniah Chetty & Sons, gets broadly two kinds of footfalls in their retail stores—sales coming from repeat purchases of its previous customers and the sales coming from new walk-in customers. The former set of customers belong to the older generations, look for long-term value and usually purchase in bulk, while the latter are the new-age fashion-conscious customers who look for trendy designs and are essentially deal driven. Both sets of customers have different expectations and hence different engagement touch points. The jewellery chain uses different jewellery designs and marketing techniques to provide both kind of shoppers a delightful shopping experience.

Dynamic Touch Points

The engagement touch points are not always static. ITC continuously experiments with its biscuits and creamy range of biscuits to bring in new flavours and tastes to its very demanding set of millennial consumers, whose tastes and choices keep changing very fast.

The dynamic nature of the touch points can also be looked at from the perspective of speed with which a brand delivers on the engagement touch points. Take Club Mahindra for instance; they have installed touch screen kiosks in their resorts to gather feedback from their customers on a continuous basis and make corrections or amend. This ensures that feedback is collected from the customer before the customer leaves the resort, rather than waiting for him/her to arrive next time. Considering that their millennial customers are very tech-savvy, such ways of collecting instant feedback work well.

Discovering, understanding and delivering on these engagement touch points become primal to engaging customers. However, it is pertinent to note that such engagement may not be possible without engaging the 'internal customers' or the employees.

As we come to the end of the book, let us revisit where we started from. I took a very common sense route to millennial engagement to be very frank. Of course it followed years of serious research and speaking to countless millennials, but all of it started with two very basic understandings. One that the word 'engagement' has genesis from couples and hence the best way to interpret engagement is to explore what really engages or bonds two people. I discovered that it was the degree and depth of understanding between them. The greater the understanding, the lesser were the chances for any misunderstanding to creep in between them and hence the bond grew only stronger as the days passed. The reverse was also true. With couples lacking understanding and efforts towards the same, every opportunity of interaction turned out to build mistrust and misunderstanding only grew, thereby weakening the bonds and rupturing them quite often. It would not be wrong to say that understanding not only precedes engagement but also builds it. Second, my opportunities to speak to millennials and to company leaders, HR heads and parents left me with a deep certainty about the poor understanding that other generations have about millennials, often giving rising to myths about their behaviour and rough edges in relationship, irrespective of the context. With these two basic foundations in place, I set out on a journey to first understand the genesis of the millennial mindset, their behaviour and their life to credibly suggest/prescribe with assertion and authenticity a way forward to build a strong engagement with this cohort. But this book is only a beginning towards helping companies and societies to better understand millennials and engage with them. Each one of you who has read this book can be a medium to spread this word and make 'mission millennial' a success.

REFERENCES AND SUGGESTED READINGS

Agarwal, S. (2015, 1 December). The rise of the rent economy. *Live Mint.* Retrieved 14 April 2017, from http://www.livemint.com/Companies/ YGsj788q0scuhYYFY1WOaL/The-rise-of-the-rent-economy.html

Anders, G. (2014, 17 September). Millennials' zesty new identity: The 'burning man' generation. *Forbes.* Retrieved 22 May 2017, from https:// www.forbes.com/sites/georgeanders/2014/09/17/millennials-zesty-new-identity-the-burning-man-generation/#269ae9ae3ffe

AXA. (2016, 17 August). Two years on: How Reverse Mentoring has developed at AXA. Retrieved 17 May 2017, from http://www.discoveraxa. com/articles/two-years-on-how-reverse-mentoring-has-developed-at-axa

Barnikel, M. (2005, 20 May). Generation Y media habits show tide is turning in favour of internet. *Media*, p. 12.

Bauman, Z. (2003, April). *Liquid Love: On the frailty of human bonds.* Polity Press.

Bazaarvoice. (2012, June). Talking to strangers: Millennials trust people over brands. Retrieved 19 May 2017, from http://resources.bazaarvoice. com/rs/bazaarvoice/images/201202_Millennials_whitepaper.pdf

BDA (Bensinger, DuPont & Associates). (n.d.). Depression and work. Retrieved 25 April 2017, from http://www.bensingerdupont.com/ depression-and-work-download

Bentley University. (2014, 11 November). Millennials at work. Retrieved 29 May 2017, from http://www.bentley.edu/newsroom/latest-head-lines/mind-of-millennial

BigCommerce. (2017). Ecommerce trends: 135 stats revealing how modern customers shop in 2017. Retrieved 18 May 2017, from https://www. bigcommerce.com/blog/ecommerce-trends/#cmtoc_anchor_id_0

Burns, J. (2016, 16 August). Millennials are having less sex than other gens, but experts say it's (probably) fine. Retrieved 4 July 2017, from https://www.forbes.com/sites/janetwburns/2016/08/16/millennials-are-having-less-sex-than-other-gens-but-experts-say-its-probably-fine/#-2299f21ad958

Business Insider. (2016, 1 September). Millennials reveal 100 brands they love. Retrieved 7 July 2017, from http://www.businessinsider.in/Millennials-reveal-100-brands-they-love/99-DC-Shoes/slideshow/53966676.cms

———. (2017, 3 April). America's hottest CEOs are devoting more time than ever to hiring. Retrieved 8 May 2017, from http://www.businessinsider.in/Americas-Hottest-CEOs-Are-Devoting-More-Time-Than-Ever-To-Hiring/articleshow/21033579.cms

Buxton, O. M., Cain, S. W., O'Connor, S. P., Porter, J. H., Duffy, J. F., Wang, W., & Shea, S. A. (2012). Adverse metabolic consequences in humans of prolonged sleep restriction combined with circadian disruption. *Science Translational Medicine*, 4(129), 129–143.

Chandna, H. (2016, 14 April). 93% Indians want to be entrepreneurs: Study. *Hindustan Times*. Retrieved 29 May 2017, from http://www.hindustantimes.com/business/93-indians-want-to-be-entrepreneurs-study/story-jQVuvPnDuUGxKofMfJKxQL.html

Cherlin, A. J., Talbert, E., & Yasutake, S. (2014). *Changing fertility regimes and the transition to adulthood: Evidence from a recent cohort*. Paper presented at the Meetings of the Population Association of America, Boston. Retrieved 26 April 2017, from http://paa2014.princeton.edu/papers/140559

Clark, D. (2000). Learning styles & preferences.

Claxton, C. S., & Murrell, P. H. (1987). *Learning styles: Implications for improving educational practices*. Washington, DC: Association for the Study of Higher Education.

Compass. (2016, 15 July). Bangalore is world's 2nd fastest growing startup ecosystem, has youngest entrepreneurs, says study. *The Huffington Post*. Retrieved 29 May 2017, from http://www.huffingtonpost.in/2015/07/29/bangalore-global-startup-_n_7893924.html

Cone. (2008). Civic minded millennials prepared to reward or punish companies based on commitment to social causes. *CSR Wire*. Retrieved 15 September 2017, from http://www.csrwire.com/News/6641.html

Consumerist. (2015, June 3). Nearly 70% of consumers rely on online reviews before making a purchase. Retrieved 19 May 2017, from https://

REFERENCES AND SUGGESTED READINGS

consumerist.com/2015/06/03/nearly-70-of-consumers-rely-on-online-reviews-before-making-a-purchase/

Daily Mail. (2017, 4 April). Time to grow up? Millennials are shunning marriage in favour of living with their parents. Retrieved 5 May 2017, from http://www.dailymail.co.uk/sciencetech/article-4379620/Young-people-killing-marriage-live-parents.html

Dallas Business Journal. (2017, 19 April). Millennials boost American Airlines over Delta for brand of the year. Retrieved 22 May 2017, from http://www.bizjournals.com/dallas/news/2017/04/19/millennials-boost-american-airlines-over-delta-for.html

Deloitte. (2014, January). Big demands and high expectations—The Deloitte Millenial Survey. Retrieved 19 August 2014, from http://www.deloitte.com/assets/Dcom-Italy/Local%20Assets/Documents/Pubblicazioni/gx-dttl-2014-millennial-survey-report.pdf

———. (2016). The 2016 Deloitte Millennial Survey winning over the next generation of leaders. Retrieved 19 May 2017, from https://www2.deloitte.com/content/dam/Deloitte/global/Documents/About-Deloitte/gx-millenial-survey-2016-exec-summary.pdf

———. (2017). The 2017 Deloitte Millennial Survey Apprehensive millennials: seeking stability and opportunities in an uncertain world. Retrieved 19 April 2017, from https://www2.deloitte.com/content/dam/Deloitte/us/Documents/about-deloitte/deloitte-millennial-survey-2017-executive-summary.pdf

Denton Record-Chronicle. (2016, 27 August). Companies turn to 'reverse mentoring' to tap millennials' knowledge. Retrieved 17 May 2017, from http://www.dentonrc.com/business/business/2016/08/27/companies-turn-to-reverse-mentoring-to-tap-millennials-knowledge

Dowdy, Landon. (2015, 8 December). Millennials are more generous than you think. *CNBC.* Retrieved 25 May 2017, from http://www.cnbc.com/2015/12/08/millennials-are-more-generous-than-you-think.html

Doyle, E. M. (2015, 10 March). Why 84% of millennials don't trust traditional advertisers. *Bandt.* Retrieved 22 May 2017, from http://www.bandt.com.au/advertising/84-millennials-dont-trust-traditional-advertisers

Dunn, R., & Waggoner, B. (1995). Comparing three innovative instructional systems. *Emergency Librarian, 23*(1) 9–15.

The Endocrine Society. (2017). Prolonged sleep disturbance can lead to lower bone formation. *Science Daily.* Retrieved 4 August 2017 from https://www.sciencedaily.com/releases/2017/04/170402111317.htm

ENS Economic Bureau. (2014, 28 February). Mandatory 2% CSR spend set to kick in from April 1. *The Indian Express.* Retrieved 15 December 2014, from http://indianexpress.com/article/business/economy/mandatory-2-csr-spend-set-to-kick-in-from-april-1/

ET. (2015, 27 July). Accenture too drops bell-curve appraisals. Retrieved 3 May 2017, from http://economictimes.indiatimes.com/news/international/business/accenture-too-drops-bell-curve-appraisals/articleshow/48230902.cms

———. (2017, 9 May). To tap into Gen Y ideas, leaders become mentees. Retrieved 17 May 2017, from http://tech.economictimes.indiatimes.com/news/corporate/to-tap-into-gen-y-ideas-leaders-become-mentees/58588035

FlightView. (2017). Convenience & choice: What travelers want most (and are willing to pay for) throughout their journey. Retrieved 22 May 2017, from http://cdn2.hubspot.net/hubfs/278711/Convenience-and-Choice-in-Travel-July2015.pdf?t=1437574555227

Forbes. (2014, 9 November). The rising wave of millennial travelers. Retrieved 19 May 2017, from https://www.forbes.com/sites/tanyamohn/2014/11/08/the-rising-wave-of-millennial-travelers/#2b-c896b12bc8

———. (2016, 13 September). The complicated truth about millennials and credit cards. Retrieved 19 May 2017, from https://www.forbes.com/sites/robertharrow/2016/09/13/the-complicated-truth-about-millennials-and-credit-cards/#404aa035404a

Gallup. (2016, 15 June). Brands aren't winning millennial consumers. Retrieved 17 May 2017, from http://www.gallup.com/businessjournal/192710/brands-aren-winning-millennial-consumers.aspx

Garner, R. (2015, 3 August). EY: Firm says it will not longer consider degrees or A-level results when assessing employees. Retrieved 6 July 2017, from http://www.independent.co.uk/news/education/education-news/ey-firm-says-it-will-not-longer-consider-degrees-or-a-level-results-when-assessing-employees-10436355.html

Giliberti, C. (2016, 8 March). 3 reasons why millennials want long form storytelling over 'snackable' content. *Forbes.* Retrieved 22 May 2017, from https://www.forbes.com/sites/under30network/2016/03/08/3-reasons-why-millennials-want-long-form-storytelling-over-snackable-content/#51eb7cc8380e

REFERENCES AND SUGGESTED READINGS

Goldstein, A. N., Greer, S. M., Saletin, J. M., Harvey, A. G., Nitschke, J. B., & Walker, M. P. (2013). Tired and apprehensive: Anxiety amplifies the impact of sleep loss on aversive brain anticipation. *The Journal of Neuroscience, 33*(26), 10607–10615.

Gratton, L. (2011, 14 October). The Skill Gap: Asian Style. *Forbes.* Retrieved 16 May 2017, from https://www.forbes.com/sites/lyndagratton/2011/10/14/the-skill-gap-asian-style/#12f641be3405

Gustafson, K. (2016, 9 June). The next wave of online shopping is about to hit. *CNBC.* Retrieved 5 July 2017, from http://www.cnbc.com/2016/06/09/the-next-wave-of-online-shopping-is-about-to-hit.html

Harris Poll EquiTrend. (2017). 2017 Harris Poll EquiTrend® Rankings. Retrieved 22 May 2017, from http://www.theharrispoll.com/equit-rend-rankings/2017

Hawk, T., & Shah, A. (2007). Using learning style instruments to enhance student learning. *Decision Sciences Journal of Innovative Education, 5*(1), 1–19.

Hsee, C. K., Yang, A. X., & Wang, L. (2010). Idleness aversion and the need for justifiable busyness. *Psychological Science,* 21(7), 926–930.

Investopedia. (2016, 26 July). Money habits of the millennials. Retrieved 27 April 2017, from http://www.investopedia.com/articles/personal-finance/021914/money-habits-millennials.asp

Jacobs, E. (2017, 24 February). Millennial women confident they can close the gender gap. *Financial Times.* Retrieved 4 August 2017, from https://www.ft.com/content/1767b740-f2bd-11e6-8758-6876151821a6

Jones Day. (2014, April). India's new corporate social responsibility require-ments—Beware of the pitfalls. Retrieved 15 December 2014, from http://www.jonesday.com/indias-new-corporate-social-responsibili-ty-requirements--beware-of-the-pitfalls-04-15-2014/

Kharb, P., Samanta, P. P., Jindal, M., & Singh, V. (2013, June). The learning styles and the preferred teaching—Learning strategies of first year med-ical students. *Journal of Clinical & Diagnostic Research, 7*(6), 1089–1092. Retrieved 5 October 2015, from http://www.ncbi.nlm.nih.gov/pmc/articles/PMC3708205/

Kirkova, D. (2014, 13 March). Who cares about Facebook friends? We only have FIVE true pals and they're from childhood, work or the school gates. *Daily Mail.* Retrieved 26 April 2017, from http://www.dailymail.co.uk/femail/article-2579193/Who-cares-Facebook-friends-We-FIVE-true-pals-theyre-childhood-work-school-gates.html

Lee, M., Crofts, T., McGovern, A., & Milivojevic, S. (2015). *Sexting among young people: Perceptions and practices.* Canberra: Australian Institute of Criminology.

Leung, A., McGegor, M., Sabiston, D., & Vriliotisi, S. (2014). VARK learning styles and student performance in principles of micro- vs. macro-economics. *Journal of Economics & Economic Education Research, 15*(3), 113–120.

Lin, N., Simeone, R., Ensel, W., & Kuo, W. (1979). Social support, stressful life events, and illness: A model and an empirical test. *Journal of Health and Social Behavior, 20*(2), 108–119.

Litauen, B. C., & Miller, J. (2012, August). Corporate social responsibility and Generation Y, pp. 43–44.

Litzinger, M. E., & Osif, B. (1993). Accommodating diverse learning styles: Designing instruction for electronic information sources. In L. Shirato (Ed.), *What is good instruction now? Library Instruction for the 90s* (pp. 73–81). Ann Arbor, MI: Pierian Press.

LOKNITI–CSDS–KAS. (2017, 3 April). LOKNITI–CSDS–KAS survey: Mind of the youth. *Indian Express.* Delhi. Retrieved 4 July 2017, from http://indianexpress.com/article/explained/lokniti-csds-kas-survey-mind-of-the-youth-4597199/

Mallick, P. K. (2011). *Staff system in the Indian Army, time for change.* New Delhi: Centre for Land Warfare Studies and K. W. Publishers Pvt. Ltd.

Marriott, N. (2004). Using computerized business simulations and spreadsheet models in accounting education: A case study. *Accounting Education, 13*(1), 55–70.

Marsick, V. J., & Watkins, K. E. (2001). Informal and incidental learning. *New Directions for Adult and Continuing Education, 2001*(81), 25–34.

Marta, E., Gulielmetti, C., & Pozzi, M. (2006, September). Volunteerism during young adulthood: An Italian investigation into motivating patterns. *Voluntas: The International Journal for Voluntary and Nonprofit Organizations, 17*(3), 221–232.

MarTech. (2015, 28 October). Infographic: 46% of consumers use social media in purchase decisions. Retrieved 18 May 2017, from https://martech.zone/social-media-infographic/

McAllister, D. C. (2014, 09 September). What's Behind Millennials' Trust Issues? *The Federalist.* Retrieved 12 April 2017, from http://thefederalist.com/2014/09/09/whats-behind-millennials-trust-issues/

REFERENCES AND SUGGESTED READINGS

McCrindle Research. (2006). *New generations at work: Attracting, recruiting, retraining and training Generation Y*. Sydney: Author.

McGlone, T., Spain, W. J., & McGlone, V. (2011). Corporate social responsibilities and millennials. *Journal for Education for Business, 86*(4), 195–200.

Meyer, M. I. (2016). Let's talk about sext: Gendered millennial perceptions of sexting in a cyborg society (mini-dissertation). Retrieved 15 September 2017, from https://open.uct.ac.za/bitstream/handle/11427/20774/thesis_law_2016_meyer_melissa_isabella.pdf?sequence=1

Milgram, S. (1974). The perils of obedience.

Money. (2015, 22 July). Millennials will pay more for these air-travel extras. Retrieved 22 May 2017, from http://time.com/money/3967624/millennial-flyer-spend-money-air-travel-extras/

MSL. (2014). Asian millennials expect business to solve important social issues and empower Gen Y to drive change together. Retrieved 15 December 2014, from http://asia.mslgroup.com/news/asian-millennials-expect-business-to-solve-important-social-issues-and-empower-gen-y-to-drive-change-together/

National Employability Report. (2012). National Employability Report, MBA Graduates 2012. Retrieved from http://www.aspiringminds.com/research-articles/national-employability-report-mba-graduates-2012

NCFMR (National Center for Family and Marriage Research). (2017, 10 April). Fewer and fewer millennials tying the knot. *The Times of India*. Retrieved 4 August 2017, from http://epaperbeta.timesofindia.com/Article.aspx?eid=31808&articlexml=Fewer-and-fewer-millennials-tying-the-knot-10042017013032

Nielsen. (2017, 3 August). Want more, be more: When it comes to gender equality, millennial women are more optimistic about closing the gap. Retrieved 5 August 2017, from http://www.nielsen.com/us/en/insights/news/2017/when-it-comes-to-gender-equality-millennial-women-are-more-optimistic-on-closing-the-pay-gap.html.

Noble, K. (2013, 15 March). Replacing traditional teaching methods. Imperial College, London. Retrieved 10 July 2017, from http://www3.imperial.ac.uk/newsandeventspggrp/imperialcollege/newssummary/news_12-2-2013-15-9-5

OECD (Organisation for Economic Co-operation and Development). (2015). Hours worked. Retrieved 25 April 2017, from https://data.oecd.org/emp/hours-worked.htm

Oesterle, S., Johnson, M. K., & Mortimer, J. T. (2004, March). Volunteerism during their transition to adulthood: A life course perspective. *Oxford Journals, 82*(3), 1123–1149.

O'Leary, C., & Stewart, J. (2013). The interaction of learning styles and teaching methodologies in accounting ethical instruction. *Journal of Business Ethics, 113*(2), 225–241.

PCQuest. (2017, 03 02). India's digital marketing has grown at 33% annually in last 6 years. Retrieved 22 May 2017, from http://www.pcquest. com/indias-digital-marketing-has-grown-at-33-annually-in-last-6-years/

Perlow, L. A., & Porter, J. L. (2009). Making time off predictable—and required. *Harvard Business Review*. Retrieved 5 July 2017, from https:// hbr.org/2009/10/making-time-off-predictable-and-required

Petrilla, M. (2016). 'Millennipreneurs' are starting more businesses, targeting higher profits. *Fortune*. Retrieved 29 May 2017, from http://fortune. com/2016/02/20/millennial-entrepreneurs-study/

Phadnis, S. (2012, 17 October). Companies use online games as hiring tool. Retrieved 6 July 2017, from http://timesofindia.indiatimes.com/business/india-business/Companies-use-online-games-as-hiring-tool/articleshow/16844791.cms

Pooley, E. (2005). Kid these days. *Canadian Business, 78*(12), 9–26.

Prasad, A. (2014, 11 August). India's new CSR law sparks debate among NGOs and businesses. *The Guardian*. Retrieved 15 December 2014, from http://www.theguardian.com/sustainable-business/india-csr-law-debate-business-ngo

PrincetonOne. (n.d.). Understanding Generation Y: What you need to know about the millennials. Retrieved 26 April 2017, from http://www. princetonone.com/news/PrincetonOne%20White%20Paper2.pdf

Prithishkumar, I., & Michael, S. (2014, April–June). Understanding your student: Using the VARK model. *Journal of Postgraduate Medicine, 60*(2), 183–186. Retrieved 5 October 2015, from http://www.ncbi.nlm.nih. gov/pubmed/24823519

PTI. (2014, 19 June). Govt provides clarity on CSR activities under Companies Act. *The Times of India*. Retrieved 15 December 2014, from http://timesofindia.indiatimes.com/business/india-business/Govt-provides-clarity-on-CSR-activities-under-Companies-Act/articleshow/36833349.cms

PTI. (2017, 24 January). Over 80% engineering graduates in India unemployable: Study. *Financial Express*. Retrieved 25 May 2017, from http://

www.financialexpress.com/jobs/over-80-engineering-graduates-in-india-unemployable-study/201150/

Puntam, R. D. (2000). *Bowling alone: The collapse and revival of American community*. New York, NY: Simon & Schuster.

Rai, S., & Khatri, S. (2014). Learning styles among the outstanding physiotherapy undergraduates students. *Pravara Medical Review*, 6(4), 14–17. Retrieved 5 October 2015, from http://www.pravara.com/pmr/pmr-6-4-5.pdf

Raisinghani, M. S., Chowdhury, M., Colquitt, C., Reyes, P. M., Kadivi, N. B., Ray, J. M., & Robles, J. E. (2005). Distance education in the business aviation industry: Issues and opportunities. *International Journal of Distance Education Technologies*, 3(1), 20–43.

Rana, P. (2012, 12 December). Study: Less than 10% of Indian MBA graduates are 'employable'. *The Wall Street Journal*. Retrieved 10 July 2017, from http://blogs.wsj.com/indiarealtime/2012/12/12/study-less-than-10-indian-mbas-employable/

Renger, R. F., Midyett, S. J., Mas, F. G., Erin, T. E., McDermott, H. M., Papenfuss, R. L., & Hewitt, M. J. (2000). Optimal living profile: An inventory to assess health and wellness. *American Journal of Health Promotion*, 24(6), 403–412.

Sakaal Times. (2017, May). Millennials rent household items instead of buying them, says website. Retrieved 19 May 2017, from http://sakaaltimes.com/NewsDetails.aspx?NewsId=5142929303114499907&SectionId=4924098573178130559&SectionName=Top%20Stories&NewsTitle=Millennials%20rent%20household%20items%20instead%20of%20buying%20%20them,%20says%20website

Scaling Green. (2014, 7 June). McCarthy Group Study: "Millennials trust their friends, not advertising". Retrieved 1 May 2017, from http://scalinggreen.tigercomm.us/2014/06/mccarthy-group-study-millennials-trust-their-friends-not-advertising/

ScienceDaily. (2016, 17 October). Will millennials ever get married? Retrieved 8 May 2017, from https://www.sciencedaily.com/releases/2016/10/161017124248.htm

Scroll.in. (2016, 30 October). An Indian startup that lends furniture raised $30 million—proving that millennials hate permanence. Retrieved 19 May 2017, from https://scroll.in/article/820205/an-indian-startup-that-lends-furniture-raised-30-million-proving-that-millennials-hate-permanence

Seager, C. (2014, 19 February). Generation Y: Why young job seekers want more than money. *The Guardian.* Retrieved 19 August 2014, from http:// www.theguardian.com/social-enterprise-network/2014/feb/19/generation-y-millennials-job-seekers-money-financial-security-fulfilment

Security Magazine. (2009, 1 January). Gen Y: Help and Hindrance. Retrieved 22 May 2017, from http://www.securitymagazine.com/articles/79561-gen-y-help-and-hindrance-1

Siegel, R. L., Fedewa, S. A., Anderson, W. F., Miller, K. D., Ma, J., Rosenberg, P. S., & Jemal, A. (2017). Colorectal cancer incidence patterns in the United States, 1974–2013. *Journal of the National Cancer Institute, 109*(8), djw322. doi:10.1093/jnci/djw322

Singh, N. (2015, 22 September). Indians hike time and spend on beauty salons. *The Times of India.* Retrieved 4 July 2017, from http://timesofindia. indiatimes.com/city/mumbai/Indians-hike-time-and-spend-on-beauty-salons/articleshow/49052647.cms

Singh, R. (2013, 22 August). Now, boys spend more on cosmetics than girls! *The Times of India.* New Delhi. Retrieved 4 July 2017, from http://timesofindia.indiatimes.com/life-style/relationships/love-sex/Now-boys-spend-more-on-cosmetics-than-girls/articleshow/21797622.cms

SiteAdWiki. (2015). Latest average CPM 2015. Retrieved 17 May 2017, from http://www.siteadwiki.com/2015/02/latest-average-cpm-2015.html

Skidmore Studio. (2015, 10 June). Airlines need to go above and beyond to win millennials. Retrieved 22 May 2017, from http://www.skidmorestudio.com/airlines-need-to-go-above-and-beyond-to-win-millennials/

Stanford Business. (2004, 1 January). MBA graduates want to work for caring and ethical employers. Retrieved 25 May 2017, from https:// www.gsb.stanford.edu/insights/mba-graduates-want-work-caring-ethical-employers

StarTribune. (2016, 25 July). Target, UnitedHealth and other companies turning to 'reverse mentoring' to tap millennials' knowledge. Retrieved 17 May 2017, from http://www.startribune.com/target-unitedhealth-and-other-companies-turning-to-reverse-mentoring-to-tap-millennials-knowledge/388085972/

Startup Genome. (2017). *The 2017 global startup ecosystem report.* Retrieved 29 May 2017, from https://startupgenome.com/thank-you-enjoy-reading/

Statista and Glassdoor. (2017, 28 May). Top 10 ways bosses lose team's respect. *The Times of India*, p. 19.

REFERENCES AND SUGGESTED READINGS

Sundar, R., Mookharjee, D., Babar, M., & Ravikumar, U. (2011). A study of single mothers in four metro cities of India. Ministry of Women and Child Development. Retrieved 26 April 2017, from http://wcd.nic.in/ Schemes/research/dtd14092015/Single%20Mothers-%20Executive %20Summary%20WCD.pdf

Sustainable Brands. (2015, 24 September). Study: Millennials are strongest CSR supporters in U.S. Retrieved from http://www.sustainablebrands. com/news_and_views/marketing_comms/mike_hower/study_millennials_are_strongest_csr_supporters_us

Telefónica. (2013, 5 June). Indian millennials value being an entrepreneur: Survey. Support Biz. Retrieved 29 May 2017, from http://www.support-biz.com/articles/news/indian-millennials-value-being-entrepreneur-survey.html

The Conference Board of Canada. (2014, 25 June). *Workplace preferences of millennials and Gen X: Attracting and retaining the 2020 workforce.* Retrieved 4 July 2017, from http://www.conferenceboard.ca/e-library/abstract. aspx?did=6270

The Telegraph. (2015, 15 May). Humans have shorter attention span than goldfish, thanks to smartphones. Retrieved 17 May 2017, from http:// www.telegraph.co.uk/science/2016/03/12/humans-have-shorter-attention-span-than-goldfish-thanks-to-smart/

Time. (2014, 24 September). Why 25% of millennials will never get married. Retrieved 8 May 2017, from http://time.com/3422624/report-millennials-marriage/

Tsui, A. H. H. (2008). Asian wellness in decline: A cost of rising prosperity. *International Journal of Workplace Health Management*, (2), 123–135.

Uggen, C., & Janikula, J. (1999, September). Volunteerism and arrests in the transition to Adulthood. *Oxford Journals, 78*(1), 331–362.

UPS. (2016, June). UPS pulse of online shoppers. Retrieved 18 May 2017, from https://solvers.ups.com/assets/2016_UPS_Pulse_of_the_Online_ Shopper.pdf

Uthra, V. (2014, January–March). A study on teaching pedagogies among MBA-school faculty. *International Journal of Business and Administration Research Review, 2*(3). Retrieved 5 October 2015, from http://ijbarr.com/ downloads/2014/vol2-issue3/10.pdf

VoucherBin. (2015, 13 October). *Social media: The largest international expo* (Infographic). Retrieved 18 May 2017, from http://www.voucherbin. co.uk/social-media-the-largest-international-expo-infographic/

WHO (World Health Organization). (2017). *Depression and other common mental disorders: Global health estimates.* WHO. Retrieved 25 April 2017, from http://www.who.int/mental_health/management/depression/prevalence_global_health_estimates/en/

Williams, R. (2014, 19 March). How the millennial generation will change the workplace. *Psychology Today.* Retrieved 19 August 2014, from http://www.psychologytoday.com/collections/201403/misunderstood-millenials/how-millennials-are-changing-the-workplace

World Economic Forum. (2015). Persistent jobless growth. Retrieved 29 May 2017, from http://reports.weforum.org/outlook-global-agenda-2015/top-10-trends-of-2015/2-persistent-jobless-growth/

ZDNet. (2013, 18 March). Millennials will soon dominate travel spending. Retrieved 22 May 2017, from http://www.zdnet.com/article/millennials-will-soon-dominate-travel-spending/

Zephoria. (2017). The top 20 valuable Facebook statistics (Updated May 2017). Retrieved 22 May 2017, from https://zephoria.com/what-we-do/

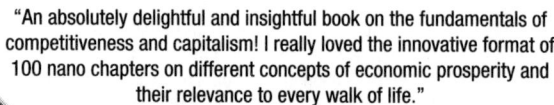